THE WORK OF WORK

THE WORK OF WORK:

SERVITUDE, SLAVERY, AND LABOR IN MEDIEVAL ENGLAND

edited by

Allen J. Frantzen and Douglas Moffat

1994
GLASGOW

CRUITHNE PRESS

1994

© Cruithne Press
197 Great Western Road
George's Cross
Glasgow G4 9EB
Great Britain

British Library Cataloguing in Publication Data

Work of Work: Servitude, Slavery, and Labor in Medieval England
I. Frantzen, Allen J.   II. Moffat, Douglas
306.3620942

ISBN 1-873448-03-1

Set in Palatino, by Cruithne Press typesetting
and printed and bound in Great Britain by BPC Wheatons, Exeter.

Cruithne Press gratefully acknowledges the financial support of the
University of Michigan for the publication of this volume.

CONTENTS

Allen J. Frantzen — Department of English, Loyola University Chicago

Ruth Mazo Karras — Department of History, Temple University

Elizabeth Stevens Girsch — The Middle English Dictionary, University of Michigan

John Ruffing — Medieval Studies Program, Cornell University

George Ovitt, Jr. — Sidwell Friends' School, Washington, D.C.

Ross Samson — Cruithne Press, Glasgow, Scotland

Niall Brady — Medieval Studies Program, Cornell University

Douglas Moffat — The Middle English Dictionary, University of Michigan

David Aers — Department of English, Duke University

Louise M. Bishop — Department of English, University of Oregon

Madonna J. Hettinger — Department of History, College of Wooster

THE WORK OF WORK: SERVITUDE, SLAVERY, AND LABOR IN MEDIEVAL ENGLAND

Allen J. Frantzen

Replying to her niece's complaint that Jane Austen was irrelevant, the novelist Fay Weldon wrote, "I want you to conceive of England, your country, two hundred years ago":

> A place without detergent or tissues or tarmaced roads or railway trains, or piped water, let alone electricity or gas or oil; where energy (what a modern term) was provided by coal, and wood, and the muscle of human beings, and that was all. Where the fastest anyone could cover the ground was the speed of the fastest horse, and where, even so, letters could be posted in London one evening and be delivered in Hereford the next morning. Because people were so poor — most people — they would run, and toil, and sweat all day and all night to save themselves and their children from starvation.[1]

Labor that so taxed poor workers' bodies had, however, redeeming merits for their souls. "Your reward would be in heaven," Weldon noted. "The Bible rather rashly claimed that that was where the poor went, thus giving the rich every justification for preserving their poverty."[2] Weldon's depressing description reminds us of the grinding poverty and suffering that are among the least appealing aspects of pre-modern life. But that is not, in the main, how scholars have chosen to view the Middle Ages. Nor was it always Weldon's preferred view of the eighteenth-century world of Jane Austen. "I was brought up, as were many of my generation," she writes, "with a vague knowledge of how and where she lived, and a general association between her and elegant Regency Bath, all dandies, coaches, balls, finery and elopements. The child's view of history."[3]

Although they do not entertain a "child's view of history," medievalists have been quite willing to overlook the dirt and grime of medieval culture in favor of shining surfaces — glittering manuscripts rather than plain ones, swords rather than plowshares. High culture, not mass culture, is in the main the stuff of our research. This collection of essays on labor, slavery, and servitude in the English Middle Ages seeks to refocus attention on the mundane working world.[4] Our title, "the work of work," itself works in several senses. For one, these essays discuss labor's role in a three-part structure familiar in descriptions of the medieval world: the division of society into those who ruled, prayed, and worked. This model, an enduring commonplace that has had considerable influence in medieval studies, was a powerful expression of what David Aers calls "the leading ideology," the normative description of social structures in the English Middle Ages. That ideology supplied boundaries of identity and shaped them into a persuasive theology of rank and class. "The leading ideology thus made the inherited social world, with its distribution of power, work and wealth, so natural that any opposition to it seemed literally monstrous, as well as iniquitous," Aers writes.[5] The tripartite model both articulated and controlled social tensions; it valorized the status quo and damned the discontent of those who did not know — and keep — their places.

Two other aspects of our title are equally important. Douglas Moffat and I want to call attention to the misery of work, the burden of physical labor, the sweat acknowledged in Weldon's comments. We also want to emphasize the hidden power of work to demean those who perform it. That is why we have chosen to characterize labor in terms of slavery, serfdom, and servitude: nobody was slave, serf, or servant by choice unless the slavery or servitude in question was metaphorical. Slaves of love and servants of God were not, in most cases, also physical laborers. Labors of love, even Herculean labors, were different from the hard physical labor that was routine for most people in the Middle Ages.

Metaphorical labors are widespread among medievalists, too, but most of us have had little direct experience of the need to labor physically to stay alive. Our labors, when we describe them as such, are work, but they are far from slavery and servitude. We are, however, beneficiaries of the physical labor of others, as we can see every day rushing into our offices as the cleaning staff leaves, or crowding into airplane seats as the cleaning crew is shuffled out the back door. Those of us who come from laboring families — farmers, factory workers — may find that we enjoy the social status that academia confers. True, its material rewards do not compare favorably to other prestigious occupations, such as law or medicine. But then academic employment is not as demanding as brain surgery; nor is academic work as directly accountable to external forces as are routine legal procedures — divorce, for example, or selling or buying a house. Our work in the classroom has more immediate consequences (or so we like to think), but in most cases they are difficult to trace.

As we see our own world, so do we tend to see the Middle Ages: a place where work was done if not off stage then so far in the background as to require no attention. Yet reminders of labor are everywhere in medieval texts. The Wife of Bath's "Citees, burghes, castels, hye toures" for example, are, in the very next line, paired with "thropes, bernes, shipnes, dayeryes" (villages, barns, stables, dairies), humble structures on whose productivity the exalted structures depended (III, 870–71).[6] The Wife is a good witness for the proximity of the glamorous to the mundane, for she is, by any standard, an extraordinarily popular reference for the one form of medieval ugliness that contemporary scholarship gazes upon willingly: misogyny. So singular and concentrated is this gaze, R. Howard Bloch observes, that "medieval misogyny" might seem to be a redundant phrase, since misogyny "participates in a vestigial horror practically synonymous with the term *medieval*, and because one of the assumptions governing our perception of the Middle Ages is the viral presence of antifeminism."[7] Few topics are so widely discussed in medieval scholarship these days as feminism,[8] and in English literary studies in particular it would be difficult to find a literary character more prominent than the Wife.

Slavery and servitude are also horrors of medieval cultures that persist into modern times; they are hardly vestiges (Bloch, let me note, is at pains to stress the persistence of antifeminism). But I believe that for most medievalists servitude and slavery are remote institutions, experienced indirectly through novels and research materials and therefore much less likely than misogyny or other directly-experienced forms of sexual discrimination to impinge on consciousness. The Wife reminds us that hard work was needed to supply ecclesiastical and aristocratic needs in Chaucer's time. But her reminder comes offhandedly, part of a scene-setting gesture, and offhandedness is one way in which labor was treated by authors in the period, even though medieval people, like the poor in the eighteenth century, worked all the time. Authors including Chaucer also treated the subject indirectly, using irony and humor that express contempt, subtle and otherwise, for those who worked. Here too medieval scholars seem to follow authorial gazes. In the scholarly tradition, particularly in its contemporary stages, the emphasis falls on the author's cleverness or, in the Wife's case, on the female character herself rather than on her view of the economic landscape.

The same is true of a male character used by Chaucer to comment on labor, the repulsive and proud old knight in *The Merchant's Tale*, January, consumed by passion for May, his beautiful young wife. This fine and "hidden" reference to the work of work juxtaposes labor to sexual play. January spends their wedding feast imagining how he will make love to her. But first he must clear out the wedding guests:

> And finally he dooth al his labour,
> As he beste myghte, savynge his honour,
> To haste hem fro the mete in subtil wyse. (1765–67) [9]

When they are gone and the newlyweds are in bed, the narrator again uses "labor" ironically, this time to ridicule the old man's apparent impotence. January says to his wife,

> "Ther nys no werkman, whatsoevere he be,
> That may bothe werke wel and hastily;
> This wol be doon at leyser partifly.
> It is no fors how longe that we pleye." (1832–35)

The narrator satirizes January's sexual ambitions by describing sexual "play" as "labor." January is a "werkman" and his wife is an object (a "sex object") on whom work is performed. Sexual intercourse is parodied not as play, as Chaucer elsewhere describes it (*The Miller's Tale*, for example), but as labor: it is an effort for the old man to make love. Then a reference to real labor intrudes to underscore the old man's folly:

> "A man may do no synne with his wyf,
> Ne hurte hymselven with his owene knyf." (1839–40)

But a man can easily hurt himself with his own knife, and a man can still, the Church maintains, sin sexually with his wife. The joke instead would appear to be how a man can injure himself instead of his partner with his penis, a reversed image of intercourse that mocks the old man's pretensions to potency. The humor depends not only on our remembering that January is very old (he's sixty, a great age in Chaucer's time) but also that he is a "worthy knyght" (1246) and therefore someone whose age and class should keep him from being compared to a laborer, especially in his own speech. The powerful figure is twice shamed by the narrator's recourse to the language of the powerless: the old man is ridiculed because he thinks and acts like a young one; the knight is ridiculed because he thinks and acts like a laborer. It is true that such humor does not necessarily indicate a lack of respect for labor or laborers themselves, but it does render labor itself invisible, reducing it from a force in culture to a figure of speech.

If we turn from figures of speech to work itself, we must ask where in medieval sources slavery and servitude are represented. In reference to medieval England, we find that the later period is far richer in scholarship than the earlier, Anglo-Saxon centuries. We know from Bede's *Ecclesiastical History*, *Beowulf*, the Exeter Book riddles,[10] and elsewhere that slavery was an institution of fundamental importance to Anglo-Saxon England. But there is little bibliography to help us discover the meaning — the cultural work — of this work. The major history of the period by Sir Frank Stenton makes only a few passing references to it. As David Pelteret has noted, scholars have until recently had to rely almost exclusively on the discussion written by John Mitchell Kemble over one hundred years ago.[11] The issues of forced labor and the lives of the unfree contradict the Christian benevolence that some scholars like to think ruled the Middle Ages. These issues also undercut the view, so dear to early students of the Anglo-Saxon language, that Anglo-Saxon society was free and democratic and therefore superior to later feudal cultures. There are many reasons why slavery and servitude, however important they were as social and economic institutions in medieval life, have failed to interest scholars, among them the scholarly tradition itself.

This is true for more than the tradition of Anglo-Saxon studies. Discussing research on the slave populations of Roman villas, Ross Samson writes, "I believe that scholars have been led subconsciously to accept that slaves were infrequent on villas simply because of the almost total lack of literature on the subject." Elsewhere he finds a scholar asserting that studies of slavery in early medieval Gaul "are many," when, according to Samson, the "exhaustive bibliography" in 1989 comprised all of four works.[12] It would seem that slavery, servitude, and labor continue to be undervalued in our understanding of medieval life in part because they have long been undervalued in scholarship about the Middle Ages.

Discussions of slavery and servitude are becoming more numerous in a scholarly climate newly attuned to the lives of disenfranchised social classes. Slavery and servitude have come into clearer focus as historians have broadened their analysis of medieval culture beyond the categories defined by political dynasties and have begun to consider the evidence of less prestigious categories and voices, what Carolyn Walker Bynum has called history in the "comic mode."[13] Working from Scandinavian evidence, Ruth Mazo Karras has analyzed slavery as a social category that was not merely the function of an economic system, but rather a social classification that persisted through changes in dynasties and political relations.[14] As historically-oriented gender studies and gay studies have become more numerous, the intersection of economic and sexual exploitation has become more apparent. Early Germanic, Scandinavian, Irish, and Anglo-Saxon societies were slave-holding but were not "slave societies" to the extent that either ancient societies, such as Rome, or New World societies (the American South) were.[15] That is why fuller analysis of other social structures, including sexual roles, increases our understanding of the role of slavery in those cultures.[16] Class-structured homosexuality and the link between slaves and sexual exploitation have been examined by David F. Greenberg, who notes that male and female slaves were sexually used by their owners "with impunity," and that male prostitutes were usually, but not always, slaves (i.e., some were free men).[17] Greenberg has observed that studies of homosexuality have flourished with the increased tolerance for homosexuality. "The partial success of the gay-liberation movement's efforts to refute popular beliefs that homosexuality is harmful has done much to stimulate the study of its prohibition," he writes.[18] Most medievalists are not descended from enslaved peoples, however, and most scholars of that ancestry do not study the Middle Ages. Hence it is important to rely on multiple disciplines and cultures in order to learn about medieval slavery. Connections between medieval and modern institutions are important sources of help, and models and patterns for inquiry can be drawn from studies in pre-medieval eras, especially from studies of classical periods.[19]

Given the enormous and obvious importance of what Richard Lefebvre des Noëttes called "imperious material conditions,"[20] it would seem that the history of labor in all its forms is at least as important as the diplomatic, military, and ecclesiastical history that fills our bookshelves. Historians working outside English materials have long thought so. "Throughout medieval Europe men spoke of personal liberty and of servitude, i.e., of the deprivation of liberty," Marc Bloch wrote (women too, of course). "The courts investigated carefully, sometimes agonizingly, who was free and who was not."[21] Philosophical questions of personal liberty have created rich and varied scholarly discourses both traditional and poststructuralist. Studies in the former category debate the rise of the individual;[22] those in the latter contemplate the relation of "the construction of the subject"[23] to our notion of medieval people. But the material conditions of labor, whether of slavery, of servitude, or of the manual work of free people, have not, outside economic history, been adequately explored.

Another French scholar who has long recognized the hidden importance of work in the medieval period, and who continues the powerful developments of behavioral history known as the "Annales" school,[24] is Georges Duby, whose great study, *Les trois ordres ou l'imaginaire de féodalisme* (*The Three Orders: Feudal Society Imagined*), is one of the most influential written on the subject, and one of the most sympathetic — not to say polemical.[25] Recent studies which emphasize medieval France include Michel Mollat's *The Poor in the Middle Ages*. Pelteret's work, and Christopher Dyer's *Standards of Living in the Later Middle Ages*, with its emphasis on England from 1200–1500, are among the few that assist us in learning about servitude and slavery in earlier English periods.[26]

Of the historiographical models available, none has more immediate appeal than Duby's. More plainly than any who have followed after him, Duby probes the fundamental injustices that linked Christian conceptions of labor to patterns of social organization. He emphasizes the importance of money and trade, and the nexus of those elements in the city. He never allows his focus to stray from the powerful marriage of Church and State in the control of the things of this world. Duby's point of entry into the topic is textual, a point of entry that also serves in some of the essays included in the present collection. Through a reading of an unfinished poem by Adelbero of Laon, "Carmen ad Rodbertum regem" (c. 1031), Duby explains the immense importance of "the category of the 'vulgar'": the people whose function was to toil and whose subjugation was hereditary. This "toil," Duby writes, was

> A sad word, evoking sweat, affliction, poverty — exploitation. Assigned to fulfill this function were those who, by nature, because their blood was not the blood of kings, and because they were not ordained, were compelled to alienate their strength in the service of others.[27]

Some commanded, others obeyed, and birth determined the category to which each belonged. Those who sought holy lives could overcome the conditions of birth, however, so it was among the laity that the crucial distinction between leading and following was registered: there were those who ruled and the "vulgar," the people who served. Those who served inherited their condition, and the painful toil Duby describes was an essential part of it. Their condition was governed by "the principle of necessary inequality" that sustained a society "in which the high reigned in perfection and the low grovelled in sin." [28]

By the eleventh century it was taken for granted that the third order, the "people" who worked, was itself divided into two groups. These were the artisans and merchants who dwelled in cities, and the *agricolae*, peasants who lived in the countryside. The peasants were seen as childlike in their simplicity and assured of salvation because, as Honorius Augustodunensis wrote, "they feed the people of God by their sweat."[29] The logic of this concept, which we have already seen in Weldon's statements, was perverse.

Duby says that the assumed salvation of the poor affirmed the already desirable link between the clergy and the cities. If they could be considered categorically saved, the rustics need only be exhorted to obey. At the same time, those most in need of prayer (and most capable of giving donations to ensure prayer in perpetuity) were merchants and others who lived and worked in cities, free men and women of means in whom the clergy could most profitably invest their time.[30] Assurances of their salvation, however, did not save the peasants from the most withering scorn. Lee Patterson has demonstrated that peasants were described as subhuman, likened to animals, and even demonized.[31] "Needless to say," Patterson cautions, "any argument that stigmatizes the vast majority of the population as damned beyond redemption . . . can hardly enter the mainstream of medieval political thought." But Patterson also suggests that the image of the damned, demonic peasant established itself in popular art — the drama, for example — even as theological discourse proclaimed the peasant's simple and therefore saved nature.[32]

Some of the most powerful imagery in the literature Duby surveys does not distinguish between merchants and agricultural peasants. Instead it lumps them together at the lowest levels of architectural and bodily metaphors of which medieval authors were fond. Honorius's *Jewel of the Soul* construes the bishops as pillars, princes as arches, and doctors as windows through whom light streamed; knights formed the protective roof over this structure, and then, prostrate and "huddling together to form the floor that the others trod underfoot," were the *laboratores*. In the organic bodily image that formed the counterpart to the architectural metaphor, peasants were also the feet.[33]

Medievalists wishing to consider the implications of such imagery can do no better than to consult the art of medieval cathedrals, products of the conjunction of piety and labor, urban wealth and political might, monuments incorporating portraits of labor in action, including such commonplaces as the "labors of the seasons." Henry Kraus — basing his discussion almost entirely on French sources — argues that the Church permitted its artists to incorporate peasant life into cathedral decoration as a way of keeping the unruly laboring masses in check. He comments on "the Democracy of the Blessed," a procession of the saved led by a peasant, pilgrim, or monk rather than a member of the powerful classes:

> One can see the local priest making the rounds of his church's art with his parishioners, as was indeed the established practice, urging home the subject of "redemption through work." It would be a sure solace to the peasants, weighted down by their worldly burdens, to see their familiar labors exalted upon the house of God.[34]

Part of the work of work, therefore, was to preserve medieval systems that ensured the unequal distribution of wealth and reconciled the most miserable to their abjection and subjugation. About these systems we medievalists seem to know less than we should. Medieval texts tell us about laborers and their activities rather than categories of production. The economic systems functioning behind and within those ideas are difficult to detect, although the ideas that framed material circumstances are commonplaces that all medievalists recognize. These include, in addition to the assumed salvation of the poor, the identification of labor as the wages of sin and the link between sexual identity and work.

What one finds missing in the mainstream of work on the Middle Ages, outside the research of political economists, is familiarity with theories of labor, Marxist or otherwise, in the period (the exception, of course, is the theory associating labor with punishment for sin). This is very unfortunate, since medieval evidence strongly influenced Marx's theories of slavery and serfdom in particular. Marx developed the concept of "wage-labor" in contradistinction to other, feudal forms of labor, and the vast literature that has developed around his analysis continues to merit attention.[35] In medieval texts, "labor" incorporates a series of abstractions that traditional political economics describes in language that sees labor as always and everywhere the same. An introduction to the debate about forms of labor can be found in the work of Raymond Williams, which also provides a strong model for writing about labor in the pre-modern period, especially remarkable because Williams recognized the importance of the personal in this scholarly endeavor.[36]

"Labor," Williams observes, is a term that "is not often used outside two specific modern contexts": "the economic abstraction of the activity" of work, and "the social abstraction of that class of people who performed it."[37] These economic and social abstractions are familiar; they include "labor force," "labor relations," and "laborer," which is still in current use to indicate those who perform certain kinds of physical work, chiefly unskilled. "Labor" in reference to organized labor in the United States often refers to "blue collar" work only. "Working" usually means "working for pay," so that people who are not working for hire (e.g., the traditional housewife, or the child who belongs to a working-class family and works on a farm or in another family-owned business) could be described as "out of work," even though they work all the time.[38] We refer to one's "work" rather than one's "labor" because the former term is less likely than the latter to connote pain or trouble. That association, which had enormous importance for the status of the working poor in the Middle Ages, today survives chiefly in reference to "labor" in childbirth.

Like "labor," "work" had an early association with pain and toil, and the history of both words indicates the relationship between modern attitudes and medieval institutions. In the example of *The Merchant's Tale* above, labor is only a pretext for sexual humor. January's sexual work is humorous in part because it is not likely to result in "labor" of a different kind — childbirth, that is — for his bride. The sexual division of labor, instituted at what medieval people believed was the origin of history in the book of Genesis, fuels Chaucer's humor. As seen in Scripture, and widely represented in medieval art and literature, that division is no laughing matter:

> To the woman he said, "I will greatly multiply your pain in childbearing; in pain you shall bring forth children, yet your desire shall be for your husband and he shall rule over you."
> And to Adam he said, "Because you have listened to the voice of your wife, and have eaten of the tree of which I commanded you, 'You shall not eat of it,' cursed is the ground because of

you; in toil you shall eat of it all the days of your life; thorns
and thistles it shall bring forth to you; and you shall eat the
plants of the field. In the sweat of your face you shall eat bread
till you return to the ground, for out of it you were taken; you
are dust, and to dust you shall return."

Genesis 3.16–19

Of this passage, Susan Stanford Friedman writes, "God's punishment of Adam and Eve in Genesis has provided divine authority for
the sexual division of labor. Adam's *labor* is to produce the goods of
society, by the 'sweat of his brow,' an idiom that collapses man's
muscular and mental work. Eve's labor is to reproduce the species in
pain and subservience to Adam."[39] The sexual division of labor, we
know, created lasting stereotypes. Following the iconography
suggested by the description of Adam and Eve being driven from
Eden, medieval artists associated Adam, the father and prototype of
Christ, with gardening, and Eve, the mother, with domestic activity,
including weaving and spinning, but most of all with the labor of giving birth to children.[40]

I have emphasized words and literary representations here, and it is
plainly with the evidence of words that most of the contributions in
this volume are primarily concerned. The essays nonetheless take
various approaches to slavery and servitude, ranging from Marxist
economic history to lexicography and to medieval labor itself, ranging
from the *opus Dei* of monastic life to the litigation against servants in
the fifteenth century. Several of the essays began as papers read as part
of a day-long interdisciplinary seminar on "The Work of Work" at the
International Congress of Medieval Studies at Western Michigan
University, Kalamazoo, in May 1992 (participants included Bishop,
Brady, Frantzen, Karras, Moffat, Ruffing, and Samson). Other essays
were solicited to balance the emphasis and expand the scope of the
collection (Aers, Girsch, Hettinger, and Ovitt). The session brought
cross-cultural perspectives to bear on problems of slavery and labor
and drew attention to the processes of material production that have
traditionally been slighted. The contents of the collection testify to the
diversity of the seminar and demonstrate why inquiries into questions
of work must inevitably be raised from multiple perspectives, including archaeological, feminist, historical, and literary.

Our collection centers on medieval England, Anglo-Saxon to
fifteenth century. We include three papers that address work in more
general medieval contexts, however, each taking up evidence from an
important culture in contact with England. The essay by George Ovitt

[11]

discusses the place of work in the early medieval period and examines the monastic concept of manual labor. Early links between slavery and the status of women in Scandinavia are examined by Ruth Karras, who includes some Anglo-Saxon evidence. The Anglo-Saxon vocabulary of slavery is discussed by Elizabeth Stevens Girsch. John Ruffing analyzes the construction of labor in the monastic paradigms found in the *Colloquium* attributed to Ælfric, a Latin text best known through the Old English interlinear gloss in the single surviving manuscript. Ross Samson analyzes the idea of the "end" of slavery in the early medieval period and related social changes created by the Church. The conceptualization of labor in early Ireland is discussed by Niall Brady, who emphasizes agricultural evidence.

Servitude was not only a category of labor in the Middle Ages, as Douglas Moffat reminds us in his discussion of servility as the result of military defeat and hence as a condition forced on the English after the Norman Conquest. Moffat sees servitude as a politically and racially motivated category that expressed English resentment against descendants of the Normans in the period before the Black Death. In the later fourteenth century the most powerful expressions of concern about labor and social justice belong to William Langland. Two essays, David Aers' discussion of Langland's concept of wage labor and Louise Bishop's on the role of "vocation" in the poem, examine labor's role from perspectives located in larger social contexts in which the poem is immersed (Aers) and centered within the text (Bishop). Madonna Hettinger's essay on the status of the servant in the fifteenth century, focused like Aers' on legal considerations and based on court records heretofore unexamined, bridges the distance between medieval and early Renaissance relations between masters and servants.

The scholarly tradition, up to this point inhospitable to discussions of servitude and slavery, is changing, as gender studies demonstrate, and this change bodes well for the study of material conditions more generally. As scholarship grows to include topics of sexuality previously taboo, it will inevitably include social topics that have also been shunned (although for less interesting reasons). It might once have seemed entirely reasonable that studies of the Middle Ages should ignore the degrading aspects of medieval cultures and focus instead on those cultures' most beautiful artifacts — frequently textual, rarely material. Some years ago I suggested that the study of Anglo-Saxon penitential literature had been impeded by the high Anglicanism of such formidable scholars as Charles Plummer. "It is hard to see how anyone could busy himself with such literature and not be the worse for it," he wrote.[41] Today such disdain for mundane subjects would, in most if not all quarters, be considered narrow and elitist. Many if not most medievalists now acknowledge the need to look behind the elegant artifacts of medieval culture, themselves the products of skilled workers, masters and mistresses of their crafts, to other material and working conditions that were neither memorable nor glamorous and indeed as grim as those described by Weldon.

Douglas Moffat and I thank the authors for their participation in the seminar and their cooperation and patience as this volume took shape. We thank the University of Chicago Press for permission to reprint Ovitt's essay from *Technology and Culture* (1986). We are grateful to Joseph Lambin of Loyola University for his technical assistance. We also thank the Office of the Vice President for Research of the University of Michigan for a generous subvention.

NOTES

1. Fay Weldon, *Letters to Alice on First Reading Jane Austen* (New York, 1984), p. 34.

2. Weldon, *Letters*, p. 35.

3. Weldon, *Letters*, p. 43.

4. My comments have benefitted from discussion with several colleagues, including David Aers and Christopher Kendrick, and especially Douglas Moffat, whose work on the vocabulary of slavery in Middle English was the start of this volume.

5. David Aers, *Chaucer, Langland and the Creative Imagination* (London, 1989), pp. 1–37 at p. 3. On the "trifunctional" model see also Britton J. Harwood, "The Plot of *Piers Plowman* and the Contradictions of Feudalism," in Allen J. Frantzen, ed., *Speaking Two Languages: Traditional Disciplines and Contemporary Theory in Medieval Studies* (Albany, 1991), pp. 91–114 at pp. 93–94.

6. Quoted from *The Riverside Chaucer*, ed. Larry D. Benson (Boston, 1987), p. 117.

7. R. Howard Bloch, "Medieval Misogyny," in R. Howard Bloch and Frances Ferguson, ed., *Misogyny, Misandry, and Misanthropy* (Berkeley, 1989), p. 1.

8. Not everyone will agree with this assessment, of course. Judith M. Bennett observes that "although *women* are better assimilated into medieval studies in the 1990s [than previously], *feminist scholarship* is not." See Bennett's "Medievalism and Feminism," *Speculum* 68 (1993): 309–31, at 314. In "When Women Aren't Enough," my essay in the same volume, I assert that "feminist scholarship pervades the disciplines of art, history, law, literature, and religion" (445–71, at 445). these essays are reprinted in *Studying Medieval Women: Sex, Gender, Feminism*, ed., Nancy Partner (Cambridge, Mass., 1994).

9. These passages from *The Merchant's Tale* are quoted from Benson, ed., *The Riverside Chaucer*, pp. 160–61.

10. See, among others, John Tanke, "*Wonfeax wale*: Ideology and Figuration in Sexual Riddles of the Exeter Book," in *Class and Gender in Early English Literature: Intersections*, ed. Britton Harwood and Gillian Overing (Bloomington, 1994), pp. 21–42.

11. For an informative recent survey of the Anglo-Saxon evidence, see David Pelteret, "Slave Raiding and Slave Trading in Anglo-Saxon England," *Anglo-Saxon England* 9 (1981): 99–114. John Mitchell Kemble, *The Saxons in England* 1 (London, 1849, rev. by Walter de Gray Birch, 1876).

12. Ross Samson, "Rural Slavery, Inscriptions, Archaeology and Marx: A Response to Ramsay MacMullen's 'Late Roman Slavery'," *Historia* 38 (1989): 99–110; see p. 102 for the first quote and p. 99 note 4 for the second. For a more recent discussion of the decline of slavery, see Adriaan Verhulst, "The Decline of Slavery and the Economic Expansion of the Early Middle Ages," *Past and Present* 133 (1991): 195–203.

13. Carolyn Walker Bynum, *Fragmentation and Redemption* (Cambridge, Mass., 1989), pp. 11–26.

14. Ruth Mazo Karras, "Servitude and Sexuality in Medieval Iceland" in *From Sagas to Society*, ed. Gísli Pálsson (Enfield Lock, 1992), pp. 289–304; *Slavery and Society in Medieval Scandinavia* (New Haven, 1988); "Concubinage and Slavery in the Viking Age," *Scandinavian Studies* 62 (1990): 141–62.

15. Clare A. Lees, ed., *Medieval Masculinities: Regarding Men in the Middle Ages* (Minneapolis, 1994).

16. Karras, *Slavery and Society in Medieval Scandinavia*, p. 5.

17. David F. Greenberg, *The Construction of Homosexuality* (Chicago, 1988), pp. 119–21.

18. Greenberg, *The Construction*, p. 4

19. See, for example, Aline Rousselle, "Personal Status and Sexual Practice in the Roman Empire," in *Fragments for a History of the Human Body*, vol. 3, ed., Michel Feher, with Ramona Naddaff and Nadia Tazi (New York, 1989), pp. 300–333.

20. Richard Lefebvre des Noëttes, *L'attelage et le cheval de selle à travers les âges* (Paris, 1911), p. 12, quoted by Henry Kraus, *The Living Theatre of Medieval Art* (Philadelphia, 1972), p. 40.

21. Marc Bloch, *Slavery and Serfdom in the Middle Ages* (Berkeley, 1975), p. 33.

22. See Rodney Hilton, *Class Conflict and the Crisis of Feudalism* (London, 1984), for an excellent survey of recent scholarship on the question. Here and elsewhere, Hilton argues a point of view challenged Alan MacFarlane, *The Origins of English Individualism* (Oxford, 1978). MacFarlane's view (that "peasant" was a term the English properly used only of foreign peoples) has been severely criticized by Hilton and others.

23. Lee Patterson, *Chaucer and the Subject of History* (Madison, 1991), pp. 3–13.

24. The "Annales" school of behavioral history was co-founded by Bloch and Lucien Febvre. On this development, see Norman Cantor, *Inventing the Middle Ages* (New York, 1993), pp. 132–35.

25. Georges Duby, *Les Trois ordres ou l'imaginaire de féodalisme* (Paris, 1978), translated by Arthur Goldhammer as *The Three Orders: Feudal Society Imagined* (better translated as "The Imaginary of Feudalism") (Chicago, 1980).

26. Christopher Dyer, *Standards of Living in the Later Middle Ages: Social Change in England c. 1200–1500* (Cambridge, England, 1989); Michel Mollat, *The Poor in the Middle Ages: An Essay in Social History*, trans. Arthur Goldhammer (Paris, 1978; New Haven, 1986).

27. Duby, *Three Orders*, p. 59.

28. Duby, *Three Orders*, p. 59.

29. Honorius, *Elucidarium*, PL 177:1147:49, quoted in Duby, *Three Orders*, p. 250.

30. Duby, *Three Orders*, pp. 251–52.

31. Patterson, *Chaucer and the Subject of History*, pp. 256–70. See also Michael Camille, "Labouring for the Lord: The Ploughman and the Social Order in the Luttrell Psalter," *Art History* 10 (1987): 423–54, and *Image on the Edge: The Margins of Medieval Art* (Cambridge, Mass., 1992), pp. 118–20, 132–43.

32. Patterson, *Chaucer and the Subject of History*, p. 267.

33. Jacques Le Goff, "Head or Heart? The Political Use of Body Metaphors in the Middle Ages," *Fragments for a History of the Human Body*, ed. Feher, pp. 13–26.

34. Kraus, *The Living Theatre*, pp. 109–10, 118; quotation from p. 109.

35. The terms of Marxist analysis are readily defined in Tom Bottomore, et al., *A Dictionary of Marxist Thought* (Cambridge, Mass., 1983); see p. 265 for the quote.

36. Raymond Williams, *The Country and the City* (1973; Frogmore, 1975). For a discussion of the personal in Williams writing, see comments by David Wallace, "Carving Up Time and the World. Medieval-Renaissance Turf Wars; Historiography and Personal History," *Working Papers* 11 (1990–91), The Center for Twentieth-Century Studies, University of Wisconsin-Milwaukee, pp. 11–12.

37. Raymond Williams, *Keywords* (New York, 1976), p. 179.

38. Williams, *Keywords*, p. 335.

39. Susan Stanford Friedman, "Creativity and the Childbirth Metaphor: Gender Difference in Literary Discourse," in *Speaking of Gender*, ed. Elaine Showalter (New York, 1989), pp. 73–100, quote from p. 76.

40. For a brilliant survey of some relevant images, see Kraus *The Living Theatre*, pp. 41–62.

41. Allen J. Frantzen, *The Literature of Penance in Anglo-Saxon England* (New Brunswick, 1983), p. 3.

2

Desire, Descendants, and Dominance: Slavery, the Exchange of Women, and Masculine Power

Ruth Mazo Karras

	Sceolde forht monig
blachleor ides	bifiende gan
on fremdes fæðm.	

Many a frightened white-cheeked woman
had to go trembling into a stranger's embrace.[1]

During the Middle Ages large numbers of women and men were removed from their homes by force and taken to other parts of Europe, North Africa, and the Middle East as slaves.[2] As one would expect, given the gender division of labor in the Middle Ages, the personal experiences of enslaved men and women were quite different.[3] It was not only the subjective experience of male and female slaves that differed, but also the effect of men's and women's enslavement on the enslaving society.

Most scholarship on slavery and serfdom, especially in Europe, tends to treat the institution of servitude as ungendered. Relative numbers of male and female slaves, the gender division of labor, and slave marriage and reproduction have always been topics of investigation, but few scholars have called into question the function of the whole institution within the broader system of gender relations of a given society.[4] I propose to approach the wider impact of servitude on society by suggesting how masters used the enslavement of women as a tool to dominate both women and men, slaves and free.[5]

Three reasons may be identified for men having sexual relations with their women slaves — the gratification of their privileged (upper-class, heterosexual, masculine) sex drive, the production of offspring (especially sons) in order to assure the continuity of the lineage, and the assertion of power, symbolic as well as practical, over the en-slaved. These three reasons might be termed desire, descendants, and dominance, and of the three dominance was the most important motivating factor; it fit into a system of masculine purchase and con-trol of women's sexuality generally.

Orlando Patterson has recently argued that personal freedom was a value for women before it became one for men. Once a man suffered the social death of slavery, he might as well be physically dead; there was no way for him to regain his lost honor. A woman, however, could recover hers: "with them the possibility of the restoration of their status as legitimate members of their master's or their own former community existed." Thus a slave man would not yearn for freedom, which was not a possibility, but a woman would. "What could be more personal than the fear of rape and captivity? . . . And what could more forcefully impress upon the individual consciousness the value of freedom than to be released from this condition?"[6] Patter-son speaks here of Homeric Greece, but his words about the import-ance of freedom to women because of the impact of slavery on them ring true for the Middle Ages too.

Stories of slaves in medieval literature do not stress the psycholog-ical impact of slavery on women, or their desire for freedom. In Anglo-Saxon literature the stories of captured slaves tend to be about men, even though the more typical victim of enslavement by capture was probably a woman.[7] The story of the enslavement of a woman would not allow authors the same play with notions of servility, humility, dominance, and inversion, since women's enslavement did not much change the sort of work they did, and they were already assumed to be submissive as women. In medieval Europe the symbolic power of the enslavement of women came from their sexual use rather than from the imposition of forced labor or other servile treatment.[8]

Slavery was different for women and men largely because women were more commonly exploited sexually as well as economically.[9] Both genders experienced a loss of rights, personal autonomy, honor, and kin. Women slaves, however, were far more likely than men to experience what we would consider rape (although in most legal systems master-slave intercourse was not treated as rape).[10] Given the sorts of marriage arrangements prevalent in ancient and medieval Europe, slavery was far from the only circumstance under which a woman might find herself having sexual intercourse with a man not of her own choosing. But marriage was considered an honorable arrangement for the woman as well as her family. The slave woman was dishonored as well as forced.

The majority of female slaves were probably not purchased primarily for sexual purposes, even though they may have been used in that way.[11] There are no statistics on total numbers of women slaves in medieval Europe, let alone their use, sexual or otherwise. In the case of people enslaved following a battle or raid, the majority could well have been women, as men would have been killed in the fighting. Individuals kidnapped and sold into slavery were not necessarily disproportionately female, but surplus family members sold into slavery by their kin probably would have been. The slave trade in the medieval Mediterranean comprised mostly women, because where slavery was primarily domestic, as in high medieval Italian towns, it was predominantly female.[12] In agricultural populations, where the prevalent form of unfree labor was serfdom rather than slavery, the ratio of men to women was often much higher, probably because females were less valued and subject to infanticide.[13] In both rural and urban European society, numbers of women slaves depended on the existence of demand for their labor and their availability at attractive prices, not in most cases on the presence of men rich enough to acquire multiple sex partners by purchase. Nevertheless, once purchased they were sexually available to their masters, in the case of slaves legally, in the case of serfs perhaps less so.

Desire is superficially the least problematic of the three reasons for the sexual exploitation of female slaves: one might assume that in a society where there were no restrictions on sexual object choice for a free man, men would have sex with anyone attractive and accessible, and slaves by definition are accessible to their masters. Social norms may restrict opportunity or object choice, as with the medieval church's disapproval of non-marital sex. In the Middle Ages, though, a double standard meant that men breached these norms with impunity. In those medieval societies where there were slaves, hardly an eyebrow would be raised if a man had sex with his female slave (and possibly not with his male one either).[14] In Anglo-Saxon penitential literature, for example, one finds penances for sex with one's female slave, but no worse, indeed in many cases much lighter, than for other types of fornication and adultery. Whether or not she consented made little difference.[15] Acculturated to take what he wished from the lower classes, a medieval master would have no reason not to use sexually any slave woman who appealed to him. Desire becomes both more problematic and more interesting historically, however, if we examine the social framework that channeled it in particular directions. It is too simple to say that in the absence of constraints people will have sex with anyone to whom they are attracted: both the nature of the constraints and the nature of the attraction are culturally conditioned. Desire can be both historicized and complicated by viewing it in the context of descendants and dominance.

Only in modern society is sexual desire completely separable from procreation.[16] It may have been to some extent separable in premodern times, at least for men, because of a simple lack of concern for the children they may have engendered, but anthropologists have tended to treat polycoity (where one man has sexual relations with a number of women) as primarily motivated by male wishes to maximize reproductive potential.[17] In any case, when the woman was the man's own slave he was forced to deal with the resulting offspring, even if only to decree that they be exposed. Nor, in a hierarchical, slaveowning society, could sexual liaisons across class lines be entirely separated from dominance; a man might be attracted to any woman but relative social position plays a role in attraction, and only if he was in a superior social position could he avail himself of her sexual services other than through marriage.

In some slave systems, the production of offspring is a primary function of female slaves. These are not necessarily the children of the master himself; they may simply be desirable as a cheap source of additional labor. Even where it is not the primary function of slave women, the production of children can be a distinct economic advantage.[18] Often, however, slave women are valued for their ability to provide heirs for the master. In Islamic law a slave woman who had borne a son to her master was freed after the master's death.[19] Slave women may have performed something of the same function in early medieval Europe, although in European law codes sons by slave women, although recognized, would generally not inherit unless there were no sons by the wife.[20] As the church, and under its influence secular law as well, came to prohibit inheritance by "illegitimate" children, this motivation for sexual exploitation of slaves lost importance.[21] Among working people, to whom inheritance did not matter so much, there might have been a greater advantage to having many sons, but those families would have owned few if any slaves.

Dominance, more than desire or descendants, was the most important factor in the sexual exploitation of slave women. By exercising his right to sexual relations with a slave, a free man could exert his power not only over the slave women involved, but also over the slave men whose women he was appropriating, the other free men with whom he might be competing for multiple sexual partners, and the free women whom he could threaten by preferring slave women to them. Sex as an assertion of power over subordinate women is hardly unique to slavery. It is an important issue, for example, in the current controversy over sexual harassment in the workplace. It was an important component too of hierarchical relations in the Middle Ages, when it was generally assumed that men of the upper classes would have sexual access to women of the lower.[22] That sexual exploitation of subordinate women is connected to the assertion of hierarchical power can clearly be seen in the myth of the *droit du seigneur* or *ius primae noctis*. As a formal custom, the lord's right of defloration of his female serfs probably never existed, and to derive inheritance customs or other legal relations from it is highly dubious.[23] In England, evidence for lords' sexual exploitation of their female serfs is surprisingly scanty.[24] Nevertheless the development of the myth of the *droit du seigneur* is a sign of the fear of this sort of seigneurial power and the way lords tried to make their power felt.

In the case of slaves, sexual use by masters was not only accepted but legal: in most slaveholding societies there was no mechanism to punish a master who used his slaves sexually. And in some slave societies it is clear that masters did so as a way of asserting authority over all slaves, humiliating men slaves who thought of themselves as married to the women slaves, punishing particular women slaves, and humiliating the masters' wives. It could also be used to assert one's place within the hierarchy of the master class. As one scholar of American slavery puts it, "Within the slaveowner's world, the sexual supremacy of dominant males subsumed the interests of all women and the men of the subordinate nation, race, or class."[25] In medieval Iceland, magnates accumulated female slaves, and controlled sexual access to them, as a mark of prestige and perhaps also as a way of rewarding their followers.[26] In Anglo-Saxon England, masters' control over their slave women operated in much the same way. Their monopoly over sexual access to those women was not simply a matter of protecting their rights to the slaves' labor and reproductive potential. In seventh-century Kent, the fines for having sex with someone else's slave varied not only according to the status of the slave but also according to the status of the master, indicating a significant honor or prestige component in the master's maintenance of control over the sexual activity of his slave.[27] Christine Fell discusses these provisions in a paragraph concerning "the protection of women against rape and seduction," but in the case of slaves it is clearly the master who is being protected.[28]

The use of slave women as a tool to assert control over slave men and superiority over other free men must be viewed in the wider context of gender relations. Men also asserted their dominance over women, for example, through marriage. Marriage had many other meanings and functions, notably the formation of an alliance between families, in which the woman was instrumental but personally irrelevant. One of the important functions of marriage, however, was the assertion of a particular man's control over a particular woman's sexuality. In many cases, as in early medieval Europe, he was purchasing this control. Even if the woman's family was also contributing a dowry, or he was giving her a morning-gift, the man had to make a payment to the woman's family, and the meaning of this payment was the acquisition of control over her reproductive potential.[29] Diane Hughes suggests that the morning-gift too represents "a man's formal claim to sexual rights over his wife — no longer purchased from her kin, but gained from the woman herself."[30] This control would be felt by the woman; she was the one married off to him, often without her opinion being considered (although women at some times and places in medieval Europe had more say than others).[31] But it was an assertion of control over the behavior of other men as well; they were the ones to whom a man signaled status by acquiring a prestigious wife and fathering a large number of children. Although slaves were less useful as breeders of children, sexual control over multiple women could still serve as an indicator of status in relation to other men.

In many cultures, men have exchanged women with men of other lineages in return for material goods. Unlike the case of slavery, where the price of a slave presumably bears some relation to her economic value to the purchaser, the price of a wife may be set by largely symbolic considerations. The transaction is considered a reciprocal exchange of gifts, rather than a purchase and sale. The exchange, however, is necessary in order to validate the marriage and to create the proper relationship between the two parties (the father and the husband, or the father's lineage and the husband's lineage). In addition, the fact of exchange establishes that the men doing the exchanging have rights over women that women do not have over either themselves or their male kin.[32]

If we analyze the marriage transaction as a purchase, what exactly is the husband buying? He is not buying the wife outright as property; he still possesses her in a different way from the way he possesses his slave. In Rome he had the power of life and death over his wife as he did over his slave, but he had the same power over his adult children; it was a result not of purchase, but of his patriarchal status. Certainly one of the things he purchased was control over her person and property; this can be clearly seen in the two types of Roman marriage, with and without *manus*, in the latter of which the woman's father or brother retained certain rights over her, or in the Lombard laws where bride-price purchased the *mundium*.[33] In Scandinavia, what a husband was in effect purchasing at marriage was the legitimacy of his children. For a marriage to be valid in early Iceland, a *mundr* had to be paid, and if it was not, the children were not able to inherit.[34] The children of a looser relationship, which could be termed concubinage, were at a disadvantage in terms of inheritance even before the church began to lay such stress on the notion of legitimacy. Only if the appropriate price had been paid was the relationship of the sort to produce heirs; it was as though only a properly purchased woman could be under strict enough control to guarantee the paternity of her children.

The evidence is not so clear for Anglo-Saxon England as to what exactly a man was purchasing at marriage. The laws of Æthelberht assumed a payment for a valid marriage. They did not specify to whom it was paid, but the implication is that it went to her relatives, who had to return it if she was returned to them: "Gif mon mægþ gebigeð, ceapi geceapod sy, gif hit unfacne is. Gif hit þonne facne is, ef þær æt ham gebrenge, ⁊ him man his scæt agefe." ("If a man buys a maiden, the bargain shall stand, if there is no dishonesty. If however there is dishonesty, she shall be taken back to her home, and the money shall be returned to him.")[35] The same laws also required that a payment be made to the *agende* of a young woman who has eloped, implying that the *agende* (which in other contexts may be translated as "owner") had some rights over her which were compensable in money.[36] The laws of Ine of Kent also presupposed a payment for marriage: "Gif mon wíf gebyccge" ("if a man buys a wife") and the marriage does not take place, the bride's guardian shall give back the payment and pay as much again ("agife þæt feoh ⁊ forgielde").[37] The laws of Cnut, in prohibiting a woman from being forced to marry someone whom she dislikes, or sold for money, indicate that women were in fact being sold in marriage by their kinsmen.[38] In one text on the proper method of betrothal, the payment to the family is referred to as a payment for rearing the woman (*fosterlean*), although there was also a payment directly to the woman and a grant of support if she should outlive him.[39]

The terminology of sale and payment used of marriage does not necessarily imply the same kind of purchase as would be understood with livestock, for example. In gnomic verse, Christine Fell argues, the phrase *cyning sceal mid ceape cwene gebicgan* should not be translated "a king shall buy a queen with property," because *bicgan* means "to pay for," and the man actually paid the morning-gift to the woman herself; similarly, *agende* does not necessarily imply ownership, simply responsibility.[40] To the extent that payment went to the woman rather than her family, this argues for a high status for women and against the notion of their being purchased. Although the payment may not be a bride-price, however, and in any case bride-price is very clearly different from the purchase price of a slave, it still remains true that a payment for the woman is considered a crucial step in the formation of marriage, and that one of the main things it acquired was sexual rights. After her marriage, the woman's husband collected the fine if another man had sex with her; for example in Æthelberht's laws a man who lay with another's wife had to pay his (or possibly the woman's) wergeld and provide another wife out of his own money, and in Alfred's he paid compensation to the husband.[41] In Alfred's Wessex a man also had the right to attack with impunity any man found in bed with his wife.[42] It is possible in the case of rape that the woman received the fine herself.[43]

The bride-price, then, like the slave price, represented the purchase of control over the woman's sexual behavior — prompted both by the wish to control her procreative capacity and the wish to monopolize her vis-à-vis other men as a way of asserting power over them. In both cases financial exchange was a symbolically important part. This similarity in the situation of wives and slaves suggests some comments upon the origins and function of merchet, the payment upon marriage of a villein in high medieval England, about which there has been a good deal of discussion.[44] Searle is no doubt right that it functioned largely as a fiscal measure for the lords. But it may also have had the symbolic meaning of the purchase of sexual control over the woman — not specifically buying out the lord's right to deflower her, since that never formally existed, but acquiring from the lord the rights to her over against other men. The use of demeaning language such as "ransom of blood" for merchet, which became the test par excellence of villein status,[45] could create an implication of the right of the lord over his villeins' bodies, and thus was a way for him to assert his power that struck home for both male and female villeins.

Men's sexual exploitation of women slaves in the early Middle Ages, which was among other things a mode of asserting dominance over other men, was one segment of a whole cultural system by which men exchanged women and used their control over those women's sexuality to assert their status vis-à-vis other men. Captors metaphorically emasculated the vanquished by taking their women; purchasers of slaves added to their prestige (and to the productivity of their household or estate) by accumulating slave women. Men could be dishonored by enslavement, and by owning them masters could exert control over them directly; but the ownership of slave women, because it fit into the whole system of masculine purchase of control over women's sexuality, was of greater ideological significance. This essay has spoken in very general terms and sketched only the broad outlines of trends; details of the system varied over time and place. Nevertheless the general relation held true and was an important one for northern European slaveholding societies.

Viewing the sexual exploitation of women slaves as part of the ideological significance of slavery, as well as part of the system of purchase of sexual control over women, may provide one clue to the shift away from slavery in England, and perhaps elsewhere in Europe as well. The explanations usually given for this shift are economic, and make good sense: for various reasons slavery was no longer profitable. However, the fact that the purchase of sexual control over women was no longer so important to men of the master class may also have played a role. Bride-price gave way to dowry by the twelfth century — about the same time slavery was ending.[46] Men no longer purchased sexual control over their wives, in part because the church's teaching on sexuality, which was becoming more codified and more thoroughly disseminated, guaranteed them that control without the need for a symbolic exchange.[47] The wider system of purchase of sexual rights over women, into which the sexual exploitation of slave women fit, was no longer in operation. This is not to say that where slaves still existed they were not exploited, nor to say that serfs were not similarly exploited. But the process may have lost much of its symbolic impact as the wider system of gender relations evolved.

NOTES

1. *Genesis A: A New Edition*, ed. A. N. Doane (Madison, 1978), ll. 1969–1971; trans. Christine Fell, *Women in Anglo-Saxon England* (London, 1984), p. 67.

2. For the best synthesis on the slave trade in the Middle Ages see William D. Phillips, Jr., *Slavery from Roman Times to the Early Transatlantic Trade* (Minneapolis, 1985).

3. On the gender division of labor in the Middle Ages, and the tasks of women slaves, see David Herlihy, *Opera Muliebria* (Philadelphia, 1990).

4. A list of all the studies of slavery in Europe and elsewhere that have ignored or underemphasized this aspect of the institution would be pointless, but it would surely include my own previous work: Ruth Mazo Karras, *Slavery and Society in Medieval Scandinavia* (New Haven, 1988). A recent exception, which has provided an important stimulus for this paper, is Orlando Patterson, *Freedom*, vol. 1, *Freedom in the Making of Western Culture* (New York, 1991), although it approaches the problem from another direction.

5. I will be drawing here on evidence from Anglo-Saxon England and Scandinavia. For detailed studies of slavery in these areas see David A. E. Pelteret, "Late Anglo-Saxon Slavery: An Interdisciplinary Approach to the Various Forms of Evidence," dissertation, Centre for Medieval Studies, University of Toronto, 1976; Pelteret, "Slavery in Anglo-Saxon England," in *The Anglo-Saxons: Synthesis and Achievement*, ed. J. Douglas Woods and David A. E. Pelteret (Waterloo, Ont., 1985), pp. 117–33; Karras, *Slavery and Society*. For France, Spain, and Italy, see Charles Verlinden, *L'Esclavage dans l'Europe médiévale*, 2 vols. (Bruges, 1955; Ghent, 1977).

6. Patterson, pp. 54–55.

7. See David A. E. Pelteret, "Slave Raiding and Slave Trading in Early England," *Anglo-Saxon England* 9 (1981): 102–105, for some examples, including both men and women.

8. This may have been much less true, for example, in American slavery, where enslavement often entailed doing a very different kind of work (plantation labor) than free women did, or in situations involving slave trade over long distances, where the salient feature for both male and female slaves would have been the uprooting from their home.

9. The ancient world provides plenty of examples of sexual use of male slaves, and there may have been medieval cases too, but it was certainly much less common than the sexual use of women slaves.

10. Male slaves were sexually exploited as well, notably in cultures like those of ancient Greece and Rome where to be the active partner in a homosexual relationship was no shame to an adult free man. See David Greenberg, *The Construction of Homosexuality* (Chicago, 1988), pp. 157–58; John Boswell, *Christianity, Homosexuality, and Social Tolerance* (Chicago 1980), pp. 77–78. This phenomenon was not as universal, however, as the sexual exploitation of women slaves.

11. On their use in the textile trade, and their sexual availability, see Herlihy, *Opera Muliebria*, p. 85; Susan Mosher Stuard, "Where Slavery Meets Gender," paper presented at the Medieval Academy of America meeting, Princeton, April 1991, discusses sexual use of women slaves not bought for that purpose.

12. See e.g. Susan Mosher Stuard, "To Town to Serve: Urban Domestic Slavery in Medieval Ragusa," in *Women and Work in Preindustrial Europe*, ed. Barbara Hanawalt (Bloomington, 1986), pp. 39–55. For statistics on the Mediterranean slave trade see Verlinden, vol. 2.

13. Emily Coleman, "Infanticide in the Early Middle Ages," in *Women in Medieval Society*, ed. Susan Mosher Stuard (Philadelphia, 1976), pp. 47–70, makes this

argument; see also Carol Clover, "The Politics of Scarcity: Notes on the Sex Ratio in Early Scandinavia," *Scandinavian Studies* 60 (1988): 147–88.

14. The focus of this paper is on women, and the sexual exploitation of male slaves was less significant at least quantitatively (besides having left no record) than that of female slaves. Nevertheless it is important not to lose sight of the possibility of a similar dynamic at work between masters and male slaves as between them and female slaves, although the degree of social acceptance may not have been the same. The angelic English boys Bede describes Gregory encountering on the Roman slave market might well have been understood as intended for sexual purposes. *Bede's Ecclesiastical History of the English People*, 2:1, ed. Bertram Colgrave and R. A. B. Mynors (Oxford, 1969), pp. 132–34; see Allen J. Frantzen, *Desire for Origins* (New Brunswick, 1990), p. 47, for the way sixteenth-century authors interpreted this passage. Boswell, *Christianity, Social Tolerance, and Homosexuality*, remains the standard on medieval attitudes towards sex between men.

15. Poenitentiale Theodori, 1:14:12, in F. W. H. Wasserschleben, *Die Bussordnungen der abendländischen Kirche* (Halle, 1851), p. 198 (six months' penance for having sex with one's own slave, compared to three years for adultery and a year for fornication with a virgin); Poenitentiale Bedae 3:15, in Wasserschleben, 222 (one year and three forty-day periods for sex with one's slave, compared to three years for adultery or repeated fornication and seven for deflowering a virgin [n.b. this penitential is wrongly attributed to Bede]). See also Robert Spindler, ed., *Das altenglische Bussbuch (sog. Confessionale Pseudo-Egberti)*, V.6.h–6.i (Leipzig, 1934), p. 177. I am indebted to Allen Frantzen for this reference as well as for others on slavery in the penitentials.

16. Although some would argue that masculine sexual behavior (notably seeking to maximize the number of sexual partners) is an adaptation for maximizing the number of offspring, most biologists recognize that the reason a behavior evolved is not necessarily the reason that people engage in it today. See Donald Symons, *The Evolution of Human Sexuality* (New York, 1979), for the evolutionary point of view. In modern Western society there are social and financial reasons why most men do not wish to maximize the number of their offspring, even if one were to concede that they have a genetic predisposition to behave in ways that (absent modern technology) have that effect.

17. Jack Goody, *Production and Reproduction: A Comparative Study of the Domestic Domain* (Cambridge, 1976), p. 42.

18. See Claire C. Robertson and Martin A. Klein, "Women's Importance in African Slave Systems," in *Women and Slavery in Africa*, ed. Robertson and Klein (Madison, 1983), pp. 5–11, for an argument that the reproductive functions of slaves have been overemphasized.

19. See further discussion of the role of reproduction in servitude in Ruth Mazo Karras, "Servitude and Sexuality in Medieval Iceland," in *From Sagas to Society*, ed. Gísli Pálsson (Enfield Lock, 1992), pp. 289–304.

20. Margaret Clunies Ross, "Concubinage in Anglo-Saxon England," *Past and Present* 108 (1985): 3–34, has argued that there was a major distinction in Anglo-Saxon England between sons of free concubines and those of slaves. She draws on Old Norse parallels to prove her case, however, and I have argued that in early medieval Scandinavia concubines were presumed to be slaves and that the children of a slave or free concubine both had the same rights upon specific action by their father and the agreement of his heirs. Ruth Mazo Karras, "Concubinage and Slavery in the Viking Age," *Scandinavian Studies* 62 (1990): 141–62.

21. See Jack Goody, *The Development of the Family and Marriage in Europe* (Cambridge, 1983), pp. 75–77, although I would disagree that "it was this crucial distinction between freeborn and slave-born that the Church changed into one between legitimate and illegitimate children."

22. To give just two literary examples of this general assumption: Andreas Capellanus suggests that if a man should fall in love with peasant women, "be careful to puff them up with lots of praise and then, when you find a convenient place, do not hesitate to take what you seek and to embrace them by force." Andreas Capellanus, *De Amore*, ed. E. Trojel, 2d ed. (Munich 1964), p. 236, trans. John Jay Parry (New York, 1941), p. 150. Although Andreas may be using satire to criticize this sort of behavior, it indicates the kind of access to which men of the upper class would feel themselves entitled. In the Miller's Tale Chaucer suggests that Alisoun is "a prymerole, a piggesnye,/For any lord to leggen in his bedde,/Or yet for any good yeman to wedde." *The Riverside Chaucer*, ed. Larry D. Benson (Boston 1987), p. 69, ll. 3268–70. She is an appropriate marriage partner for a yeoman, an appropriate sexual partner for someone of a higher rank; one reading of Chaucer's description might be that he finds this quite routine.

23. The best summary of scholarship on the subject is Wilhelm Schmidt-Bleibtreu, *Jus Primae Noctis im Widerstreit der Meinungen. Eine historische Untersuchung über das Herrenrecht der ersten Nacht* (Bonn 1988). See also W. D. Howarth, "'Droit du Seigneur': Fact or Fantasy," *Journal of European Studies* 1 (1971): 291–312.

24. Paul Hyams, the leading authority on English villeinage, has looked for such evidence and has not found it: "Chattel Ownership and Humans: Ideas of Servitude in Medieval England," paper delivered at the 27th International Congress on Medieval Studies, Kalamazoo, May 1992, a paper which very much stimulated my thinking on this topic. When Hyams' work on the subject is published it will greatly advance the discussion of some issues only touched on here.

25. Catherine Clinton, " 'Southern Dishonor': Flesh, Blood, Race, and Bondage," in *In Joy and Sorrow: Women, Family, and Marriage in the Victorian South, 1830–1900*, ed. Carol Bleser (New York, 1991), p. 55. For further discussion of this phenomenon in American slavery, where it has been best documented, see Jacqueline Jones, *Labor of Love, Labor of Sorrow: Black Women, Work, and the Family from Slavery to the Present* (New York, 1985), p. 28; Elizabeth Fox-Genovese, *Within the Plantation Household: Black and White Women of the Old South* (Chapel Hill, 1988), p. 297; Catherine Clinton, "Caught in the Web of the Big House: Women and Slavery," in *The Web of Southern Social Relations: Women, Family, and Education*, ed. Walter J. Fraser, Jr., R. Frank Saunders, Jr., and Jon L. Wakelyn (Athens, Ga., 1985), pp. 19–34.

26. Karras, "Servitude and Sexuality."

27. Æthelberht 10–11, 14, 16. All citations to law codes are from F. Liebermann, *Die Gesetze der Angelsachsen*, vol. 1 (Halle, 1903).

28. Fell, p. 62. As she points out, in the case of injury to a male slave the master also received the fine. She sees women slaves as being thus treated because they are slaves, not because they are women; see below for discussion of the situation with regard to free women.

29. See Diane Owen Hughes, "From Brideprice to Dowry in Mediterranean Europe," *Journal of Family History* 3 (1978): 265–96, on the various marriage payments among the Germanic peoples in Europe; see also David Herlihy, *Medieval Households* (Cambridge, Mass., 1985), pp. 73–74, 98–100. For a general theoretical discussion see Jack Goody and S. J. Tambiah, *Bridewealth and Dowry*, Cambridge Papers in Social Anthropology no. 7 (Cambridge, 1973).

30. Hughes, p. 276.

31. See Fell, p. 58; Clunies Ross, pp. 8–9; Jenny Jochens, "Consent in Marriage: Old Norse Law, Life, and Literature," *Scandinavian Studies* 58 (1986): 142–76. Although the church did make an effort from the twelfth-century on to guarantee the woman's right to refuse consent (see John T. Noonan, "Power to Choose," *Viator* 4 (1973): 419–34), it took a very strong-minded twelve-year-old indeed to refuse the bridegroom her family selected.

[27]

32. Gayle Rubin, "The Traffic in Women: Notes on the 'Political Economy' of Sex," in *Towards an Anthropology of Women*, ed. Rayna Reiter (New York, 1975), p. 177.

33. Sarah B. Pomeroy, *Goddesses, Whores, Wives, and Slaves: Women in Classical Antiquity* (New York, 1975), pp. 152–55; Hughes, p. 269.

34. Karras, "Concubinage and Slavery," pp. 144–45, 156.

35. Æthelberht 77, 77.1, trans. F. L. Attenborough, *The Laws of the Earliest English Kings* (Cambridge 1922), p. 15. Liebermann translates "ceapi geceapod sy" as "sei sie durch [Braut]kaufgeld [giltig] erkauft," which without his bracketed interpolations seems more precise than "the bargain shall stand." However, in either case it is clear that the payment validated the marriage.

36. Æthelberht 82.

37. Ine 31.

38. 2 Cnut 74 (although she got a morning-gift too: 2 Cnut 73a).

39. "Be wifmannes beweddunge," Liebermann 1:442.

40. Fell, pp. 16–17, 56–57; Gnomic Verses, ed. W.S. Mackie, *The Exeter Book*, part 2, Early English Text Society O.S. 194 (London 1934), p. 38, l. 81. Liebermann (1:8) glosses *agende* in Æthelberht 82 as "Eigenthümer [der Vormundschaft über sie]." Anne Klinck, "Anglo-Saxon Women and the Law," *Journal of Medieval History* 8 (1982): 109, argues that even if terms are translated so as to speak of guardianship rather than ownership, the fact that Anglo-Saxon language did not differentiate between the two is significant. I would agree with Fell that people would have understood a wife as being "owned" in a different way from a slave, but nevertheless there was some link.

41. Æthelberht 31 (it is unclear whose wergeld is to be paid: see Liebermann 2:9); Alfred 10.

42. Alfred 42.7. Compare 2 Cnut 53, in which an adulterous woman forfeits all her property to her husband, and her nose and ears are cut off; the husband no longer gets compensation from the lover. The woman is treated as a responsible party rather than as a possession.

43. Alfred 11.2: "Gif he mid gehæme, mid IX scill. gebete," which Liebermann glosses as "büsse er [ihr] mit 60 Schill." He suggests that this is in addition to a fine, arguing that in Alfred 25, for the rape of a slave a man pays five shillings to the owner plus a 60-shilling fine. However, even if the 60 shilling compensation here is in addition to a fine (or even if it went to the king), there is nothing to indicate that it went to the woman rather than her kin. Similarly in Alfred 26: if a girl not of age is raped, "sie ðæt swa ðæs gewintredan monnes bot"; there seems no warrant for Attenborough's translation (77), "the same compensation shall be paid *to her* as is paid to an adult" (italics added). In 2 Cnut 52.1, if anyone rapes an unmarried woman, "gebete þæt be were" ("let him compensate for that with wergeld"), but again it is not clear to whom.

44. Jean Scammell, "Freedom and Marriage in Medieval England," *Economic History Review* 27 (1974): 523–37; Eleanor Searle, "Freedom and Marriage in Medieval England: An Alternative Hypothesis," *Economic History Review* 29 (1976): 482–86; Jean Scammell, "Wife-Rents and Merchet," *Economic History Review* 29 (1976): 487–90; Eleanor Searle, "Seigneurial Control of Women's Marriage: The Antecedents and Function of Merchet in England," *Past and Present* 82 (1979): 3–43; Paul Hyams, Paul Brand, and Rosamond Faith, "Debate: Seigneurial Control of Women's Marriage," *Past and Present* 99 (1983): 123–48; Eleanor Searle, "A Rejoinder," *Past and Present* 99 (1983): 148–60.

45. Faith, p. 134; Hyams, "Chattel Ownership and Humans."

46. No firm date can be put on either one. Slavery per se seems to have declined rapidly in England after the Conquest; dowry (gifts *in maritagium*) was known by 1086 but became more common in the course of the twelfth and thirteenth

centuries. See Frederick Pollock and Frederic William Maitland, *The History of English Law Before the Time of Edward I*, vol. 2 (Cambridge, 1968), pp. 15–16.

47. Ironically, hot upon the heels of this development would come the monetization of the economy and the bringing into the cash nexus of all sorts of relationships that had not previously been there — including the widespread purchase of sex through prostitution, which functioned as a different sort of control of women. See Ruth Mazo Karras, *Common Women: Prostitution and Sexuality in Medieval England*, in progress.

3

Metaphorical Usage, Sexual Exploitation, and Divergence in the Old English Terminology for Male and Female Slaves

Elizabeth Stevens Girsch

Old English, like most languages spoken by slave-holding societies, had an extensive vocabulary expressing the notions central to the institution of servitude; and no student of historical semantics will find it surprising, given both the nature of language in general and the sweeping social changes that overtook medieval England, that the terms constituting this vocabulary underwent significant semantic change over the course of the Anglo-Saxon period. All the same, the development of the set of OE words signifying "slave" is remarkable: the particular changes that it undergoes suggest that an unusual combination of internal linguistic forces and external pressures on the lexicon acted to produce the realigned system that emerged on the threshold of Early Middle English (EME). The purpose of this paper is to explore those changes and, by pointing to some of the social realities that they appear to illuminate, to offer some possible explanations of the mechanisms that brought them about. Of special interest in regard to the mechanisms of change is the impact of metaphorical language; most striking overall, perhaps, is the divergent development of masculine and feminine terms.[1]

Early OE, as exemplified in the works of the Alfredian circle, the Lindisfarne and Rushworth Gospels, and a few other texts generally conceded to be contemporaneous with these, employed four principal terms to signify "a slave of unspecified gender" and "a male slave":

þeow(a), þræl, þegn, and esne. A fifth term, wealh, occurred far less frequently but becomes established in a significant role in later OE.[2] The same terms remain in later OE, as typified primarily by the writings of Ælfric, Wulfstan, and a few anonymous contemporaries, although all have undergone changes in usage. By the latter part of the transitional period, however, and in EME, as defined primarily by Layamon's Brut, the Katherine Group, the Bodley, Trinity, and Vespasian homily collections, and a few additional works ascribed to the late twelfth and early thirteenth centuries, the set of five terms has been reduced, essentially, to three: esne has dropped entirely from the language, and the survival of wealh is extremely dubious.[3]

The other three terms have more complicated fates, and summarizing them will necessitate anticipating in brief my discussion of their usage in OE. Through most of the period, þeow(a) was the primary word for "slave," regularly and clearly referring to persons in the legal condition of servitude in the Anglo-Saxon law codes as well as rendering the Latin term servus and somewhat less commonly translating famulus, mancipium, and empticio.[4] Þræl had been in the early period essentially confined to the Aldredian glosses on the Gospel, where it rendered servus; it re-emerged in the writings of Wulfstan but was still quite narrowly distributed, never appearing, for example, in the works of Ælfric, glosses on the Psalter, or the West-Saxon Gospels, all of which boast numerous occurrences of þeow(a). Þegn had signified "slave" in a rather restricted group of texts in early OE; other senses of the word had always predominated, and by the late OE period its uses as a slave-word are very rare indeed.[5] Thus up through late OE, þeow(a) occupied the central position in the vocabulary of servitude, overshadowing its remaining rivals, þegn and þræl, which are quite restricted in their use at this point.

The feature perhaps most significant in the development of these words as a group is their potential for various sorts of ambiguities. Þegn of course also means "retainer" or "king's liegeman, "nobleman," "warrior"; esne also means "hired workman, laborer, man"; and wealh also means "foreigner, Briton, Welshman." Simply put, each of these terms can equally well — and in the case of both þegn and wealh, probably more readily — refer to free men as well as to slaves.[6] Thus any instance of these terms may, in the absence of clarifying contextual elements, elicit the contradictory notions of free man and slave. The result is a lexically unstable situation.

The ambiguity of þeow(a) takes a different form. While the word lacks additional denotations, it appears regularly in metaphorical expressions like *þeow(a) godes*, the typical referents of which are saints, bishops, and people in the religious life. I will argue that this aspect of the word's usage, which grew increasingly prominent over the OE period, exerted a powerful influence on its sense — and indeed on the entire set of the vocabulary to which it belongs. *Þegn* and *esne*, in addition to the ambiguities afforded by their competing non-slave senses, shared the duality resulting from this metaphorical usage as well; *wealh*, although virtually never used metaphorically, retains the duality that it displayed in early Old English throughout the period, as the two uses of its ME reflex would indicate. *Þræl*, in contrast, never signifies free men or appears — with only two exceptions — in the metaphorical usages so typical of *þeow(a)* and *þegn*. Thus of all the terms it alone unambiguously and literally means "slave" from the early OE period into EME.

This semantic single-mindedness would appear to have paid off, for despite the term's always restricted distribution, *þræl* comes to supercede the vastly more common *þeow(a)* as the principal slave-word by the transitional period and stands, practically unchanged, as the group's sole survivor in Present-Day English (PDE). Although *þeow(a)* and *þegn* maintain a tenuous presence in the slave-vocabulary of EME, this apparent continuity in fact masks a break in their development, inasmuch as both had been undergoing a shift away from the sense "slave" before the transitional period, when the process halted and a sort of reversion to senses more common in the earlier period took place. Both disappeared, in any case, by late ME, apart from the specialized development of *thane* familiar to readers of *Macbeth*.[7]

Women of the Anglo-Saxon period having enjoyed equal opportunity, as it were, in the field of enforced servitude, OE possessed a full set of feminine slave-terms. Related semantically and morphologically to the grammatically masculine terms just enumerated, they co-existed alongside them from earliest OE on, also undergoing a series of changes during the period. The changes that they underwent differed strikingly, however, from those that affected their masculine counterparts, and I will argue that the different conditions under which male and female slaves lived were in part responsible for these divergent developments.

The principal terms signifying "female slave" included *þinen*, *þeowen*, *wyln*, and *mennen*, corresponding to *þegn*, *þeow*, *wealh*, and *mann*, respectively.[8] In the early period, *þinen*, *þeowen*, and *mennen* occurred, all serving as renderings of or glosses on a large number of Latin terms, among them *ancilla*, *serva*, *servula*, *famula*, *pedisequa*, *abra*, and *dula*, in contexts ranging from Biblical translations to glosses on the Silver Latin poets. Although the most common of the terms over-all, *þinen* appears slightly less frequently than *þeowen* and *mennen* in early texts and is entirely lacking in legal texts of all periods; by the time of Ælfric and Wulfstan, it has superceded both of these in most uses. *Mennen*, the favored term in legal usage, grows increasingly re-stricted from early OE on and is not to be found in either the Ælfrician or Wulfstanian canons; *þeowen*, though relatively common in Ælfrician saints' lives, is also lacking in Wulfstan. *Wyln* belongs exclusively to the late Old English period and even in that era is quite uncommon outside Ælfric's canon.

Wyln differs from its fellows not only in this aspect of its distribution but in another very significant one: the other three terms signifying "female slave" all find their way into metaphorical expressions parallel to the phrase *þeow godes* cited above, referring, like their masculine counterparts, to saints and holy women. The metaphorical usage of feminine terms, however, displays distinctive features that belie this seeming parallelism. The feminine terms, in fact, clearly develop somewhat independently of the masculine terms; most strik-ingly, all four disappear virtually without a trace by the end of the OE period.[9] Thus while *þræl* prevails over two other survivors from the masculine set, *þeow* and *þegn*, the feminine terms all go the way of *esne* — but not, I believe, by the same route.

As always in cases of lexical and semantic change, various explana-tions might account for developments in the OE slave vocabulary, and in this instance it would be as well to address at once the question of historical circumstances and their influence on the lexicon, since several would appear to bulk large in any hypothesis regarding the development of terminology for slaves. First, there is the disappear-ance of slavery as a legal entity and social institution in England, a process that must have affected the lexicon, to the extent that it re-duced the pool of potential referents of any term signifying "slave." According to Pelteret, the institution was in decline during the final years of the Anglo-Saxon period.[10] A gradual movement toward new forms of land-management and agricultural practice was nudging the slaves along toward the new status of *villeins*, while at the same time it was exerting a downward pressure on the small farmers and free laborers, who eventually merged with the freed slaves in a more loosely defined social group unified by common disadvantages: lim-ited mobility, highly restricted legal rights, heavy burdens of taxation, and, doubtless, justified but ineffectual resentment of the landholding nobility. Linguistic change often occurs when a word's referents undergo significant change of this sort, and such may have been the case here, although it must be clear that, whatever the actual conditions of their lives, in their legal position former slaves became less like the former referents of the surviving term *þræl*, rather than more. Such a circumstance would perhaps favor an alternative explanation for the realignment of the masculine terms. The same might be said for the total loss of the feminine terms, which would seem to suggest, improbably, some hitherto unobserved acceleration of the emancipation process for women. The decline of slavery as a feature of Anglo-Saxon society does not supply a sufficient or even entirely fitting explanation for the changes that occur in the terminology referring to slaves.

The second, more cataclysmic event of the period under consideration, the Norman Conquest, was itself largely responsible for that decline and for the institution of villeinage, a new system of land tenure affecting many who had borne the name of slave under the previous system. Its primary effects were not, of course, as history has shown, linguistic; yet the imposition of these new social structures undoubtedly produced lexical changes, and many new terms entered the language.[11] Traditionally, linguists observe that in such situations terms from the higher-status language tend to displace those from the lower-status language. Yet, as slave-terminology refers exclusively to persons and positions of low status, the native terms might well have struck the Normans as good enough for the natives.[12] Numerous terms do arise in the twelfth century to signify members of the newly-developed group of former slaves and former small farmers now serving as tenants on the great estates granted to fiefholders — *villein, churl, bonda, gebur, cottager*, and so on — but they are of diverse origins. The two important French loans, *servaunt* and *slave*, central as they are to the vocabulary of servitude and slavery in the later Middle Ages, enter the language well after the English terms that they might have displaced have disappeared; neither is certainly attested much before 1300.[13] Thus while no doubt the Conquest hastened and intensified some linguistic processes already occurring within this vocabulary, it could not have served as a major mechanism of change: neither the chronology nor the results quite fit.

What, then, accounts for the combination of lexical loss and semantic repositioning that a glance backward from the thirteenth century reveals? If these external factors are insufficient as the sole agents of change, they were perhaps more effective when they joined forces with internal linguistic pressures on the vocabulary of slavery — pressures which, I contend, the characteristic usage of these terms in OE produced. The ensuing linguistic responses to ambiguity, quasi-homo-nymic conflict, and, in the case of the feminine terms, a subtle form of semantic marking, I will argue, conditioned the development of the entire set of nouns signifying "slave."

Establishing the semantic features essentially associated with the notion of "slave" in OE, though imperative if the discussion is to pro-ceed, is fraught with practical difficulties and methodological pitfalls. The vocabulary to which the slave-terms belong contains more than a hundred terms occurring in more than 5,000 citations. Furthermore, the overlap between some of its terms and many very common words that share forms or senses complicates any treatment of it. The words themselves exhibit varying degrees of complexity, and all undergo changes over the course of the OE period. Obviously, this brief examination of a small subset of the terms cannot stand as a substitute for a full study of the whole.

More troublesome than any logistical difficulties, however, are the methodological problems, and in an effort to circumvent at least some of them, I have taken a subjective and non-technical approach. My in-tent is to clarify those features that must, under normal linguistic con-ditions, describe any referent of any of these terms.[14] To rephrase this in terms of PDE, we use the word "slave" when we wish to indicate, refer to, or label a person who matches the following description: he (or she) must be legally unfree and owned by another person; he must have little or no autonomy, he must be disenfranchised, or closed out of the social systems whereby free persons derive their status, and, finally, he must be in some way marked as a slave. I will use the ad-jective "humbled" to capture the sense of this final feature, but that is only a kind of abbreviation for a rather elusive concept. The feature may be manifest in physical signs like brands or shackles; it may be revealed in nothing more than the acknowledgement of slave status. If the person whom we intend to signify fails to match this description fairly closely, we do not call him or her a slave, at least if we are speak-ing factually and without metaphorical or ironic intent.

Although we cannot know how closely the Anglo-Saxon concept of the slave matched our own, I think we may assume a fair degree of overlap; that is, when speakers of OE employed one of these terms, they presumably referred to a person characterized by features much like these. One may evince the regular correspondence, in texts from all periods, between the Latin *servus* and these terms in contexts in-arguably requiring interpretation of the Latin word as "a person in the condition of involuntary servitude"; evidence from untranslated texts, however intuitively persuasive, is inevitably circular.

The semantic field covered by these terms extends from a notion of "slave" as a person minimally characterized by the features isolated above to its converse, that is, from a notion that would, in PDE, more naturally find expression in the word "servant" to its opposite, the despised and degraded "slave" who is barely accorded human status. Its crucial feature, however, is one so obvious that it might, if not pointed out, go unnoticed: it has no naturally positive realm. Literally understood, slavery is not a desirable condition. True slaves are unenviable persons — or even non-persons — and it is difficult to imagine circumstances in which anyone would gladly claim the label of slave for himself or bestow it upon someone else as a compliment. In literal use, terms signifying "slave" should carry neutral overtones at best, and one would expect many occurrences to bear strongly negative connotations, a circumstance which might be expected to color the set of terms as a whole. Certainly the development of positive connotations would seem unlikely, if not impossible. Yet this is precisely what occurred in one significant area of usage, the metaphorical, with enormous consequences.

To appreciate the effect of this phenomenon, however, one needs a sense of the literal usage of slave-terms. An example useful for its probable absence of polemical purpose or even self-consciousness is the following passage from Ælfric's *Grammar*, in which Ælfric offers a paradigm to illustrate forms of the possessive pronoun:

> *Meus seruus* min þeowa, *mei serui* mines þeowan, *meo seruo* minum þeowan, *meum seruum flagello* minne þeowan ic swinge; *o mi serue, ara bene* eala min þeowa, era wel; *a meo seruo monitus sum* fram minum þeowan ic eom gemyngod; ET PLURALITER *mei serui laborant* mine þeowan swincað, *meorum seruorum labor* minra þeowna geswinc, *meis seruis cibo do* minum þeowum ic sylle mettas, *meos seruos diligo* mine þeowan ic lufige, *a meis seruis ditatus sum* fram minum þeowum ic eom gewelgod. [AeGram 100.10–20].[15]

Although the illustration of the accusative case with *flagello* as its governing verb naturally strikes the modern reader most strongly, in all its elements, from the constant repetition of the possessive phrase *min þeowa* to the admonition to work well to the final claim of wealth conferred by the ownership of slaves, this passsage reinforces virtually every semantic feature associated with slavery. Even the illustration of the dative case by means of the verb *do* (*sylle*) in an expression of seeming beneficence serves to underline the dependence of the slave upon his master. The fact that it is Ælfric, furthermore, who is so casually invoking these negative implications lends weight to the assertion that the enumerated features are essential to the terms, for we generally accept him as a clear-headed, humane, and generally sympathetic figure who would hardly have served as or approved of an Anglo-Saxon Simon Legree.

Legal uses of the unmarked terms are often even more revealing; the law codes are replete with references to the slave as property, clear indications of the owners' power of life and death over these possessions, explicit mentions of the slave's lack of social rank and legal standing, and specifications of humiliating physical punishments for slaves guilty of various — and in some cases trivial — offenses. A citation from the statutes promulgated by King Ine shortly before 700 is illustrative:

> Ne þearf se frige mid þam þeowan mæg gieldan, buton he him wille fæhðe ofaceapian, ne se þeowa mid þy frigean [LawIne 74.2].

> (A freeman need not associate himself with a relative who is a slave, unless he wishes to ransom him from a vendetta; nor need a slave associate himself with a relative who is a freeman.)[16]

Despite some uncertainties of interpretation, several points are clear: first, that the condition of slavery may affect one member of a family and not another, a circumstance that implies the possibility of passing from servitude to freedom and the converse; second, that the loss of social status incurred by a person in entering the state of slavery is apparently so great as to outweigh the usually powerful obligations of kinship; and third, that the legal distinction between the free and the unfree manifested itself in day-to-day social relations. An immediately preceding law specifying the disposition of a *þeowwealh* who kills a free man makes the slave's unenviable position even clearer: his owner may, according to his whim, ransom the miscreant for a cash payment or hand him over to the kinsmen of his victim, who presumably will exact blood revenge.[17]

Several uses of *esne* in legal texts are equally informative; the first three decrees of Hlothhere and Eadric, two seventh-century Kentish kings, concern the *esne* who kills an *eorlcundne mannan* or a *frigne mannan.* In such cases his *agend* must, like the owner of the homicidal *þeowwealh* mentioned above, pay for damage done by his property and surrender the *esne* in compensation.[18] The laws of Wihtred, another early Kentish king, prescribe a fine for the *esne* who *ofer dryhtnes hæse* does *þeowweorc* on the Sabbath.[19] For more serious offenses committed by the *esne* or *þeow*, however, it is proclaimed, *gebete his hyd*; that is, "let him make amends with his hide" by being lashed — invariably a servile penalty.[20] In the early laws, clearly, the presentation of the *esne*, like that of the *þeow*, takes on quite unfavorable coloration. Such uses demonstrate the sort of negative associations that naturally accrue to nouns signifying "slave."

Yet even in the early period, and especially later, the more common usage of all the slave-words is typified not by the legal materials but by Scriptural, homiletic, and liturgical texts. Although these are, almost without exception, derived from Latin originals and thus reflect Latin-influenced usage of slave-words, it is useful to recall that these are also the sorts of materials most likely to have reached the ears of the ordinary speaker of OE, who, after all, probably seldom heard expounded the laws of earlier eras. The average Anglo-Saxon villager, indeed, although he may well have been familiar with standard legal terminology touching upon his own status and that of his neighbors, probably heard little formal legal discourse and still less literature. But he doubtless heard homilies and the Scriptural passages on which they were based, as well as the saints' legends recounted from the pulpit as exempla or inspiration and perhaps retold as local history or exotic entertainment. Directed at the common churchgoer, their language, accordingly, must have reflected — and helped to shape — the common lexicon.

In this group of texts, usage of the principal slave-words differs quite markedly from legal usage; a great many, dependent upon source texts, render Latin *servus*, and many or most refer to Biblical or historical, rather than contemporary, slavery. The distinction may scarcely matter in passages such as Ælfric's rendering of Genesis 30:43, which dilates upon God's favoring of Jacob:

> Iacob wæs þa swiðe welig, hæfde manega heorda & þeowas & þeowena, olfendas & assan [Gen 30.43].

> (Jacob was then very prosperous; he had many flocks and slaves, male and female, and camels and asses.)

Nothing here would seem out of place in a contemporary Anglo-Saxon account, apart from the camels. Perhaps that could not be said of

Alfred's Exodus-based specifications for the conferring of perpetual slave status by the piercing of the slave's ear with an awl.[21] But it is probably safe to say that slave-words in Biblical and historical contexts nonetheless evoked concepts essentially similar to those evoked by contemporary usage.

Greater in its significance, I think, is the frequent occurrence in these texts of the collocations *godes þeow(a)*, *cristes þeow(a)*, *cristes þegnas*, and the like. Such phrases refer, of course, to persons in a condition of metaphorical slavery; *þeow(a)* and *þegn* signify literal slaves relatively infrequently in the religious and homiletic materials, and even their literal referents are often the near-figurative slaves of gospel parables. *Esne* also frequently renders *servus* in Scriptural materials; most notably, it is Alfred's choice to express the Psalmist's self-referential *tuus servus*, a locution which recurs hundreds of times. *Þræl*, in contrast, is conspicuously lacking in collocations expressing metaphorical slavery; only two such locutions occur, and both are negatively charged — *þræl ... synnes* in a rendering of Jesus's admonition regarding the imprisoning effects of sin and, in the later period, *antecristes þrælas* in a Wulfstanian homily.[22]

The character of these metaphorical applications of slave-terms is various, but most display a feature evident in the citation below:

> Nu, Petrus, us syndon to sceawienne niwe campas & gewin þæs ealdan feondes ongæn þone Godes þeow, on þam he gebrohte his willum manige gefeoht, ac swa þeh genyded he gedyde bigias & fleam fore þæs halgan mannes sigore [GD 2(C) 8.122.21].

> (Now, Peter, are to be shown to us new battles and strife of the old fiend against that *Godes þeow*, on whom he brought many a fight by his will; but nevertheless, bowed, he [made obeisance and took] flight in the face of the holy man's victory.)

It should be immediately apparent that the connotations attached to the phrase *godes þeow* can hardly have been negative; no lowly, subservient wretch, this saint is a champion, a victorious combatant against mankind's enemy, the devil. Although the martial imagery in this passage is a little more extreme than usual, the basic presentation is not uncommon; in many cases the phrase *Godes þeow*, referring to a saint or martyr, is varied within a few lines by *godes cempa* or similar locutions.[23] The submissiveness and passivity that should mark a slave are entirely absent in these and many other cases. There can be no doubt, I think, that the attributes of a good *þeow godes* overlap with those of a good *mennisc þeow* only minimally, a point which must affect the connotations of the term. *Þegn*, which often replaces *þeow* in these phrases, is even more susceptible, given its pre-existent associations with the military.

Another common collocation, *cyninges þegn*, also contributes to this ameliorative process. In non-religious materials, such as the Chronicle and vernacular charters, especially, it is by far the most common use of the term *þegn*. This pattern, which persists for much of the OE period, reinforces the positive connotations that accrue to the word in its non-slave senses. Thus when in religious texts a parallel usage of *þegn* develops early in this period, the resonance of the secular phrase may affect it. In, for example, the *Martyrology*, *þegn* occurs almost exclusively in the phrase *Cristes þegnas*, the referent of which is the twelve disciples or apostles — and the connotations of which must be positive. In combination with an increasingly frequent use of *þegn* to render Latin *minister* in translations of Scripture, both Old and New Testament, this usage no doubt discouraged the use of *þegn* to signify "slave," which had grown rather limited as the word's other senses gained greater prominence and naturally grew even more so as the phrases in which it tended to occur developed positive connotations unsuited for a term signifying "slave."

The features associated with the concept "slave" are, as enumerated above, the lack of freedom, autonomy, and social status, the state of being possessed by someone else, and the manifestation of slave status through some form of humbling. It quickly becomes obvious that in metaphorical application of slave-words, these features are all thoroughly undercut: their typical referents are well-born, well-regarded, and often themselves masters of households and religious houses or even warriors and kings. In short, *þeow* in *Godes þeow* is too much at odds with the defining features of the concept "slave" to signify "slave." The collocation has a sense — the terminology of slavery remains so interwoven with theological language that even now we can comfortably render it "servant of God" — but the features that describe it are altogether unlike those that characterize the literal slave.

The central concept mediating between the literal and the metaphorical is of course the notion of submission, of subjugation of the self to another. Yet it is rare for that aspect of metaphorical servitude to receive much emphasis except in conventional and pious descriptions of saints; equally common or perhaps more so, and certainly more memorable, are descriptions of the martyrs' proud defiance in the face of emperors, their stern admonitions to their persecutors and the like. It is true that the ideal *þeow godes* is blessed with complete absence of self-will, and his meekness is praised as a virtue. But what Anglo-Saxon, hearing St. Andrew termed *godes þeow*, would immediately focus on that saint's submission to God's will rather than on his warrior-like defeat and subsequent conversion of the Anthropophagi?

Many saints and holy men are presented as strong, bold, even arrogant — at least in their defense of the Faith and their fellow-Christians — and a still larger number as free-born or even of noble family. Many act decisively and authoritatively, and sometimes on their own behalf, in the face of threats or danger; and even those who ultimately lose their lives do so with positive enthusiasm. If they are humbled, it is by choice; their persecutors are never able — despite often lavishly depicted attempts — to impose humility upon them. The inherent contradictions are striking, even given the nature of metaphor: the features called up by these sorts of portrayals cannot readily be grafted onto the features characterizing the notion "slave." The locution *godes þeow* becomes virtually self-contradicting, and the effect on the term in isolation is, I think, to undermine its ordinary denotation. [24]

Other ambiguities built into the usage are slightly subtler. It is probably apparent that metaphorically-used slave-terminology most commonly appears in the form of noun-plus-genitive phrases such as *godes þeow*, which parallel, at least on the surface, such typical locutions as *folcesmannes esne* and the like.[25] Yet the two differ sharply. One of the principal features of the slave is his status as property; it is reinforced again and again by these genitive constructions and by modification with possessive pronouns. As long as the referent is understood as property, the relationship between slave-term and governing word is clear; how, though, is one to analyze *godes þeow*? The ascription of literal ownership is impossible. I suggest that the common collocation *cyninges þegn*, by way of the phrase *godes þegn*, provided the model for an unconscious analysis as "a *þeow* who has sworn allegiance to God" — with the concomitant shift in connotation from "possession" to "associate, liegeman."

The notion of "association" calls up another point: to the Anglo-Saxon mind, I think, the concept of a God surrounded by slaves would have seemed vaguely Oriental, decadent, or unbecoming. His model for lord and liegemen, however romantically removed from the everyday life of the ordinary agricultural laborer or villager, would surely have been the *comitatus*. A shift from "God's servant" to "God's liegeman" would thus have been natural in the case of *godes þeow*; it would have been even likelier, I think, in the case of the familiar collocation *cristes þegnas*, referring to the Apostles. Even if in origin the phrase was to be understood "Christ's servants," it would quite naturally have gravitated toward an interpretation as "Christ's comitatus," particularly given their eagerness to die in his name, if not in his defense.

The elusive feature of markedness, or of being humbled, might be mentioned in this same connection; I have already noted the near-arrogance of some persons termed *godes þeowa*, and it is clear that those termed *cristes þegnas*, too, are not to be confused with those whose status subjugated them to earthly masters. A subtler manifestation of this feature's undercutting is to be found in the frequent instances of self-identification: saints, bishops, popes, and martyrs, from the Venerable Bede to Gregory the Great, regularly announce *ic eom þeow godes*. There are dozens of occurrences of this utterance or equivalent ones; in contrast, there are but a handful of instances in which real slaves claim the name of slave.[26] Of course, because it is uncommon for real slaves to have speaking roles in OE stories, the paucity of such statements is not altogether surprising; even so, the alacrity with which those who in reality sported mitres or the tonsure rather than brands or chains embraced the title of slave seems noteworthy. It cannot, whatever the intent of the speaker who so identified himself, have evoked in the hearer the sense of superiority that he might have felt regarding someone truly beneath him in rank and status. Instead, it must have seemed a legitimately prideful claim — martyrdom and sainthood were, after all, noble endeavors, and these were the designated and approved hero-substitutes for the pagan heroes of Germanic legend who spoke of themselves thus. Such a usage, especially common in the narratives of saints' lives that to a great extent served as popular literature, cannot but have contributed to the weakening of the literal sense of *þeow*.

Developments in the use of the term *þegn*, which frequently alternated with *þeow*, also contributed to this process. *Þegn*, in divesting itself of the sense "slave," as it had done almost completely by the late OE period, had lost its only consistently pejorative, or potentially pejorative, use. Meanwhile, its long-standing use as "man of a rank between *ceorl* and *eorl*" was being upgraded to "nobleman, princeling," and the like in Ælfric's and Wulfstan's lexicons.[27] The long-standing and already positive sense as "king's attendant, royal retainer" may have profited by the positive development of *cristes þegnas* as "the

Apostles" that it had itself encouraged and, less significantly, by the word's frequent use as "minister" in contexts implying close association with people at the top of the ecclesiastical or civil hierarchy. Taken together, the effect on *þegn* might well have been a virtually complete separation between these more prominent and more positive senses and the possibly almost archaic-seeming sense of "slave." Thus the collocation *godes þegn* might have begun to approach the status of *Godes cempa* rather than merely that of an alternate locution signifying a metaphorical slave as *þegn* underwent this amelioration. It would have been natural to supply the positive senses in the context of a phrase like *godes þegn*, and if such a phrase then varied *godes þeow*, both, presumably, would profit from the amelioration, a further assault on the literal sense of *þeow*.

If one accepts the premise that the metaphorical usage of *þeow* undermined the term's ability to evoke the characteristic features of the slave and that this, in combination with ameliorative pressure from *þegn*, might have produced a blurring of the word's original sense and a conflict with its ameliorated secondary sense, one can then see how the rest of the system might in turn have been affected. Conventional linguistic wisdom dictates that languages resist excessive ambiguity. In the system of unmarked terms there would have existed, by the late OE period, a complex of ambiguities: the positive and negative senses of *þegn* in quasi-homonymic conflict, both *esne* and *wealh* capable of signifying either slaves or freemen, and *þeow* used repeatedly and regularly — even occasionally without modification — to refer to persons who unambiguously were not slaves. Only *þræl* was, and had consistently been, essentially free of ambiguity of any sort. Thus *þeow*, under pressure from *þegn* and the amelioration of its metaphorical senses, lost its position as the principal unmarked term expressing the concept "slave." Neither *wealh* nor *esne*, both of which had their own ambiguities, could fill the partial void left by the shift of *þeow* toward the purely metaphorical realm. Nor could *þegn*, which had essentially lost its sense as "slave" through the replacement of it in some of the term's most common uses by a notion akin to "associate." Only *þræl*, which had consistently been applied to literal slaves since its entry into the language, could readily absorb the uses for which *þeow* no longer seemed suitable. It may have been unconsciously felt to be particularly suited to the essentially negative concept "slave" because of its associations with the Danes and all that they represented. In any case, it prevailed and, alone of all these terms, endured, even becoming productive of derivatives such as *þraldom*.

As dangerous as it is to speculate on the mental furniture of the average OE speaker, it is probably safe to say that the effect of this primarily religious language was no doubt intensified by the complex, theologically based ambivalence toward slavery common to the western medieval world. Medieval Englishmen, clergy and lay, believed that slavery was divinely ordained and, as a consequence of original sin, part of the human condition; as Ælfric remarks, God grants that it is some men's lot to be born sons of slaves, others' to be born sons of queens.[28] Ælfric would have asserted, furthermore — despite the apparent sympathy he displays in the "ploughman" section of his *Colloquy* — that earthly slavery is illusory, that only servitude to sin is real, and that voluntary enslavement of the self in Christian service is perfect freedom; at least, as an orthodox churchman he must have accepted these premises, because they were based in Scripture, especially John 8:34, taught by the Fathers, and incorporated into the doctrine of the Church.[29]

Ordinary people would have heard these same propositions preached in sermons like the ones cited above; and if their notion of slavery was based on their own experience and observation, it is still perhaps true that they might have absorbed something of this paradoxical construct, this reversal of the ordinary notions of slavery and freedom. The full effects on their conceptualization of the institution and the degree to which the theological position might have seemed a justification for injustice are unknowable. Whether they would have perceived — or appreciated it, if they did — an attempt at humility on the part of those who adopted the terminology of slavery to name themselves and others who had undertaken the religious life is impossible to determine. But it is certain that the notion of "slave" called up in reference to archangels, patriarchs, bishops, or warrior saints cannot have been precisely that evoked by reference to dung-bedaubed fellow laborers, or even the children of Israel groaning beneath the whips of the Egyptians. And it seems to me equally certain that the employment of the same terms to name all of these cannot but have affected the perception of those terms, particularly in combination with the other ambiguities characteristic of their use.

But a set of forces even subtler in their manifestation acted upon the ostensibly parallel set of feminine terms. These words, despite their occurrence in similar constructions and contexts, do not undergo blurring of sense. Nor do they display the duality that is so prominent a feature in the set of unmarked terms: that is, while a *þegn* may be a nobleman, an *esne* a free laborer, a *mann* any male of any degree, and a *wealh* a Welshman, for better or worse, no *þinen*, *þeowen*, *mennen*, or *wyln* is ever, except in metaphorical applications, anything other than a female person in the condition of servitude.[30] Even in metaphorical applications, the terms frequently appear in conjunction with contextual elements emphasizing humility and passivity — sometimes seemingly gratuitously; a conventional introduction of a women's name in a charter shows the tendency at work in an environment probably quite untouched by stylistic concerns, reading *ic Luba eadmod godes ðiwen* (I, Luba, humble *þeowen* of God).[31] Even more strikingly, the repeated rendering of the verse *quia respexit humilitatem ancillae sue* from the Canticles of the Psalter is the most typical use of the feminine terms in reference to the Virgin Mary. The importance of this circumstance is not, I think, to be underestimated.

It is perhaps appropriate to begin, however, by taking up briefly the question of the feminine terms' status in relation to that of the unmarked terms. Modern usage provides a model for comparison of unmarked and feminine terms that, while useful, may also be misleading if applied too rigorously to earlier stages of the language. It has often been observed that in such pairings the feminine term carries overtones ranging from the mildly to the strongly pejorative; familiar examples include *poet—poetess*, *sculptor—sculptress*, *author—authoress*, and *waiter — waitress*. The argument regarding these terms, at least those with agentive force, has traditionally been that the marking implies a violation of the natural expectation and thus a presumption that the marked member of the pair will exhibit some inferiority in the activity indicated by the term. In other words, an authoress is expected to write less well than an author, inasmuch as it is surprising for her to write at all.[32]

One might assume that the feminine slave-terms exhibited the same tendency, and yet, one might ask, if the crucial factor in pejoration is naturalness and the violation of the natural expectation, what could be more natural — in early England, of course — than for women to be servile? If the terms are in fact more pejorative than the corresponding unmarked terms, the explanation must lie elsewhere. But I am not entirely certain that they are. I think that the unmarked terms may actually bear stronger negative connotations than the feminine terms, at least on the surface.

First, the attributes that the terms evoke are not so far removed from those associated with any woman, whether enslaved or free. For a man to be owned, deprived of his autonomy, unable to seek legal redress for wrongs done him, or deprived of his dignity would have been a degradation; to impose those conditions on him, a humiliating and in some sense unnatural act. For a woman, the set of conditions defining servitude would have been not altogether removed from the existence she might expect as a free woman — the property of her father until he gave her to a husband, largely without autonomy except in trivial affairs, without legal standing in many or even most situations, and almost certainly required to display, and probably impelled to feel, humility. Thus, paradoxically, the feminine terms might be genuinely less pejorative as applied to their referents than the unmarked terms, but as a group they would still indicate persons of low status and thus occupy the more negative regions of the semantic field.[33]

The metaphorical uses might seem to constitute an exception, since the Virgin Mary and female saints are, after all, persons of very high status and serve as the referents of these terms on numerous occasions. While it is true that the feminine terms are capable of signifying very well-regarded women, even their metaphorical uses are less susceptible to amelioration by this means than are their unmarked counterparts: the difference between the two may lie in the extent to which the metaphorical application negates the attributes of the slave attached to the term in its literal use. As I noted above, many contexts in which feminine terms in metaphorical use appear emphasize the submissiveness and humility of their referents. Of course this contextual emphasis is not confined to the feminine terms, but these traits appear more consistently as elements in the presentation of female metaphorical slaves than in those of males, and the degree to which their referents seem to throw off the mantle of slavery in their adoption of the label is consistently less pronounced. The *þeowen godes*, though she is often well-born and may defy persecutors or withstand attacks of fiends, less often resembles a medieval Wonder Woman than she does a menaced innocent, with Christ as her rescuing hero.

The image of the menaced innocence, furthermore, embodies the feature that may be most powerfully, if subtly, affecting the connotations of these terms; the implication of the fate that the *þeowen godes* often barely escapes is generally quite clear. A strikingly high percentage of the marked terms, in both literal and metaphorical use, occur in contexts that draw attention not just to their referents' sex but, explicitly or implicitly, to their sexuality. In the end, this tendency may be among the most significant determinants of the terms' overall usage, their development, and perhaps even their ultimate disappearance. These terms, I believe, are marked for sexual availability rather than merely for sex in the sense of gender, and this marking is a primary reason for their negative value.

In a sense, such an underscoring of sexuality is hardly surprising; as Ruth Mazo Karras points out elsewhere in this volume, vulnerability to sexual exploitation was an unfortunate fact of life for the female slave.[34] Yet in another respect it is unexpected because it occurs not just in the obvious settings — the laws dealing with the rape of slave-women, the penitentials in which penalties are mandated for cohabitation with one's slave, and so on. In these cases the reference to the sexuality of the female slave is overt, and so is the tacit recognition of her victimization on account of it. But there are subtler instances that imply a deeper and less conscious awareness that the *þeowen*, the *wyln*, the *mennen*, or, to a somewhat lesser extent, the *þinen*, was a sexual being — and endangered by the potential for sexual subjugation thereby implied.

As an example, one may take the case of St. Agatha, who in Ælfric's account attracts the lustful attention of the Emperor. He commissions the wicked Aphrodisia and her nine whorish daughters to corrupt the saint; failing in the attempt, they complain of her steadfast virtue to the Emperor, who summons her and demands to know why, if she is *æþelboren* as she asserts, she demeans herself by behaving as though she were a *wyln*. By this he presumably refers to her rejection of the earthly rank that he offers her and her expressed desire to suffer *for cristes naman ða cwealm-bæran wita* rather than enjoy the voluptuous pleasures that he can provide. Her response to this characterization is the claim *ic eom godes þinen*, whereupon the rebuffed Emperor begins to rail at Agatha, now termed *cristes mædene*; the rest of the narrative follows the usual course, through attempted humiliation, torture, and death.[35] The saint triumphs, of course, through her glorious martyrdom, but I think that her earlier victory is not to be discounted; she transforms the potential label of forced concubine into an equivalent to *cristes mæden*, "virgin of Christ," turning away the sexual threat.

In many of the lives of female saints similar situations present themselves. St. Lucy, having identified herself as *þæs ælmihtigan þinen*, is immediately threatened with sexual violation by the vicious Paschasius.[36] St. Margaret catches the attention of the wicked Olibrius, who inquires whether she is *þeow*, in which case, he says, *ic sylle feoh for hire & heo biþ me for cyfese* (I shall give money for her and she will be as a concubine to me.)[37] Once again, though, it quickly becomes apparent that while she will not be his *þeowen* she already is God's; she identifies herself in subsequent prayers as *þinre þeowen*, driving the spurned Olibrius to destructive fury.[38]

Similar passages abound, but perhaps equally interesting are cases in

which the metaphorical expressions refer not to holy virgins but to females who came to sainthood after a walk on the wild side. Among
these, St. Pelagia is explicit; referring to herself as *deofles þinen*, she ad-
mits to having been filled with lust.[39] The notorious penitent St. Mary
of Egypt is hailed by St. Zosimus as *þu Godes þeowen* in a passage that
may hint at her checkered past; in any case, the designation of the former
courtesan as *þeowen godes* forges another link between the two notions. [40]

I do not mean to imply that the metaphorical expressions used to
signify female saints evoked specifically sexual images; I merely wish
to point out that the potential victimization or former exploitation of
these holy women is often emphasized in the neighborhood of expressions conjoining them, as it were, with literal female slaves, who
clearly did suffer indignities of this sort, if the evidence of the laws and
penitentials is to be trusted.[41] It is worth observing that a high percentage of the feminine slave-words in the Old Testament refer to female
slaves who were given to husbands of infertile women as concubines
and that the predominant use of such terms in the psalms is in renderings of the phrase *filius ancillae tuae*, emphasizing indirectly the sexuality or at least the procreative function of the *ancilla*. And perhaps it is
significant as well that even the repeated rendering of Mary's response
to Gabriel contains hints of the same; when she speaks these words —
in one of Ælfric's several versions, *Ic eom godes þinen: getimie me æfter
þinum worde* (I am God's *þinen*; deal with me according to thy word) —
she is expressing submissiveness to the will of God, but, more to the
point, she is also being impregnated.[42]

The association between the names for female slaves and the sexual
submissiveness imposed upon them by their state would certainly
have remained below the surface, but it might still have helped to
doom these terms. The decorous Ælfric, who occasionally interrupts a
lurid saint's legend to chide his flock for their prurience, may have
been sufficiently aware of it that he preferred not to employ *mennen*,
the term most commonly found in specific statutes dealing with sexual
abuse of slave-women, and to restrict his use of *þeowen* fairly sharply;
whereas he employs the phrase *godes þeow(a)* dozens of times to refer
generally to men in the religious life, he virtually never employs the
phrase that would be the feminine equivalent.[43]

Ælfric's implicit characterization of the *wyln*, his preferred term for
the literal female slave, which is provided by his paradigm for *mea
ancilla*, dwells upon her role as a worker, omitting a phrase that he
used in a parallel paradigm employing *þeow(a)*: *meos seruos diligo*, or
mine þeowan ic lufige.[44] Since he virtually coined the term, or at least

resurrected it from obscurity, he could be certain that it carried very little baggage, and it seems that he might have extended it to metaphorical applications. Yet he does not; there is no *wyln godes*. This may be because the term is thoroughly literal. God would not, in Ælfric's theology, have desired or needed slaves — though he seems to have had liegemen in his *þeowas* and *þegnas*, a company from which females would almost certainly have been excluded as a matter of course in Anglo-Saxon England. Thus if *mennen* and *þeowen* bore the taint of sexual suggestion and *wyln* the mantle of literal slavery incapable of amelioration through the means available to the masculine terms, it is reasonable that none of these terms would have been suited to name nuns and consecrated virgins.

For Ælfric, at least, the role of the true female slave is to be *nytwyrthe*, as he admonishes his *wyln*, while the role of the metaphorical slave is to remain pure; *Godes mægden* is a common epithet for his female saints. He appears most comfortable with the terms least cumbered by overtones of sexual availability, which may explain his use of *þinen* to refer to the Virgin Mary when his sources required a rendering of *ancilla*: of all of the terms, it alone seems never to have been applied to literal, contemporary females in the unhappy condition of enforced servitude.[45] And Wulfstan's well-known propriety appears to have effected even more severe restraints on his usage; no feminine slave terms appear in his works at all.

But whether through the sensitivities of late OE writers or not, the terms all fell out of use in the late OE period, and I think it possible that associations with sexual servility could have helped to precipitate their loss by another means. The changing conditions may have meant little real change for many women; the passage from statutory servitude to statutory freedom was probably neither as dramatic nor perhaps even as welcome for them as it was for men, for whom the greater insecurities of this new status were offset, presumably, by their release from the stigma of servility. But in one respect freed female slaves were certainly better off: they were no longer so readily subject to forced concubinage. Furthermore, rape of free women was much more costly than rape of slaves, and the financial disincentive to commit rape — in addition to the greater freedom of the husband or father to take action against the attacker — would doubtless have served as a minor guarantee of greater safety. Genuinely less subject to exploitation in that regard, then, perhaps they no longer so readily wore the names that had connoted their involuntary sexual availability. It is even possible that they themselves would have sought to shake off those terms; and in that effort they might have been encouraged by their husbands and male kinsman, who surely would have been no more enthusiastic about having their womenfolk labeled as available than contemporary men would. In this endeavour, furthermore, both the affected women and their male defenders could well have had the support of the homilists, whose propriety — and probable influence on the language — I have already mentioned.

But the minor change in the real-life situation of the freed female slave brings into focus another interesting feature of these terms: the doubly paradoxical nature of metaphorical servitude for women. I have noted above that paradox was built into the adoption of slave-words to name male saints, bishops, and the like: voluntary enslavement of the self to God was perfect freedom. In a sense, that may have been true, but more metaphorically than literally; a man who entered the religious life and made vows of poverty, chastity, and obedience gave up some freedoms even as he gained spiritual emancipation. An ordinary slave given the choice between literal freedom and the religious life would probably have opted for the former. For women, however, this religious servitude may well have constituted a greater freedom than literal freedom from literal slavery did. In the secular world, a free woman might expect to be in the power of a man for most or all of her life. Childbearing and childrearing would have occupied much of her time and energy, whether she had sought them or not. Unless she were in the rare and fortunate position of having inherited property, she probably had little power to change her circumstances, and she may well have felt the sting of her own powerlessness.

The religious life offered her an alternative to this servitude: free of the control of father and husband, released from the burdens of bearing and raising children, ensconced in a community of self-governing women, she might well have felt herself to be freer than her sisters in the secular world. The surprising infrequency with which slave-terms signify women in the religious life in general may arise in part from this circumstance. At some level, people sensitive to language may have perceived that this locution, primarily found paired with the corresponding masculine term, was doubly incongruous, not just because of possible sexual associations but also because it defied both literal and conventional metaphoric sense in a way that its masculine equivalent did not: social realities made voluntary religious servitude, for many women, freer than ostensible freedom.

Such circumstances and tenuous hypotheses cannot fully explain the loss of these terms; perhaps simpler linguistic explanations might be adduced. The feminine terms, always without the duality of the male terms, certainly might have lacked the flexibility to accommodate new referents in the form of newly-freed female slaves. With the loss of grammatical gender, the surviving *þeu(e* and *þral* were able to serve for both men and women, and eventually *servant* arose, along with its derivatives. *Wench*, too, came into existence, shortened from the ME reflex of *wencel* "child," which had occasionally served in OE as a slave-term as well. Its subsequent development hints at the persistence of certain attitudes with regard to females in servile positions, but the terminology of the later ME period is beyond the scope of this essay.

A few facts do emerge from the foregoing discussion of developments within the system of slave-terminology, however elusive the subject and however speculative its treatment must be. Some of the terms persisted while some were lost; some genuinely appear to have undergone alterations in their customary application or semantic range. Anglo-Saxon slavery did die out in the later OE and transitional period, and a new system of land tenure did arise. The Normans conquered England, bringing new forms of social organization and imposing their language, with its inbuilt attitudes, on the substrate of OE, with all that such an imposition implies. In this paper I have offered a means of fitting all those phenomena together in a focus on the words naming a little-studied group of Anglo-Saxons caught up in those changes and suggested ways in which those changes can be seen in the words themselves. Perhaps it will also serve as a starting point for further investigations into the vast and potentially rich vocabulary of slavery in OE.

NOTES

1. This essay is based on a much longer study still in progress. Because of constraints of space, a great deal had to be excluded, in particular, many of the citations. The reader may refer to the evidence in the *Microfiche Concordance to Old English*; short titles refer to *A Microfiche Concordance of Old English: The List of Texts and Editions*, eds. Antonette diPaolo Healey and Richard L. Venezky (Toronto, 1980). I would like to thank Douglas Moffat for his extremely helpful suggestions regarding the final form of this paper and much useful criticism at every stage.

2. *Þeow(a)* stands for the grammatically strong masculine *þeow* and the weak masculine *þeowa*. No semantic distinction appears to exist between the two; they occur in free variation with one another. A few additional terms, most with only a few attestations, also occur but had to be excluded from this study because of constraints of space. For some of these, see David A. E. Pelteret, "Late Anglo-Saxon Slavery," unpublished dissertation (University of Toronto, 1976), especially pp. 398–495, "Appendix One: The Old English Terminology of Servitude and Freedom." The present study owes a great deal to Pelteret's trailblazing.

3. A single occurrence of a form *waelh* in the *Brut* almost certainly means "slave," since it appears in coordination with *þrel* as the subject of the verb phrase *wurthe*

iuroied [Brut 7412]. Layamon's penchant for archaizing is fairly well established; significantly, the term is lacking in the linguistically less conservative Otho text. A single fifteenth-century manuscript of the B-text of *Piers Plowman* contains the word *wale* in a proverbial utterance. It probably means "foreigner," an established and common sense of *wealh* throughout the OE period.

4. According to Pelteret, *servus* is the central Latin word expressing the concept "slave," "Late Anglo-Saxon Slavery," p. 93. It is equivalent, he maintains, to Hebrew *ebed* and Greek *doulos*, two other "legal status terms." Specific occupational terms are more frequently rendered by compounds such as *horswealh* or by terms not strictly within the vocabulary of servitude, such as *bydele*, even when the person performing the specified duties is clearly a slave.

5. Its primary application as a slave-word is as Aldred's rendering of *servus* in Gospel parables.

6. The same is of course true of other words that overlap with this vocabulary: *cnapa, wifmann, mægden, wencel*, and especially *mann*, the masculine counterpart of the important feminine term *mennen*.

7. See the *Oxford English Dictionary* s.v. *thegn* and *thane*. There is no evidence of the latter development in ME; it appears to have been exclusively Scots.

8. There are several others, the most important of which is *þir*, which Pelteret terms the feminine answer to *þræl*. I am not convinced that this is correct; see "Late Anglo-Saxon Slavery," p. 476, for his remarks. *Þeowe*, which Clark Hall gives as a feminine derivative of *þeow*, is morphologically ambiguous and its forms regularly overlap with those of *þeowa* and *þeow* adj.

9. A few attestations of *þinen* in transitional texts probably represent nothing more than unaltered archaisms in late reworkings of OE homilies. See a1150 (OE) *Vsp. D.Hom.* 66/9 and 148/21 and *Vsp. D.Hom. Fest.Virg.* 21/60 and 21/64 in *MED*.

10. Pelteret, "Late Anglo-Saxon Slavery," pp. 384 ff. I owe my abbreviated remarks on the conditions of late Anglo-Saxon England primarily to Pelteret's discussion in Part II of his concluding chapter.

11. One can speculate that *þræl*, of Icelandic origin, might have been reinforced by survival of a cognate form in the French of the Northmen, but I have found no evidence for such a word.

12. A factor operating in this vocabulary might have been a form of linguistic imperialism subtler than outright usurpation and replacement: the degradation of native words. No doubt everyone is familiar with the two sets of English words applied to meat animals, of which the native words designate the live animal and the French borrowings the same animal prepared for the table. The standard explanation for this linguistic conversation-piece is that the subjugated English-speaking peasantry tended, or lived cheek-by-jowl with, the beasts while their French overlords met them only as dinner. While nothing as dramatic marks the vocabulary of slavery, it is interesting that the native term *þegn*, which had been undergoing a seemingly steady course of slight amelioration or at least maintenance of a rather strongly positive value, suddenly underwent a change of course. Once again it saw an increase in uses signifying "slave" or "bound servant" and even in its other applications no longer implied the high social status that it formerly had; borrowings such as *count* and *baron* appropriated some of the concepts that *þegn* no longer covered. *Þeow*, similarly, underwent something of a reversion and partial replacement in its ameliorated senses. The explanations are somewhat more complicated than this brief treatment suggests, and I will deal with them at length elsewhere; perhaps it is sufficient for the present study to note that this aspect of the words' development may be due in part to a linguistic analog to the Conquest, the imposition of French attitudes if not French words upon a segment of English vocabulary particularly prone to reflect societal attitudes.

13. See the *Middle English Dictionary*, s.v. *servaunt* and *sclave*. A surname, *Le Serviant*, is recorded in 1242 but may well be French. A few uses of *servant* appear in early thirteenth-century mss. of the *Ancrene Riwle*. *Sclave* first appears in a text of the Becket legend dated c. 1300, where it may mean "Slav," according to Douglas Moffat.

14. A historical semanticist of a more theoretical or formal bent might legitimately ask why I did not adopt a componential analysis, setting up my features in binary terms and establishing the distinguishing features of particular terms on that basis. In this particular instance, to do so would have created a false sense of parallelism between two sets of terms only superficially alike: i.e., it would appear that *þeow* ought to be distinguishable from *þeowen* by the specification *-male* for the latter. In fact, the ramifications of what would then have to be redundantly specified as +*female* are very significant. In addition, some features that I think essential — and not necessarily identical in the two groups — are very resistant to being captured in a term suitable for a binary system.

15. I have left passages accompanied by Latin lemmata untranslated; elsewhere, unless otherwise attributed, all translations are mine.

16. See F.L. Attenborough, *Laws of the Earliest English Kings* (Cambridge, 1922), p. 60. The translation given is his.

17. LawIne 74–74.1. I have followed Attenborough's interpretation of the passages cited here. For his comments, see *Laws*, p.193.

18. LawHl 1.1–3.

19. LawWi 9.

20. Pelteret remarks on the restriction of physical punishment to slaves; see "Late Anglo-Saxon Slavery," p. 89 *et pass*. See also LawWi 10, 13 and 15 and HomU 31(Nap 39) 15 for additional evidence.

21. LawAfEl 11.5–6; cp. Ex. 21.16, Lev. 25.11.

22. JnGl(Ru) 8.34; WHom 9 123.

23. See, e.g., *Guthlac* 153–157 and Ælfric's life of St. Sebastian, lines 425–435.

24. Parallel developments in the abstract nouns *þeowdom* and *þeowet* probably exerted influence on and were influenced by the alterations in the words under discussion.

25. Significant variants include structures containing 1st- and 2nd-person possessive pronouns, such as *þin* (*min*) *þeow*.

26. The clearest example is ApT 51.21. Even here the speaker does not predicate servile status of himself, as statements such as *ic eom þegn* (*þinen*) *godes* would seem to do.

27. Ælfric uses the term to identify persons of undoubted prominence in numerous instances; see, e.g., AeLS(Basil) 358, AeLS(Eugenia) 5, etc.; furthermore, he offers forms of *þegn* as glosses for *satrapa* and *optimas* in AeGl 2.59 and AeGram 49.17, respectively. Wulfstan uses the term *þegn* as an explicit contrast to *þræl* in a formula that he repeats on several occasions; see, e.g., WPol 6.2(Jost) 137 and LawGrið 21.2. Numerous uses in the *Sermo Lupi* (WHom 20.2 92, 109, etc.) reinforce this interpretation.

28. AeCHom I 7 110.26.

29. See also AeCHom II 13.129.76, AeColl 34–35, and Pelteret, "Late Anglo-Saxon Slavery," pp. 92 ff. Useful discussion is also to be found in the opening chapters of David Brion Davis, *The Problem of Slavery in Western Culture* (New York: Oxford, 1966) and especially pp. 91–106. As Davis notes, Bracton's acceptance of the division of men into two classes, free and unfree, is illuminating; although the latter's compilation postdates the period that I am discussing, he clearly derives his distinctions from long-standing legal tradition. The absence of any such bald statements in vernacular law codes is interesting but inconclusive. Of course in God's

eyes the slave, the free laborer and the king are equal and equally empowered to choose freedom from or enslavement to sin; see AeCHom I, 19.260.23–29 and see Ruffing, below, in this volume.

30. A possible exception is the use of *þinen* to refer twice to the midwives attending the Hebrew women, who defy Pharaoh's order to kill the male babies (Exod 1.15 and 20). These women may not be slaves; the fact that they could be commanded to commit infanticide, however, does suggest that they are not entirely autonomous. Specificity of duties generally has an ameliorating effect on slave-terms.

31. Ch1197(HarmD 4) 16.

32. It is dangerous, however, to assume that these tendencies existed in earlier stages of the language, for several reasons. In languages that preserve gender in nouns, words have to be one or the other, and the effect must have been to dilute associations between feminine/masculine *forms* and perceptions of femaleness/maleness. In addition, when many ordinary words possessed derived feminine forms, the effect of these would have been less heightened than it is for PDE speakers, who have only a handful of such pairs. On the other hand, though, grammatical gender was breaking down in late OE - early ME. What could have in previous years been a formal difference with little value attached to it would have become somewhat less natural. French words entering the language were not preserving distinctions of gender; *servaunt*, e.g., entered with common gender. Thus the effect of the marked/unmarked distinction could have grown more pronounced over the course of the period.

33. Compare PDE *doctor* and *nurse*. Neither is technically marked, but the tendency is to assume masculine and feminine referents, respectively. Thus we often hear locutions like "woman-" or "lady doctor" and "male nurse." Nursing is a relatively low-status occupation, and when a man is called a nurse, it often implies mild disparagement, grounded in the assumption that as a man he ought to have been a doctor. No such assumption obtains for the woman, who would not have been expected to rise above that lower level.

34. See Karras, above, in this volume.

35. AeLS(Agatha) 45 ff.

36. AeLS(Lucy) 73 ff.

37. LS 16(MargaretHerbst) 61 ff.

38. LS 16(MargaretHerbst) 202, 264.

39. Mart 5(Hertzfield-Binz) 2277 [OC19A/09].

40. LS 23(Mary of Egypt) 2.189.

41. See LawAfEl 12.1 and 20.1, LawAf 1 25.1, LawAfRb 25, Conf 1.1(Spindler) 30, Conf 3.2 (Raith Y) 7, etc., for specific examples.

42. AeCHom I, 13 194.23.

43. The use of the phrase *þeowen (þinen) godes* to mean "women in the religious life" is least rare in Ælfric; he speaks of *halige þenas and halige þinena* in his first letter to Wulfstan and of *godes þeowum and þinenum* in CHom II, 6 56.133. A few occurrences are to be found in the RegCGl (see 2.43 and 2.68); here a Latin lemma conditioned the appearance of *þeowa and þeowenna þinre*. Overall, there are less than a dozen such uses, and the coordinate structure exemplified here is common. *Mennen* never substitutes in this usage for *þeowen* or *þinen*; nor, of course, does *wyln*.

44. AeGram 100.10. In the paradigm for *mea ancilla*, the vocative is exemplified by the admonition *eala þu min wyln, beo nytwyrthe* [AeGram 100.20]. This seems to capture the tenor of his presentation of the *wyln*.

45. The fact that such a use is not attested does not, of course, mean that it did not occur. But the total absence of *þinen* in the surviving legal materials, combined with its morphological link to the amelioration-prone *þegn*, does make it seem likely that the term resisted such an application.

4

The Labor Structure of Ælfric's Colloquy

John Ruffing

As *a cohesive* and finely-wrought dialogue on various occupations, Ælfric's *Colloquy* must have been an effective exercise for teaching quotidian Latin to monastic oblates. Mitchell and Robinson also find it "of particular value to modern readers because it offers an informal glimpse of Anglo-Saxon social structure, with representatives of various occupations explaining their function in the society in which they lived."[1] But for either group of readers, I would argue that social structure, and in particular the structure of its labor, to be no less formal and no less communicated than the grammar taught through the text. Granted, the labor structure is embedded in and thereby somewhat obscured by pleasant dialogue, the digestive aid designed to ease consumption of grammatical items, vocabulary and inflections; but in the content and arrangement of its portraits, the *Colloquy* shows a constructed balance reminiscent of more sophisticated literary catalogues like the General Prologue to the *Canterbury Tales*. [2]

In addition to its detail-laden content, the *Colloquy* possesses several formal attributes which have made it stand out in Anglo-Saxon studies, not the least its dual language. The rather literal Old English interlinear gloss is more frequently read because of its usefulness for socializing modern oblates to the ways of philology. "It is one of the most commonly read texts . . . peculiarly suited to the needs of beginners,"[3] and a favorite of readers and anthologies. But it must be variously transformed for its most usual task; thus Mitchell and Robinson:

> The charm of Ælfric's work [the original Latin] is not wholly lost in this rendering, but as it stands the translation is inappropriate for modern students of Old English to use in learning the language. . . .

The editors therefore present "an adaptation and abbreviation" of Sweet's 1897 revision "into idiomatic prose . . . normalized throughout."[4] Despite its similar use for language learning, the dominance of the vernacular version in literary consciousness tends to give prominence to its secular elements and obscure some implications of the Latin monastic exercise.[5] I wish to consider primarily those implications, but the *Colloquy*'s other formal properties make it prominent in either version, for either sociology or language study: it is short, simple, well-written, complete, and — perhaps best of all — Ælfric's, sharing the prestige of his learning and influence.

As an educational tool for an audience captive to the point of whipping (7–10, 279–83), and in the larger context of a coordinated Ælfrician intellectual program,[6] the *Colloquy* is a specifically strong indicator of views on labor, the informing principle of its carefully delineated social structure.[7] Scarcity accentuates the allure; the dialogue has little comparable company in that role, as the editor of its standard edition made clear in 1939:

> To-day the work is chiefly of interest for the picture it presents of the life and activities of the middle and lower classes of Anglo-Saxon society, concerning which Old English literature is, in the main, silent.[8]

The important word here is "literature," the category into which Garmonsway is promoting the *Colloquy*, because "its interest as a document of educational history is well established."[9] There are other sources of information, many of them non-textual, even other strictly Latin colloquies,[10] but they do not possess as high an academic profile as Old English literature, still the largest area of Anglo-Saxon studies, especially in teaching.[11] So the *Colloquy* speaks without interference from other voices largely because of its disciplinary situation: it is not just a text, it is a vernacular text, almost literature of a sort, whose content is essentially unavailable elsewhere in the vernacular. Because of its usefulness for language instruction, it is ubiquitously and conveniently edited, a very attractive and even pleasant source of information.

The temptation to tap this source is irresistible, and in the early twentieth century the *Colloquy* is cited as a transparent window on a desired proto-democratic Anglo-Saxon society. Garmonsway summarizes:

> The *Colloquy* . . . has often been culled by economists, educationalists, and social historians to brighten the early pages of their histories. But so convincing and realistic is the dialogue that many of them have misunderstood its origin and plan, and have imagined that the class for which it was intended was actually composed of the characters who take part in the discussion.[12]

Garmonsway points out the improbability of this notion on the grounds of well-known Anglo-Saxon practices, but it is a measure of the idea's strength that he can cite its presence in several well-known studies.[13] There is no less scholarly desire at stake when, in a different time and critical environment, cultural materialism clamors against silence on "the life and activities of the middle and lower classes." The *Colloquy* can then be a bulwark of redress, a (conveniently already canonical) token text which provides the sought-after quota of non-saint, non-warrior characters to assuage the class and classroom anxieties of modern language keepers.

In concert with the *Colloquy*'s other attractions, this critical desirability vaults the dialogue to a crucial position in our conception of Anglo-Saxon labor and warrants a close examination of how the text represents it. Most recent criticism has focused on the dialogue's linguistic anomalies, with less frequent interpretation looking to Ælfric's Latin sources: Colledge argues for Augustine's treatment of the merchant, while Anderson finds influences of many other authors and reads the whole "as an expression of the Benedictine monastic ideal, derived from the Rule, of an orderly and well-regulated life within the confines of an economically self-sufficient community devoted to the service of God."[14]

That economic self-sufficiency relies on the labor performed by the workers depicted in the text, which does not teach workers how to speak Latin, much less teach Latin-learning novices how to work; rather the text teaches those novices how to speak the language of work, how to constitute and manipulate it. Labor is structured around and serves a monastic life which is described twice as consisting essentially only of prayer (13–16, 266–315) and very much set apart from all the other occupations. It might be useful to frame this situation as a transformation of the monastic motto "ora et labora" into another: "orare est laborare." The first is a command of activity directed to the monks, acknowledging the separateness of the two functions while still putting prayer first; the second is a static ideal which not only lacks the urgency of imperative address, but more perilously collapses both functions in their common element *orare*. The elision of difference between the terms represents the possibility of monastic life removed from all the other labor depicted in the text. But the monks still require the fruits of that labor to live, so they must procure them from others by controlling the structure of work through language. While the *Colloquy* mostly concerns itself with physical labor, even the warring class will be included; the implicit business of the Rule has become ruling all of society, not just the monastery. This monastic assertion both generates and resolves the two dominant interpretations of the *Colloquy*. The more traditional and vernacular-biased finds a model for Anglo-Saxon society, so that the monastic text describes the world. The more recent and Latin-based finds a model of monastic textual ideals, so that the monastic text becomes the world.

The text conveys its ruling scheme by structures that distinguish both the type of labor and its attendant social values. The monks' plan for living is the societal occasion for the whole text, and that plan has a controlling and framing presence that divides the work into three sections, all marked by changes in the dialogue where the monk is conspicuously reintroduced and prompted for new directions to the discussion (203, 244). In addition, that plan is presented in the final section (a description of oblate life) as the culmination of a definite progression through the dialogue, which consists of a long sequence of workers, a dispute on the occupations (203–244), and the description of oblate life.

I will concern myself with the first section, the long sequence of workers, and its relation to the second section, the dispute on the occupations (203–44). The first is distinguished by provision of goods that are directly consumed by the community, mostly food. This function contrasts with the technology of the second section, specifically metal-dependent activities of the craftsmen, who describe themselves in support roles for the preceding workers. The craftsmen dispute their counterparts' importance because the craftsmen provide products that enable those workers to produce consumables. In fact, none of the non-craft occupations requires metal technology per se, though obviously they do as practiced in Anglo-Saxon England. That specific dependence is precisely the ironworker's point in the dispute. Despite his insistence that what they do cannot be separated from how they do it, the implicit distinction between the two is built into the dialogue's structure and its rhetoric, for that distinction is the hidden assumption that allows the plowman to be designated as the most essential worker. The last section presents a detailed account of the crowning occupation of prayer, supported by the products of the workers. Every section also contains some account of the life of prayer, beginning and ending with monastic invocation, so that both in part and in whole the monastery is the alpha and omega, the first and last word on society.

As the first in the long initial sequence of workers, the monk is supposedly one of them but is in fact set apart. Like the rest, he is interrogated by the master and describes his own daily activities, but he alone names the workers which will follow, an implicit participation in the master's ruling which makes them into a collective other:

> Quid sciunt isti tui socii?
> Alii sunt aratores, alii opiliones, quidam bubulci, quidam etiam venatores, alii piscatores, alii aucupes, quidam mercatores, quidam sutores, quidam salinatores, quidam pistores, coci. (17–21)[15]

These workers do not comprise an amorphous collection of occupations, but are themselves divided by function and are accordingly treated differently. Of most significance is the separation between those before and after the merchant: those who come before are primary providers such as the hunter, whose products come directly from natural sources; after these come secondary providers, who use others' products to make their own.

This division between primary producers and secondary providers is the frame within which are engaged the complementary issues of labor: its difficulty, its utility, and the resulting social attitudes toward it and the worker. With the primary providers, the emphasis lies in difficulty and danger, the strain of their occupations; utility is taken for granted (though it will later have to be defended through vindication of the plowman) and the tone is therefore generally solicitous. In contrast, among the secondary providers strain is not an issue, and utility — an assessment of the value they add to their source products — is paramount, accompanied by a fittingly contentious tone. As a product of these interactions, the whole sequence traces a containing arc of social freedom roughly corresponding to physical range from the monastery: the workers begin on its grounds and venture out to the edge of the known world, but they still end up in the monastery kitchen.

In order to analyze these labor issues, it is necessary to recognize one further sub-structure: each set of providers itself has two groups of workers, associated by their method of production. The primary providers consist of clearly distinguished fieldworkers and hunters; the secondary providers have an anomalous pair of goods producers and a clear trio of food preparers. Unlike the larger sections, which are appropriately marked by the rhetoric of monkish intrusions, these smaller divisions are evident only from the content and tone of the conversation, by what the workers actually do and how they do it. Rhetorically, the dialogue remains seamless: questions and answers follow each other without disruption.

First among the primary providers — as their representative plowman will be first among all workers — are the fieldworkers: plowman, oxherd, shepherd. Their occupational link is producing food with domestic animals; even the plowman's duties, and those of his assistant, are concerned with the oxen, while there is no mention of many other significant parts of the agricultural process, e.g. sowing, weeding, manuring, or the various harvest activities. The oxherd reinforces the coherence of the group when he defines his duties as complementary to those of the plowman, taking the oxen from him at the end of the day and returning them ready to go in the morning (44–7). The centrality of the domestic animals is appropriate, since they are also the material basis of monastic textual production, by means of vellum produced from their hides. The other primary providers — hunter, fisher, and fowler — produce food from wild rather than domestic animals.

The secondary providers begin with the merchant and leatherworker, who both buy what they need, an identical verb (*emo*, gloss *bicȝe* — 154, 170) reinforcing their association. Their wares also link the activities of other workers: almost half the merchant's items are smiths' raw materials ("ebur et auricalcum, es et stagnum, sulfur et uitrum et his similia" — 160–1), and the leatherworker's "cutes et pelles" (170) would come from the range of domestic and wild animals covered by the primary providers. The final group of salter, baker, and cook are linked by preparing food, which would come from the primary providers.

With these structures in place, we can begin to follow first the distinction of social freedom by range from the monastery. The fieldworkers are bound to its lands, domestic like the animals they tend; the wild animal purveyors are like their objects freer to roam nearby regions, but they are still relatively close at hand.[16] The merchant extends the reach of the dialogue "ultra marinas partes" (153–4), but after him it quickly snaps back to the domestic concerns of shoemaker and food preparers; by the time the cook ends the section, his response is precisely about trying to remain in the *collegio* (194).

Social freedom is in turn related to the themes of strenuousness and utility, which respectively dominate the treatment of primary and secondary providers. The change of emphasis corresponds to the nature of the occupations, which generally decrease in both strenuousness and utility — and societal value — throughout the section. The primary providers endure great strain, evidenced in their exchanges, but as food producers their utility is not an issue. On the other hand strain is not an issue for the secondary providers, but their assumed utility has decreased sufficiently that it becomes the focus of their exchanges. The three themes — strain, the utility of labor, and the social freedom determined by them — relate to each other in a highly structured sequence as the dialogue progresses through groups of workers, and I will demonstrate that sequence by tracing these themes through the progress of the dialogue.

The fieldworkers exhibit the least social freedom but the greatest strain and utility in their labor. The plowman clearly explains the consequences of his status: no matter how bad the weather, he dare not stay at home "pro timore domini" (25); he says he is obligated (*debeo* — 27) to plow a certain amount each day. Unlike later characters, he has no incentive to prove his utility, so the issue is moot for him — which is why the monk must later proclaim it, more for society than for the plowman; such total servitude is indeed useful to everyone but its performers, so there is great incentive to preserve it. As a fellow fieldworker, the shepherd also invokes servile obligation, though not so centrally as the plowman; he simply states "et fidelis sum domino meo" (42) as the last item in his catalogue of activities. They both address the interrogating master as *domine* in emphasizing their hard lives, thereby identifying their domination with that of the dialogue which defines them. The master himself acknowledges their effortful existence when, at the end of the plowman's catalogue of duties, the master is inspired to an utterance which prompts the plowman's concurring assessment: "O! O! magnus labor" (34). But the master stops short of the crucial connection between labor and social position, which the plowman's response must make for him. As the foundation stone of the monastic labor structure, the plowman summarizes the strain of his efforts by directly linking them with his status: "Etiam, magnus labor est, quia non sum liber" (35). The labor and social lesson would seem to be best expressed by contrapositive: if I am free, then

[61]

labor is not great.

The text's descriptive vocabulary confirms this interpretation: *labor* specifically describes actual effort, the burden of work, and is more frequent with the earlier characters. The fowler confirms the onus of *labor* when he uses it to describe precisely effort he wishes to avoid, namely feeding hawks all summer instead of opting to catch new ones each fall (146–8). Similarly, the merchant identifies *labor* as the strain and danger he goes through in risking his life over the sea (164–7). However, after the strenuous activities of the fieldworkers, occupations themselves are no longer *labor*, but either *opus* or *ars* — even that of the supposedly useless cook. The Old English glosses *deorf, weorc,* and *cræft* match respectively the Latin use of each term.

Purveyors of wild animals follow those who work with domestic animals. In keeping with their geographical range, these purveyors enlarge the scope of social freedom from servile obligation to an exchange value for their labor. The central concerns of being primary food providers (like the fieldworkers) are still present but already transforming with the new labor basis: strain remains an issue but decreases, from unavoidable drudgery to less certain danger and risk. The hunter must be brave to deal with the beasts of the forest (77–9), but the fisher stays away from the hazards of whale-catching (109–22); the fowler encounters no discernible dangers. Utility is still not an issue, but as dangers and effort decrease, the master begins to challenge occupational commitments by questioning the speakers' methods and character, which are integral parts of an occupation's social viability. The daring hunter is praised ("Ualde audax fuisti tunc" — 77), but the master does not accept the fisher's decision to avoid whales, and although the fisher attempts to rationalize it, he finally condemns himself: "Uerum dicis, sed ego non audeo propter mentis mee ignauiam" (121). The master likewise holds up alternative training methods to the fowler, who must explain that he specifically attempts to minimize the effort he expends (146–8).

The greater social freedom of this second group is not only manifest in their answering the master's challenges, but also in their laying claim to greater independence of action, and to jurisdiction over their resources. The hunter continues the spirit of the fieldworkers' servile ties by declaring himself the king's (55), but his duties also bring reward and incentive beyond sustenance:

> Uestit me bene et pascit, aliquando dat mihi equum et armillam, ut libentius artem meam exerceam. (84–5)

The fisher's reward is explicitly commerical, for he sells in a market-place, to *cives* "in civitate" (99, 97), anticipating the problem of the merchant's markup in observing that demand is greater than he can supply: "Non possum tot capere quot possum uendere" (99).[17] The idea of fairly valued trade grows further in the fowler's dialogue through the intrusion of a request (presumably the hunter's) for a hawk, the result of which is played out as a barter:

Da mihi unum accipitrem.
Dabo libenter, si dederis mihi unum uelocem canem.
Qualem accipitrem uis habere, maiorem aut minorem.
Da mihi maiorem. (133-6)

With all the workers who follow the primary providers of food, the strain of labor quickly disappears; with the secondary providers, the question of utility becomes explicit and finally dominant.[18] This reversal of strain and utility eventually forces a compensating contraction of social freedom: the occupations move back into the monastery, where utility can be regulated.

The two groups of secondary providers begin with the odd pair of merchant and leatherworker. Understanding their place benefits from a brief consideration of Latin sources, but they fit quite reasonably in the dialogue's general scheme of labor. Through his unique ability to judge and manipulate value, an activity otherwise reserved to the master, the far-roaming merchant marks the apex of social freedom. The merchant is also the master of his own family, looking after his *filios* (166) as the master does his *pueri*. He is also master of his own response (unlike the other characters), offering a largely unprompted and emphatic self-justification on the suddenly important question of utility:

Quid dicis tu, mercator?
    Ego dico quod utilis sum et regi et ducibus et divitibus et omni populo. (150-1)

This enumeration of beneficiaries is commanding, taking in the whole society — with the conspicuous exception the clerical estate — while distinguishing *divitibus*. Although the latter is not surprising for a merchant's worldview, the absence of the otherwise omnipresent monastery seems odd. One clue might lie in the Benedictine self-sufficiency for which Anderson argues, but it is also possible that Ælfric is conveniently keeping the monastery out of the potential controversy of the merchant's profit.[19] In contrast, all three estates are included when the central lesson of the dialogue is applied (233–43), and the religious estate itself is even amplified: "Siue sis sacerdos, siue monachus, seu laicus, seu milites" (240–41).

The leatherworker, who follows the merchant, brings the dialogue back into the domestic sphere and into the master's control. An additional rationale for his place might be found in the behavior of Augustine's merchant, who when challenged says that he is no worse than a shoemaker, and enumerates the shoemaker's vices. This association might explain Ælfric's placing the shoemaker just after the merchant and also providing him with a strong self-justification — "Est quidem ars mea utilis ualde uobis et necessaria" (168) — as well as a list of goods rivalling the merchant's in length. The merchant and shoemaker are also unique as the only non-trio in the first section and the only ones who have nothing to do with food.

In the relative ease of the monastery kitchen, where strain is least an issue, the food preparers bring the issue of utility to a crisis by subtle but steady escalation, finally bursting the bonds of role definition and forcing an end to the steady accrual of contributing workers in the *Colloquy*'s first section. The salter's self-justification is unchallenged; the baker concedes that although he might be theoretically dispensable, he is not practically so. But the harmonious ensemble of occupations breaks down with the cook, who interprets the whole procedure as a challenge to his marginal place in monastic society, which he appropriately labels "*uestro* collegio" (194, my emphasis). His naturalistic justification of his work is refuted outright by the master:

> Non curamus de arte tua, nec nobis necessaria est, quia nos
> ipsi possumus coquere que coquenda sunt, et assare que
> assanda sunt. (197–9)

With utility denied, there is suddenly open acknowledgement of and conflict over the social construction of occupation and status. The cook proceeds to claim his right to a place not for what he does but because *he* does it, because his position as servant is necessary for the position of master to have meaning — a unity of the social and linguistic exercise:

> Dicit cocus: si ideo me expellitis, ut sic faciatis, tunc eritis
> omnes coci, et nullus uestrum erit dominus; (200–1)

The cook identifies himself not just against the master but against the whole group as potential masters: "nullus uestrum erit dominus," the antithesis of the social aim of the exercise. At this flashpoint, the linguistically servile Old English gloss likewise subverts its Latin ruler: while the terms for master (*dominus* and *hlaford*) correspond closely, as they do throughout the text, *coci* is rendered as *prælas*, thralls, indicating that what is at stake in the cook's reply is the very "non sum liber" of the plowman. Even without appealing to the gloss, a second, complementary lesson is clear: if you do labor, then you are not a master — or again perhaps clearer in contrapositive: if you are a master, then you do not labor — not even something as supposedly trivial as cooking. And there isn't one master addressed; the whole community's potential for masterhood is threatened.

As the first section winds down, the general language of the exercise too becomes very monk-centered rather than character-centered. While the second-person pronoun had dominated all the master's speech up through the merchant, with the leatherworker the first person plural dominates, so that the master remains masked in the collective. He asserts his power in contention but never calls attention to it by speaking it directly in his own voice. Anderson notes that the question which initiates the cook's exchange (192-3) does not even address him directly, as did all previous queries.[20] It seems quite likely that this shift in verb person is part of the pedagogic strategy of the linguistic exercise; but this explanation of the most probable source of the shift does not diminish its effect on the social structure thus conveyed. This change in person requires the text to make another exception and go outside the dialogue, outside the voices that supposedly constitute its world, and acknowledge its own constructedness with stage directions to identify the cook when he speaks. "Dicit cocus" (194, 200) highlights the independent voice of the cook over against that of the master, and emphasizes the cook's dissent.

The crisis of the cook closes the long first-section litany of workers and forces a change in the *Colloquy*'s rhetorical strategy. First, control is returned to the monk as mediator of workers, with approbation redirected to those whom he controls, and who possess the desired utility:

> O, monache, qui mihi locutus es, ecce, probaui te habere bonos socios et ualde necessarios; qui sunt illi? (203-4)

The monk then names the craftsmen, just as he named the workers of the previous section. But the speaking master (addressed as *magister* by the monks, but *dominus* by the plowman and shepherd), must further mask his authority, since collectivizing did not allay the cook's threat to order. This second displacement of exercising power is an appeal to wisdom as a character, drawing *sapiens* (211) from the fictional *congregatio* of workers. The master still rules the dialogue, of course: he introduces the whole question of supremacy of professions (211–13) and resumes speaking as soon as it is settled. The purpose of wisdom is clearly to rule:

> Habes aliquem sapientem consiliarium?
> Certe habeo. Quomodo potest nostra congregatio sine consiliario regi? (208–10)

This move from authority to wisdom allows effective control of the dialogue by deflecting confrontation and appealing to an authority beyond the speaker, of which the speaker is nevertheless in control because that authority is a linguistic construct.

Scripture, of which the monks are conveniently sole proprietors, is probably the most powerful of such constructions and therefore the crown of wisdom's strategy to claim primacy for religious life. This claim insulates religious life from any comparison with the "artes seculares" (217), who are again made *alter* from the monk by their very grouping and label. Scripture itself is not explained or interpreted, merely quoted as a trumping coda to the pronouncement:

> Dico tibi, mihi uidetur seruitium Dei inter istas artes primatum
> tenere, sicut legitur in euangelio: "Primum querite regnum Dei
> et iustitiam eius, et hec omnia adicientur uobis." (213–16)

It is important that *sapiens* recites the entire verse (Mt 6:33). He requires only the first clause to make religious life the most important, but the second clause claims as a result all the worldly things which the other workers provide. When agriculture is then declared the most important secular art "quia arator nos omnes pascit" (219), the plowman is merely the most essential of all those who must supply the monastery. The deliberate blurring of who *nos* is throughout the dialogue — sometimes just the monks, but sometimes all the workers — means that the monastic life can be presented as both privileged to direct and draw on the other occupations, and yet also as belonging to them, as a real labor of its own; *orare est laborare* is its claimed work, but its real work is *dicere de labore* — so that others might labor. The challenge of the smith threatens this ambivalence, continuing the cook's acknowledgement of the interdependence and construction of social roles, in addition to pointing out the true technological dependence of the whole society.

Unlike the workers of the first section, the smiths do not provide consumable goods, but rather the tools for making those goods, tools based on the technology of iron; it is no accident that *Ferrarius* is their spokesman.[21] He rightly points out that other occupations — and hence the structure of society — depend on his tool technology, even fellow craftsman the carpenter (220–3). His tool technology is potentially as powerful as the monk's language in defining society, and the ironworker commands a similarly powerful voice in the dialogue, naming and referencing the other occupations as only the monk has done. All must eat, but the productivity of Anglo-Saxon agriculture is determined by the strength of the plow made with iron, which cultivates better than wood or stone and over a greater range of soils, most significantly some of the heaviest and most fertile ones. So while food provision is naturally a necessary condition for the existence of tool technology in any level of community, the ironworker is indirectly addressing not the philosophical ideal of the monk, but a sociological reality in which the entire condition of food production, especially the crucial surplus that feeds non-producers like kings and monks, does depend on tool technology.

Thus the counselor cannot deny the ironworker's objection and even acknowledges its truth ("Uerum quidem dicis," 224). In order to neutralize it he resorts to linguistic technology — rhetoric — preempting the ironworker's already accepted assertion of ultimate utility by appealing to the proximate utility of food provision represented by the plowman, and by ignoring the dependent relation. Specifically his obfuscation on one hand addresses the essence of the plowman's usefulness — he feeds us — while crediting the ironworker with peripheral irrelevancies:

> . . . omnibus nobis carius est hospitari apud te aratorem quam apud te, quia arator dat nobis panem et potum; tu, quid das nobis in officina tua nisi ferreas scintillas et sonitus tundentium malleorum et flantium follium? (224–8)

By privileging the social element most under his control, the worker with greatest burden and least freedom, the monk insures his continued dominance over others not so restricted. The plowman here is a cipher, otherwise discussed in the third person (219, 236), and the incongruous and gratuitous direct address hardly makes him more involved.[22] There is a small danger in recognizing the true worldly utility of the plowman, namely that the monk might be recognized to have none. But having already been set aside from the burdens of the world while still included in its benefits, the monk is relatively safe

from this danger, and he insures against it with his final pronouncement.

The final pronouncement on the secular world is an appeal for status
quo, embracing all estates. It draws together all the powerful themes
of the dialogue, attempting to immobilize them. However, the rhetoric
cannot resolve the difficulties and turns back on itself meaninglessly.
After addressing the contending parties as *socii* to efface differences,
the counselor stresses mutual service (235), reinvokes the plowman
(236–7), and asks that no one disrupt the arrangments:

> Et hoc consilium do omnibus operariis, ut unusquisque artem
> suam diligenter exerceat, quia qui artem suam dimiserit, ipse
> dimittatur ab arte. Siue sis sacerdos, siue monachus, seu laicus,
> seu miles, exerce temet ipsum in hoc, et esto quod es; quia
> magnum dampnum et uerecundia est homini nolle esse quod
> est et quod esse debet. (237–43)

The rhetorical strategy involves claiming fixed *a priori* status for the
monk's linguistic construction of an occupation as *ars*, as if it were the
only role possible, and then reifying that construction to the point of
making it act on the resisting worker, "[qui] dimittatur ab arte." The
curiously circular reasoning claims there is no place in society except
one's current one, deliberately excluding the problematic interrelations
of roles. Perhaps because it includes warriors and religious, the final
appeal invokes not just the weight and oblique authority of social
order (best expressed by *debet*), but also the self-image appropriate to
those with some power in their position, those who would not wish to
be "dampnum et uerecundia."

I hope it is clear from this analysis that there are definite groupings
and structures in the *Colloquy*'s depiction of labor, and that those
structures have a clear relation to the societal position of the workers.
In addition to acknowledging its monastic ideals and playful instruction, I think it is important to consider the tension and conflict, perhaps unavoidable, in the interplay of strain, utility, and status in the
Colloquy's labor roles, especially since they are all negotiated in a
prisonhouse of language overseen by the monastic master.

NOTES

1. Bruce Mitchell and Fred C. Robinson, *A Guide to Old English*, 4th ed. (Oxford, 1986), p. 174

2. I mention Chaucer's tour de force as perhaps the best-known medieval English example of such writing, but closer to Ælfric — and part of a larger study of this question — are the so-called Old English catalogue poems, e.g. "Deor," studied by Nicholas Howe, *The Old English Catalogue Poems, Anglistica* 23 (Copenhagen, 1985).

3. George N. Garmonsway ed., *Ælfric's Colloquy*, 1st ed. (London, 1939), p. v.

4. Mitchell and Robinson, *A Guide*, p. 174.

5. The Garmonsway edition demonstrates the dual-language situation mutely but powerfully in its visual presentation: the manuscript facsimile opposite the title page reveals Latin words in a large, dark hand, and the gloss in smaller, lighter letters above; but the edited text's typography reverse these characteristics and thus the linguistic balance of power. The different textual appearances are emblematic of one of the major questions in Old English literary criticism, namely whether Latin literary culture exerts decisive influence. See for instance Allen J. Frantzen, *Desire for Origins: New Language, Old English, and Teaching the Tradition* (New Brunswick, N.J., 1990), pp. 79–82.

6. Peter A. M. Clemoes treats the matter most completely as a part of a chronology of Ælfric's works, "The Chronology of Ælfric's Works," in *The Anglo-Saxons: Studies in Some Aspects of Their History and Culture Presented to Bruce Dickins*, ed. Clemoes (London, 1959), pp. 245–46; Kenneth Sisam, *Studies in the History of Old English Literature* (Oxford, 1953), p. 301, offers a similar opinion.

7. The centrality of labor is reinforced by David and Julia Jary in *Dictionary of Sociology* (New York, 1991), p. 236, by defining it in terms of community goals.

8. Garmonsway, *Colloquy*, p. 1.

9. Ibid., p. v.

10. The most accessible collection is that of W. H. Stevenson, *Early Scholastic Colloquies* (Oxford, 1929).

11. See for instance Allen Frantzen's survey, "A Recent Survey of the Teaching of Old English and its Implications for Anglo-Saxon Studies," *Old English Newsletter* 26.1 (1992): 34–45. The situation is not as lopsided in the United Kingdom, but is certainly not balanced. See too James Simpson, "The Enjoyment and Teaching of Old and Middle English: The Current State of Play," *Old English Newsletter* 25.3 (1992): 29–31.

12. Garmonsway, *Colloquy*, p. 14.

13. Garmonsway analyzes the problems of these studies in his edition, pp. 14–15, and in his "The Development of the Colloquy," in *The Anglo-Saxons*, ed. Clemoes, pp. 249–52. His sentiments are echoed by Earl R. Anderson, "Social Idealism in Ælfric's *Colloquy*," *Anglo-Saxon England* 3 (1974): 158–59, and Stanley B. Greenfield and Daniel G. Calder, *A New Critical History of Old English Literature* (New York, 1986), p. 87.

14. Anderson, "Social Idealism," p. 151; Eric College, "An Allusion to Augustine in Ælfric's Colloquy," *RES* 12 (1962): 180–81.

15. It is probably not accidental that there are twelve workers in the first section's list; as might be expected in a text by Ælfric, there are several deep Biblical structures which govern the *Colloquy*. I hope to treat these more completely elsewhere, but the apostolic nature of the twelve workers is reinforced by the monk's placement as first among equals, akin to Peter, and the cook's taking on the Judas role when he betrays the monastic utility which defines them. His potential replacement, akin to Matthias in Acts 1:15–26, is even present in a thirteenth (but non-speaking) worker, the humble ox-goading boy (28–30) who, appropriately enough, assists the privileged plowman and is described by him.

16. The fisher even explains that he prefers river to sea because of the latter's greater remove:

Cur non piscaris in mari?
Aliquando facio, sed raro, quia magnum nauigium mihi est ad mare. (103–4)

17. The fisher and merchant are also linked by vocabulary: *adqueror* describes how they gain from their transactions, glossed *begytan* (88, 165).

18. The only mention of *labor* among the secondary providers comes from the merchant's desire to profit for his peril in transporting goods, which is the only strain among all the occupations in that category:

    Uis uendere res tuas hic sicut emisti illic?
    Nolo. Quid tunc mihi proficit labor meus? (162–3)

19. The issue has a long history in canon law and commentary, the majority inveighing against it. Colledge posits Augustine's uncommon defense as a probable source for Ælfric's justification, which seeks to rationalize the *lucrum* claimed in line 165 (the more pejorative canon law term is *turpe lucrum*, derived ultimately from 1 Timothy 3:8). Ælfric's defense is even stronger than Augustine's: the master elicits it mildly, with none of the dramatic confrontation or controversy of Augustine's presentation; there is no mention of Augustine's central debate on misrepresentation of wares; and Augustine's positive arguments are amplified and extended. Ælfric's more favorable view of the merchant makes the dissociation from the monastery even more significant.

20. Anderson, "Social Idealism," p. 155.

21. It is also no accident that we classify societal progress in much of our history according to its dominant tool (often metal) technology, i.e. Stone, Bronze, and Iron Ages. See *Dictionary of Sociology*, q.v. Iron Age, p. 162. We tend to use other terms when societies exhibit more detailed or interesting traits, but we should not lose sight of the essential technological base. What we call the Roman world is an Iron Age civilization, despite its cultural sophistication, and the basic technological foundation is not fundamentally changed over 500 years later when the *Colloquy* is written.

22. It is not necessary for the sense of the passage and is in fact somewhat confusing given the dynamics of the exchange as a disagreement between counselor and craftsmen. If anything it creates an expectation that the plowman might have something to say for himself, and the fact that he doesn't only highlights how much he is in the counselor's linguistic control.

5

THE CULTURAL CONTEXT OF WESTERN TECHNOLOGY: EARLY CHRISTIAN ATTITUDES TOWARD MANUAL LABOR

George Ovitt, Jr.

MODERN VIEWS OF MEDIEVAL TECHNOLOGY

In *seeking* to understand why the West has been so receptive to the initiation and adaptation of technological change, the historian needs to consider the effects of the first great period of technological innovation — the Middle Ages. That the Middle Ages is the place to begin to search for the causes of this receptivity has not always been acknowledged. Beginning in the late seventeenth century, writers took an interest in the history of progress in the mechanical arts and the sciences. Yet they did not associate the first advances with what they saw as the sterile Aristotelianism of the Scholastics but rather with the prodigious scientific advances of their own age. Thus, when Thomas Sprat wrote his *History of the Royal Society* (1667), he noted that the period of domination by the Roman Catholic Church saw a "quiet as the dark of the night" descend on learning and the useful arts and saw the "sorry" philosophy of the "schole-men" take their place.[1] William Wotton wrote in 1694 that the "moderns" had outstripped the ancients in all fields of useful learning, and he wondered why the human race had been at a "full stop for 1500 years" in all areas of human enterprise except ethics.[2] In the eighteenth century, scholars were capable of forming a more balanced view of the Middle Ages, but the typical view was expressed by Turgot in his "Philosophical Review of the Successive Advances of the Human Mind" (1750). Turgot argued that from the coming of the barbarians to the cultural crescendo of the "Century of Louis, century of great men" a slow, painful progress had been made in the arts and sciences but that the Middle Ages saw human achievement all but cease.[3] Similar critiques of the intellectual and creative barrenness of the Middle Ages may be found in Condorcet, and, in the nineteenth century, in Jules Michelet, William Whewell, John Tyndall, and many others.[4]

The idea that the Middle Ages gave rise to the impetus that was to generate Western technological dynamism has been substantiated only in recent decades, in the writings of scholars such as Lynn Thorndike, Marc Bloch, Bertrand Gille, Lynn White, Jr., Guy Beaujouan, Jacques Le Goff, and Friedrich Klemm.[5] What these scholars have demonstrated is that beginning as early as the tenth century a series of original inventions, as well as an even greater number of imported and adapted technologies, began to transform the economic, social, and intellectual life of Europe. By 1400, this list of innovations and adaptations was long and impressive: water mills, projectile artillery, power saws, stirrups, eyeglasses, the spinning wheel, iron casting, the wheelbarrow, and many other objects and processes were in use and were contributing to the expansion of economic, political, and social life in Europe.[6] Equally impressive were the agricultural and demographic changes that catalyzed and then gradually helped to sustain these technological innovations. For example, changes in planting and crop cultivation, including the movement toward a system of three-field rotation and the substitution of the horse for the ox as the primary draft animal, allowed for a steady increase in crop yields between the ninth and the eleventh centuries, and these increases made it possible for Europe to undergo a population increase of roughly 100 percent between about A.D. 1000 and A.D. 1300.[7]

It is important, however, to avoid the suggestion of technological determinism implied by these remarks. While changes in agricultural techniques did help to alter the rhythm and organization of medieval life, they did not do so in a linear or progressive fashion. The history of Europe from the ninth to the fourteenth century is certainly not a history of the uninterrupted enhancement of material well-being, population growth, and technological innovation; for one thing, such a simple evolutionary model cannot account for the frequent and often quite severe periods of economic contraction that occurred throughout the period.[8] Nor, as I hope to suggest in the course of this essay, is it possible to discover a connection between technological and economic changes without taking into account a number of social and cultural variables.[9] And, finally, it is far from clear that the idea of progress — as it was formulated in the seventeenth century and reified in the nineteenth — has any real value in measuring the achievements of other times and other cultures.[10]

Nevertheless, once these necessary qualifications are entered, it is possible to state that technological innovations, expanded agricultural productivity, and the creation of new economic structures did alter significantly the quality of European life.[11] At the same time, there is some truth in the observation that equivalent technological and economic shifts either did not occur elsewhere (as was the case in the Byzantine Empire) or were not sustained (as was the case in China).[12] Given the supposition that the material conditions under which technological advance occurred could have been duplicated elsewhere, the question naturally arises as to which additional variables made the West particularly receptive to innovations in technology.

In searching for the features of medieval Western culture that enabled the initiation and perpetuation of technological change, a look eastward, toward the world of China, can be especially instructive. By the fourteenth century, Chinese inventiveness and energy had produced a technical, scientific, and material culture of extensive range and scope. Nearly every important technological innovation of the West in the realm of labor-saving devices, power transmission, and even domestic amenities was anticipated by the Chinese by anywhere from 100 to 700 years.[13] But during the long reign of the Ming dynasty (A.D. 1368–1644) — a period that saw Western Europe's consolidation and expansion of technical gains made during the Middle Ages — Chinese society partially lost its economic and technological dynamism and fell into what Mark Elvin has called a "high-level equilibrium trap."[14] In Elvin's view, both the shrinking of markets due to the closure of China to the West and the reliance on cheap labor to solve problems of production tended to eliminate the opportunities for inventiveness that had previously existed within Chinese society. Without the need for innovation, technological development came to a standstill, and when it did, the conditions that had forced this stagnation worsened.[15]

Apart from this view of the economic source of technological stagnation in fourteenth-century China, Elvin has noted another kind of change within Chinese society that also had a great deal to do with the "qualitative standstill" of the Ming period. Beginning in the fourteenth century, a philosophical reorientation occurred that had a profound effect on the course of Chinese social and economic history. The practical neo-Confucianism of the Sung dynasty gave way to a metaphysical and solipsistic system that denied the significance of the material world and undercut intellectual attempts to understand and to control the forces of nature.[16] In China, alterations in the representation of nature within the traditions of painting, poetry, and philosophy reflected — and helped to cause — changes in the perception of the human role in controlling and shaping the forces of the natural world.

Although Elvin's analysis has been the subject of considerable discussion among sinologists, his approach is provocative, for it suggests that we must look deep within a culture in order to understand fully the causes of economic or technological change. Like the cessation of technological growth in Ming China, the economic growth in medieval Europe must be analyzed from a cultural as well as from an economic perspective. It is within the context of the theological, artistic, and literary preconceptions that formed the mental landscape of the Middle Ages that one would hope to locate those factors that supported — or resisted — technological change.

One of the most provocative analyses of these cultural variables and their impact on the initiation of technological change in the West has been provided by the theologian Ernst Benz.[17] Benz argues (as Max Weber had before him) that there is a connection between Western technological achievement and "the specifically Christian premises of our Western culture."[18] According to Benz, the medieval image of the deity stressed God's role as artificer and demonstrated that in his act of fashioning human beings from matter God sanctified not only the product he produced, namely Adam and Eve, but also the process by which he did so. Isaiah 45:9–12 presents the image of God as a potter and of human beings as vessels shaped from the clay of the earth; these creatures may use the earth God has provided in order to continue to supply their needs. Likewise, the very notion of a personal, communicative Creator-God lends substance to the Western conviction that the fashioning of objects is blessed. Benz points out that other great religions, such as Buddhism, in lacking this idea of a personal creator also lack a basis on which to sanctify technology. In the West, as technology gradually grew more sophisticated and as the kinds of objects created by workmen shifted, so too did the iconography of the Creator-God shift form. According to Benz, God the potter gradually became God the master builder, and the clay used to shape human beings was replaced by the compasses used in shaping the human environment. In any case, there persisted a theological basis of support for human creativity, for human labor and technology.

The characterization of God as Creator and Architect of the universe provides Benz with the first part of an explanation for Western technological success. The second part entails the identification of human beings with God and assumes that human domination of the creation has been divinely ordained. Benz cites Gen. 1:27 and 9:6 in support of his contention that "compared to all other creatures, [human beings are] understood to be the 'image of God'."[19] The notion of human domination over the rest of the creation has often been cited as being a key factor in the history of Western technological mastery; indeed, the assumption of this domination has also been cited as being a factor in understanding Western technological disasters. Lynn White, Jr., has argued that the medieval Christian notion of human domination of the material world has provided the intellectual and moral background against which our current ecological problems must be understood.[20] "Man shares, in a great measure," White has written, "God's transcendence of nature. Christianity, in absolute contrast to ancient paganism and Asia's religions (except, perhaps, Zoroastrianism), not only established a dualism of man and nature but also insisted that it is God's will that man exploit nature for his proper ends."[21]

As persuasive as this argument might at first seem — and White is characteristically adept in drawing on a large body of material in order to suggest the historical inferences that must be drawn from these assumptions — there are other scholars who resist its inherent technological determinism and who find in Christianity just as much support for a benign, custodial view of the natural world as for an exploitative one. John Passmore, for example, has cited numerous biblical texts in support of the contention that Christianity advocated a view of nature that stressed responsibility and partnership rather than domination.[22] William Coleman argues that "the perennial Christian doctrine has been to accord man a modest livelihood in this world, not to promote his wealth or temporal power," and he suggests that the real contribution of Christianity was to apply "a new apologetic" for economic individualism during the seventeenth century.[23] Robin Attfield has recently reviewed this literature and provided a compelling argument for the view that Christian theology has consistently supported the belief that human beings are morally responsible for their stewardship of nature.[24]

To these discussions, all of which are in part responses to Lynn White's views, I would add an additional cautionary note on the use to which "paganism" and "animism" are put in discussions that find in Christianity a unique support for technological progress. Although one may find Greco-Roman texts that undervalue technological innovations and dismiss the work of laborers and craftsmen with contempt, there are equally good reasons to see these views as exceptional. One needs to look both at the actual technological achievements of the ancient world and at the compelling body of literary evidence that clearly favored the human aspiration to shape the physical world according to human ends.[25]

The third point made by Benz involves the contribution to Western technological progress deriving from the Christian conception of time.[26] Indeed, the very use of the word "progress" implies the existence of a linear conception of time, the sense that history is "going somewhere" and that events are unique and connected to one another through chains of cause and effect. Add to this the Christian expectation of a proximate eschatological event — an end to time and a consummation of all that has been achieved within the end points of creation and judgment — and a theory of meaningful action and of technological progress begins to seem compelling. "We must work . . . while it is day," writes Saint John, and we must do so in order to "redeem the time." Benz himself anticipates the obvious objection to an argument for technological progress based on the anticipation of an end of time: for, one must surely ask, would not the "work" done to prepare for the dissolution of the world be spiritual rather than material? The answer proposed by Benz is that, for the Christian of the Middle Ages, a sharp distinction between spiritual and material labor was not maintained. Labor was a form of worship, and the material and technological products of labor were manifestations of a devotion that did, indeed, prepare the Christian for the coming dissolution of time. Thus, the incentive to shape the physical world after human ideas was reinforced both by the sense of urgency that accompanies the idea of finite time and by the sense that work itself may be offered to God as a prayer.[27]

Though the arguments of Benz can by no means be accepted without reservation — we know, for example, that a theologian as influential as Augustine denied the God-as-artisan analogy — it does seem that Benz's analysis provides an appealing and persuasive explanation for the missing variable needed to account for the material successes of the Latin West during the Middle Ages. Indeed, in the hands of Lynn White, Jr., this argument has often seemed not only persuasive but predictive as well. White has argued that the Christian attitude toward work and material progress fostered a "cultural climate" favorable to technological advance, and he has also argued that traces of this formative attitude can be discovered in the art, literature, and theology of the period.[28] Yet, as White himself acknowledges, the attitudes that Benz postulates in support of technology were not universal. Some individuals resisted material change for spiritual reasons, and some rejected economic changes that implied social realignments, while others, we may assume, suffered from the generalized "technophobia" that seems to be a counterpart of technological change in every age. Indeed, M. D. Chenu has demonstrated in a compelling fashion that resistance to both material and theological "progress" was deeply ingrained in twelfth-century thought, precisely at the time when (if Benz's views are correct) one would expect to see the clearest alignment of theology with technical and social change.[29]

Jacques Le Goff provides an alternative account of the role played by Christianity in supporting technological change, an account that sees technology altering in response to the changing material conditions of Europe rather than creating the conditions under which such change occurred. Le Goff argues that the medieval church, at least until the twelfth century, viewed manual labor and craftsmanship as necessary physical burdens, as penances that could be offered as prayer.[30] As such, labor was not primarily a means of subduing the physical world but rather another discipline capable of subduing the physical self. When, in the twelfth century, the pressure of economic and social change became too great to ignore, the church developed a new theory of labor — indeed, a whole new theory of culture — that recognized the role of labor to be the subjugation of the physical world to the human will; this labor was only incidentally penitential and had as its object the material world rather than the spiritual self.[31]

Taken together, the discussions of Benz, White, Le Goff, and others point to a variety of theological convictions that seem to ratify those human activities we call "technology." Yet, in my view, what is most compelling in a variety of genres of early Christian literature is not the sanction of manual labor or craftsmanship in the interests of dominating the physical world but rather the consistent view of the centrality of labor as a means of developing the spiritual self. Although there is good reason to agree with Benz about the characterization of God as master craftsman, there is less reason to agree that this characterization convinced early medieval writers that their Christian duty entailed the subjugation of the physical world through labor. At the same time, Le Goff's view of the penitential purposes of labor needs to be balanced by the notion, found in many medieval sources, that labor served as a means of creating the conditions under which spiritual life

— which included charity as well as penance — was made possible. Indeed, I would argue that the view of manual labor presented in early Christian writers was dominated by an emphasis on the spiritual utility of work, and I would suggest that a plausible theory of how medieval Christian theology influenced medieval technology must account for the secularization of this emphasis. I would like to turn now to a discussion of some medieval texts that illustrate my point and that suggest the direction in which the analysis of the cultural context of medieval technology might proceed.

THE CULTURAL CONTEXT OF MEDIEVAL LABOR AND TECHNOLOGY

The attitudes toward manual labor expressed by writers during the Middle Ages were undoubtedly shaped by the social and economic conditions of the period; I would argue, however, that these views were also shaped by a textual tradition, specifically by the traditions of biblical commentary and by the programs for establishing normative communal rules for the governance of Christian society. The creation of these attitudes was largely undertaken ex nihilo because Greco-Roman models for the integration of manual labor into social life were either inappropriate or uninfluential.[32] Certainly Greek and Roman society had made significant technological advances. Indeed, in the areas of agricultural practice and in some craft traditions Greco-Roman models were integrated into Christian communities.[33] Yet, even though there was a great deal of intellectual continuity between the Greco-Roman and Christian worlds, theoretical support for labor and craftsmanship was re-created during the early Christian centuries in much the same way that a Christian theory of progress was constructed out of a revised view of the nature of history.[34]

Central to the bookish (if largely illiterate) culture of the early Middle Ages were religious texts, especially the book of Genesis and the Pauline epistles. Looking first at Genesis for the content of Christian attitudes toward manual labor, one notes that some commentators on the creation story did see, as Benz thought, a sanctification of human labor based on the model of God's artisanship. Saint Basil, Gregory of Nazianus, Saint Ambrose, and Bede all remind their readers that the world as the work of God brings the Worker intimately before the faithful and blesses the idea of labor itself.[35] Saint Augustine writes in De genesi ad litteram that the Creator blesses as "good" both that which he created and the work of creation itself.[36] Similar assurances are to be found in Origen's homilies on Genesis.[37]

On the other hand, nearly every commentator also noted that the most immediate consequence of the primordial sin was the condemnation of Adam and his progeny to manual labor — a labor conceived of both rhetorically and iconographically as agricultural and onerous.[38] Thus, Clement of Alexandria contrasts the innocent play of Adam before the Fall with the toil of his labor afterward.[39] Lactantius writes, in the *Divina institutiones*, that before Adam was overcome by his appetites he had only to praise God and to live freely.[40] Saint Ambrose contrasts the ease with which the earth bore fruit and supported Adam before the Fall with the pain of toil that followed it; however, Ambrose also asserts that even now, in a postlapsarian world, the earth is benign and fruitful.[41]

These observations on the relationship between sinfulness and labor must be understood within the proper context. In the hexaemeral literature, the distinction is not simply between blessed idleness and cursed labor; for one thing, commentary on the creation story (Gen.2:5 ff.) described a nonburdensome form of prelapsarian labor. Augustine makes this point clearly in his "literal" commentary on Genesis (*De genesi ad litteram*) when he writes that, before the Fall, Adam did agricultural labor of his own free will and that in this "pleasant" labor Adam merely took advantage of another blessing created by God. Likewise, in working with his hands Adam praised God and fulfilled that part of human nature that desires the rational pleasure of work.[42] Indeed, the real consequence of Adam's sin was seen, by Augustine, Ambrose, and others, not as the necessity of toil but as the estrangement from a benign natural world. Ironically, the domination and exploitation of nature is only necessary *after* the primordial sin, precisely when Adam has revealed his incapacity in a merely custodial role.

What is really described in Genesis — and what comes through most clearly in the commentaries on it — is the process of estrangement that has divided human beings from their own nature and from their function as rulers over the created world. "Man . . . who holds the principate over every living thing," is how Ambrose describes human nature; but pride has forced this natural sovereignty to become less a cooperative partnership, a benign symbiosis, and more a relationship of power and exploitation — the Golden Age becomes the Age of Iron. The hexaemeral commentaries of Basil and Ambrose in particular demonstrate the extent to which the natural world was created not for exploitation but for cooperative physical and moral sustenance. Plants and animals, which have a clear emblematic function, provide Adam with lessons in loyalty, industry and chastity.[43] Adam's sin makes work necessary because his natural power over the world is compromised: his sin also makes the organization of labor necessary, for, as Gen. 4: 17–22 indicates, the purely agrarian world — in which nature yields up its fruits freely — is transformed by Adam's sin to include a "technological" component, the domestication of cattle, the initiation of metallurgical techniques, the establishment of cities (the first was called Henoch, after Cain's son), and the institution of the arts ("[Jubal] was the father of all who play the harp and organ"). Saint Basil suggested that God has given human beings craftsmanship in order to replace the natural powers that have been lost through sin.[44] Finally, in the ultimate image of domination, God gives Noah, the second Adam, the right to kill and consume those animals with whom he once shared a peaceful, vegetarian existence. The violation of Adam's natural authority over nature removes from labor — and from human life generally — its pastoral and playful qualities and makes it instead a matter of life and death.

Apart from the theological arguments centering around the text of Genesis, numerous other biblical texts and theological commentaries suggest that manual labor was esteemed by early Christians as a source of both material and spiritual sustenance. The facts of their social lives — their marginal position in society during the first centuries of their existence as a sect, their heterogeneous background in terms of social and educational experience — tended to generate among Christians a toleration of labor and laborers not found in the Greco-Roman world. Tertullian expressed this toleration in *De testimonio animae* when he praised the "simple, and unmannered, and uncultivated, and uneducated." Similar sentiments, as well as detailed defenses of labor, may be found in Lactantius, in Origen, and in Minucius Felix.[45] Since the Christian must work in order to live — and the text most frequently cited in support of this fact is by Saint Paul ("If any man will not work, neither let him eat"; 2 Thess. 3:10) — he or she may offer up this labor as a form of praise, as a concession to social equality, as a means of social support, and as a reminder of how the labor of salvation also requires a continuous effort. Thus Cyprian writes of the risks of spiritual laziness and counsels the habit of continual labor while the third-century *Constitutiones apostolorum* warns the "idlers" (of Prov. 6:6) to learn industry from the ant because God hates the sluggard.[46]

Christianity, in fact, is seen by many of its earliest apologists as a faith that requires equal amounts of God-given illumination and human hard work. Thus, Saint Basil notes, labor is a gift from God, a means of attaining grace, and a source of praise: ". . . work itself should be a prayer of praise and thanksgiving reverently rendered to God who has bestowed on man the faculties of work and the means of exercising these faculties."[47] Using similar language, Gregory of Nazianus proclaims labor to be intrinsically valuable, materially productive, and spiritually enriching.[48] Latin writers express similar attitudes. In a letter exhorting a young novice to devotion, Jerome cites the proverb that "everyone who is idle is prey to vain desires" and reminds the young man that work is necessary not only for the support of the body but for the support of the soul as well. Hilary of Poitiers, writing midway through the fourth century, notes that bodily infirmity — that is, the need to eat, drink, and sleep — naturally prevents a religious person from practicing continual devotion but that every act, if piously performed, may be seen as a prayer.[49] This point becomes important in future discussions of the spiritual role of manual labor, especially in the context of establishing monastic ideals and rules; Hilary's assertion that ordinary life and the satisfaction of ordinary needs could be sanctified indicates the main direction that Western thought on the role of manual labor in religious life would take.

Thus in his *Institutes*, John Cassian, who had traveled to the Egyptian desert to observe the holy men living there late in the fourth century, counseled all of those committed to the religious life to engage in manual labor as a protection against the risks of sloth. Furthermore, Cassian saw in manual labor a value that lay outside the bounds of penance: "for practicing equally the virtues of the body and of the soul, a balance is struck between what the outer man needs and what the inner man finds satisfying."[50] Later on in the *Institutes* Cassian developed this theme further by showing that Saint Paul set an example by laboring with his hands and that this labor "cures many faults" of both a physical and spiritual nature.[51] Cassian, like Jerome, cited the assiduous labor of the Egyptian and Syrian monks as an example for all Christians, and he noted that the "fruits of one's hands" constitute a true sacrifice to God. However, it must be noted that by the "labor of the hands" Cassian meant not only agricultural labor but also intellectual labor, manuscript copying, and, in the purely penitential vein, redundant physical tasks whose only product was discomfort and the subjugation of the flesh.[52]

Among the earliest Christian writers, Saint Augustine's influence proved to be most influential, and his views on the role of labor and its products are therefore of particular interest. Augustine's insistence on the omnipotence of God and the dependency of man on God's grace for illumination and salvation led him to insist on the individual's responsibility for correctly evaluating the relative spiritual merit of various worldly pursuits. In *De doctrina christiana*, Augustine provides this index of relative utility: "Some things are to be enjoyed, others are to be used, and there are others which are to be enjoyed and used. Those things which are to be enjoyed make us blessed. Those things which are to be used help, and as it were, sustain us as we move toward blessedness in order that we might gain and cling to those things which make us blessed."[53] As is clear from *De opere monachorum* (On the work of monks) — a text composed in response to a group of monks who claimed that the exhortation to "live as freely as the birds" and not worry about physical sustenance was more binding than the Pauline injunction to labor — the things that can move a Christian toward blessedness include manual labor. Echoing a point made by Basil and John Cassian, Augustine writes that only those who labor and produce an excess of goods can be in a position to practice charity rather than to receive it.[54]

Despite his commitment to Christian asceticism, Augustine praised both the products of labor and craftsmanship and the process of labor that produced them; in a famous passage in *The City of God*, Augustine cites human material progress as evidence for the beneficent providence of God.[55]

This seeming paradox is part of the intellectual and spiritual outlook of many medieval writers. From Augustine and Gregory the Great to Hugh of Saint Victor and Thomas Aquinas, one finds the concurrent dismissal and affirmation of those worldly actions that produce the objects and structures that constitute Christian civilization. Indeed, it is not too much to say that the conflict that Augustine set out to resolve in *De opere monachorum* persisted throughout the Middle Ages and beyond: if the world is fallen, then actions in the world merely serve to sustain an imperfection. But with the loss of the millennial hope, the world became the theater of action for the Christian seeking salvation. The millennial hope became part of a theory of progress, and the time of waiting became a time in which to work and prepare for the delayed — but inevitable — end of time.[56] Thus labor is sanctioned, and, as *The City of God* attests, the material products of this labor were thought by Augustine to have an extrinsic value defined by their testimony to human power over nature and to human progress toward the perfection of this world — a promise thought from at least the time of Eusebius to lie at the heart of Christianity.[57]

Though Augustine avoids creating a hierarchy of labors, it seems clear that the "labor" of praise, of meditation, and of spreading the Gospel is inherently superior to the manual labor that is the duty of all those not directly involved in such spiritual occupations. In *De doctrina christiana*, he writes that "Among other arts, some are concerned with the manufacture of a product which is the result of the labor of the artificer, like a house, a bench, a dish, or something of that kind. Others exhibit a kind of assistance to the works of God, like medicine, agriculture, and navigation . . . a knowledge of these arts is to be acquired casually and superficially in the ordinary course of life unless a particular office demands a more particular knowledge."[58] Work of all kinds is of personal value to the monk, nun, or layman, for it chastens the flesh and may be offered up to God as a form of devotion; work that is productive is of value to the community of believers because it fills the intervening time of waiting and gives glory to the ingenuity of human beings. In essence, Augustine's view defines the status quo of the fourth through the twelfth centuries: some work, some pray, and some fight; all these necessary social functions glorify God and maintain the order that the early church first threatened, then rejuvenated.[59]

Augustine's recognition of the importance of manual labor—and his insistence on placing labor within a soteriological rather than a purely economic framework — reflected attitudes common to other early writers. Saint Ambrose, for example, argued that it was the desire for pleasure that led humanity into original sin and that the enhancement of the material conditions of life merely deepens one's immersion into the corruptions of the world.[60] Gregory of Nyssa counseled his readers to withdraw from "anxious toil upon the land" as part of a program to return to the prelapsarian conditions of Eden.[61] A few centuries later, in commenting on Gen. 3:17–18, Bede raised similar points: labor is the consequence of sin, a testimony to the fault of being overly concerned with the things of this world, and a means of perpetuating this concern.[62] In this recognition of the distracting nature of labor and in the insistence on the primacy of the *opus dei* over the *opus manuum*, Eastern and Western Christianity were united. Both Saint Basil and Saint Benedict, the two preeminent regulators of Christian communal life, insisted that labor must not intrude on the devotional aspects of the life devoted to God.[63] In the matter of monastic attitudes, in fact, the notion that the West was more "practical" than the East—or that Eastern devotional forms excluded labor while Western forms encouraged its practice — does not hold up. A survey of the textual background against which medieval monastic labor was practiced may perhaps help to clarify the role played by manual labor in the Christian communities established during the fourth and fifth centuries.

In fourth-century Egypt, Saint Anthony was acknowledged to have been the perfect model of the anchoristic (solitary) life, whereas Pachomius, founder of a community of monks at Tabennesi in A.D. 320, was taken to be the model of the cenobitic (communal) life.[64] At Tabennesi the monks raised their own food and worked to supply the community with all its material necessities. Crafts were practiced, trade was conducted with secular communities, and charitable functions were performed for men and women in surrounding communities.[65] Though it was not at all unusual for a religious hermit to perform manual labor — there are numerous examples recorded in the *Sayings of the Fathers* — the contribution made to the history of monasticism by Pachomius was the organization of communal labor in order to create an economic basis for the religious life.[66]

The four monastic rules known collectively as the *Regulae patrum*, composed during the fifth century and collected by Benedict of Aniane in the *Codex regularum* during the ninth century, offer some valuable insights into the consequences of this organization of manual labor during the earliest centuries of Western monasticism.[67] The first of these texts, the so-called *Rule of the Four Fathers*, discusses labor in its tenth and eleventh chapters. In chapter 10 the rule prescribes devotion to God during the first to the third hours of the day. "But," the text continues, "from the third hour to the ninth, whatever has been commanded must be done without murmuring."[68] The *Rule of the Four Fathers* next legislates that the "work of the hands" prescribed in 2 Thess. 3:10 (quoted above) nonetheless must not harm any monk overcome by weakness of the body and that the monk who is weak in spirit should work even harder in order to "restore the body to subjection." This labor was ascetic rather than productive: "Therefore, this [practice of labor] must be observed so that in nothing will the brother do his own will." Manual labor is seen here as a means of subduing the individual will by forcing the monk into a cooperative contribution to the monastery; whatever class distinctions might have existed among the monks were also extinguished through the universalizing of work usually associated with a particular social class. Indeed, a number of other regulations in other rules were included as a means of eliminating those distinctions between monks that were based on the possession of property.[69]

The *Rule of Macarius*, written late in the fifth century, adds two points to the discussion of manual labor in the *Rule of the Four Fathers*.

First of all, chapter 8 of this rule warns the monk not to hate manual labor and to avoid the dangers of idleness.[70] Second, in the last chapter of this rule, craftsmen are addressed directly: "Inside the monastery no [monk] may practice a craft, except for him whose faith is proven, and who does his work for the utility and necessity of the monastery."[71] The appearance of this regulation within the context of a set of warnings against monastic misconduct suggests that the practice of a craft, as opposed to the practice of agricultural labor, constituted a nonessential diversion from the perceived business of a monk. Although there can be little doubt that the skills of a fuller, a smith, or a carpenter would be necessary to the monastery, they were not necessary enough to compromise the commitment of the community as a whole to the work of worship; those weak in faith must first strengthen their souls before they may contribute their manual skills to the community.

The same attitude may be found in the *Rule of the Master*, composed sometime during the sixth century. In this rule manual labor is described as a cure for the spiritual tasks of idleness — the busy eye and mind are not flooded by desires. Moreover, Saint Paul's text (2 Thess. 3: 10) is cited in order to confirm the fact that there must be physical as well as spiritual labor included in the monastic schedule.[72] However, the *Rule of the Master* defines "physical labor" broadly enough to include the reading (during the winter months and until the vernal equinox) and the study of Latin. Handicrafts, when practiced in silence and under supervision, are also allowed. During the summer months manual labor in the fields is to be performed, but with restrictions:

> Field work and missions requiring travel should be considered the province of those brothers who are not skilled in the arts and have neither the desire nor the ability to learn them. The skilled craftsmen, however, are to stay at their respective crafts every day, having their daily quota of work assigned and checked. . . . Delicate and weak brothers should be assigned such work as will nourish them for the service of God, not kill them. As to the hard of heart, as also the simple brothers and those who have neither the desire nor the ability to learn letters, let them be tied down by rough labor, but in a measure consonant with justice, lest they be the only ones continually oppressed by various kinds of work.[73]

Thus, in the formulation of the *Regula magistri*, manual labor is interchangeable with intellectual labor during the inclement seasons. It includes the practice of crafts without specification of what kinds of products may be produced; it is fitted to the physical and intellectual constitutions of individual monks; and it is an introverted activity that both sustains the community and feeds the spiritual life of the individual monk. The degree of organization of manual labor appears to be far greater under this rule than under any earlier rule — the idea of daily quotas assigned and checked by superiors is not to be found in any other rules except for those that came out of the early Pachomian communities.[74] At the same time, one also notes that the "Master" explicitly warns against valuing the "profits of the flesh" too highly, and later in his text he recommends that "secular workmen" be charged with the oversight of the monastery's agricultural productivity so that "[the monks] do not let [their] thoughts wander off to worldly things."

It is thus important to note that even in this highly organized community of laboring monks, the spiritual mission of the individual and of the community was neither lost sight of nor compromised in the interests of enhanced productivity. This fact is not surprising, but it is worth stressing the ways in which the labors of the hands were consciously shaped by the labors of the soul so that one might avoid forming the impression that monastic life held inviolable the ideal of a productive social community. From its beginnings in the deserts and wadis of the Middle East, monasticism used labor to purify the individual, to sustain a community of believers, and to open up avenues of charity. The later history of medieval monasticism demonstrates that physical needs did not take precedence over the personal spiritual needs of the individual monk, and one must not lose sight of the fact that labor and productivity created a social context for the practice of religion, rather than religion creating a structure supportive of labor.[75]

This last point is particularly clear when one examines the *Rule* composed by Saint Benedict in the mid-sixth century, a text known to have been influenced by the *Rule of the Master*.[76] Benedict, first of all, saw manual labor as a necessary part of monastic life because it protects the brothers from the potentially harmful effects of leisure: "Leisure (*otiositas*) is the enemy of the soul, and for this reason the brothers must spend a certain amount of time in doing manual work (*in labore manuum*) as well as the time spent in divine reading (*lectione divina*)."[77] Manual labor supplements the true work of reading, prayer, and meditation; it assists the monks in their attempts to live "as our fathers and apostles did," and it is specifically designed so that those who are weak are not overwhelmed or driven away: "Let those who are not strong have help so that they may serve [meals] without distress. . . ." For Benedict, the very essence of monastic life entails manual labor, and, as de Vogüé has shown, the Benedictine *Rule* assumes that matters such as diet will be determined, in part, by the labor performed by a particular member of the monastic community.[78] Indeed, Benedict's discussion of manual labor occurs in a chapter of the *Rule* that outlines the basic structure of the monastic day. As Benedict says, "the labor of obedience will bring you back to him from whom you have strayed through disobedience," and the monastery is pictured as the workshop in which the monk labors to perfect his soul and to know his God.[79]

A different approach to labor and to the organization of monastic life is to be found in the Rule of Saint Columban (c. 543–615), a rule reflecting the harsher, more ascetic world of Irish monasticism, where labor was primarily a tool for the mortification of the flesh ("the main purpose of monastic rules is mortification . . .").[80] The Irish monks labored in the fields and practiced simple crafts, but "All training, according to the Apostle, for the present seems to be a matter not of joy but of sorrow; nevertheless, it yields a pleasant fruit and a peaceful increase of reward . . . for indeed what is to be learnt here without sorrow and toil . . . ? How much grief lies in the craftsman's trades? How much toil?"[81] In the rule of Columban, one encounters the ideal of labor as penance, and one sees the extent to which the eremitical ideal persisted within the structure of Western monasticism even as the Benedictines established a monastic ethic that would, by the twelfth century, accept productivity and wealth as natural by-products of cooperative labor.

CONCLUSION

The tension between the communal (cenobitic) and the solitary (eremitical) ideals in monastic rules and monastic practice was never really resolved, and manual labor, as a principal source of wealth, was always difficult to reconcile with the spiritual goals of monastic life. Labor and craftsmanship were part of monastic devotions, and in every rule but Columban's some allowances were made for the inclinations and abilities of individual monks or nuns. It is not clear from the rules alone, except for Columban's, that manual labor was viewed as being merely gratuitous or even primarily penitential; in Augustine, Basil, the "Master," and Benedict of Nursia, work was functional, a part of the Christian life lived after apostolic models, and a means of controlling rather than of punishing the flesh.

The purpose of labor — as described not only in early monastic rules but also in a wide range of apologetic and exegetical writings — was the creation of both a physical and spiritual context within which God could be more fully worshiped. Then, too, the dignity of labor in the early Christian tradition was, as Benz surmised, bound up with the creativity of God; in addition, the dignity of labor was tied by writers like Basil, Ambrose, and Augustine to the human obligation of caring for — and utilizing — the physical world.

Although Lynn White is correct in seeing human needs as central in the Christian conception of nature, the textual tradition suggests that this centrality mandated a cooperative and custodial rather than an exploitative relationship. Indeed, the realization that the "fullness of time" and the end of the world were to be delayed created a motive for the sanctification of those labors that sustained the individual Christian and the community of believers. What the monastic tradition did was to make normative what was already the case, namely, the practice of labor and craftsmanship in the interests of creating a viable community whose purpose was spiritual, whose "profit" was otherworldly, and whose interest in time was shaped by a concern for its ending rather than for its potential for sustaining progress.

In evaluating the contributions of early medieval Christianity to the subsequent history of technology, then, what emerges as most significant is the positive evaluation of labor and craftsmanship and the location of these activities within the framework of personal and communal life. Until there is a cultural consensus supporting the notions of productivity and efficiency for their own sake, there is no incentive within a social system — any social system — to concentrate on developing techniques for the elimination of the tedium of labor. Early medieval Europe spiritualized daily life, including daily labor, but until a clear-cut distinction could be drawn between acts performed for spiritual ends and acts performed for secular ends (such as profit), there could be no rationale for technological advancement.

The role played by manual labor in the medieval texts that I have summarized here suggests that the difficulty and tedium of work were not objectionable because there resided within this difficulty the potential for significant spiritual benefits. This view seems neither to support a work ethic nor to be a catalyst of technological invention; in fact, it raises the possibility that although Christianity supplied attitudes that, when joined with other economic and social factors, helped create a receptivity to technological change, Christianity was not itself responsible for creating the conditions under which such change occurred. As a religion characterized above all by adaptability, Christianity should perhaps be seen as having adjusted itself to a world being altered by technology rather than as being the decisive force behind such alteration.

NOTES

This essay originally appeared in *Technology and Culture* 27 (1986): 471–500.

1. Thomas Sprat, *History of the Royal Society* (London, 1667), pp. 11–14.

2. William Wotton, *Reflections upon Ancient and Modern Learning* (London, 1694), pp. xiv-vii, 1–3.

3. A. R. J. Turgot, *On Progress, Sociology, and Economics*, ed. and trans. Ronald L. Meek (Cambridge, 1973), pp. 41–45, 55.

4. Examples of this attitude toward medieval technology and its relationship to the history of science may be found in Condorcet, *Esquisse d'un tableau historiques des progrès de l'espirit humain* (Paris, 1795), pp. 65–77; in William Whewell, *The History of Inductive Sciences*, 2 vols. (London, 1849), 1:175–82; in John Tyndall, *Advancement of Science* (New York, 1874), pp. 28–35; and described in Jacques Le Goff, "The Several Middle Ages of Jules Michelet," in *Time, Work, and Culture in the Middle Ages* (Chicago, 1980), p. 15. For the twentieth-century history of the "dark Middle Ages," see J. B. Bury, *The Idea of Progress* (London, 1924), pp. 20–21, which provides a typical formulation of the early twentieth-century approach to the question of scientific and technological progress during the Middle Ages: "The idea of the universe which prevailed throughout the Middle Ages, and the general orientation of men's thoughts were incompatible with some of the fundamental assumptions which are required by the idea of Progress." While he takes more seriously the contributions of medieval artisans to the history of technology and science, Edgar Zilsel ("The Genesis of the Concept of Scientific Progress," in *Journal of the History of Ideas* 6 [1945]: 325–49) persists in denying to the Middle Ages any inclination to develop a consistent and progressive theory of scientific achievement.

5. I have found the following works particularly useful: Lynn Thorndike, *A History of Magic and Experimental Science*, 8 vols. (New York, 1923–58); Marc Bloch, *Land and Work in Medieval Europe*, trans. J. E. Anderson (Berkeley and Los Angeles, 1967); Lynn White, Jr., *Medieval Technology and Social Change* (Oxford, 1962) and *Medieval Religion and Technology* (Berkeley, Calif., 1978); Bertrand Gille, in *Histoire générale des techniques*, ed. Maurice Daumas, vol.1 (Paris, 1962), pp. 429–598, and vol. 2 (Paris, 1965), pp. 2–139; Guy Beaujouan, "L'Interdépendance entre la science scolastique et les techniques utilitaires (XIIᵉ, XIIIᵉ, et XIVᵉ siècles)," in *Les Conférences du Palais de la Découverte*, séries D, no. 46 (Paris, 1947); Jacques Le Goff, *Time, Work, and Culture*; and Friedrich Klemm, *Der Beitrag des Mittelalters zur Entwicklung der abendländischen Technik* (Wiesbaden, 1961).

6. I have named just a few significant innovations and ignored their chronology. For a systematic survey of inventions, see Lynn White, Jr., "Technology and Invention in the Middle Ages," in *Speculum* 15 (1940): 141–59 (rep. in *Medieval Religion and Technology*, pp. 1–22) and Gille (n. 5 above).

7. Carlo Cipolla, *Before the Industrial Revolution*, 2nd ed. (New York, 1980), p. 150; and J. C. Russell, "Population in Europe 500–1500," in Carlo Cipolla, ed., *The Fontana Economic History of Europe*, vol. 1, *The Middle Ages* (Sussex, 1976), p. 36, table 1. Russell's estimate is that population increased from 27.5 million in A.D. 500 to 50 million in 1500.

8. See, for example, Ian Dershaw, "The Great Famine and Agrarian Crisis in

England, 1315–1322," in *Past and Present* 59 (1973): 3–50; also, J. M. W. Bean, "Plague, Population, and Economic Decline in the Late Middle Ages," in *The Economic History Review*, ser. 2,15 (1963): 423–37.

9. See Lynn White, Jr., "Cultural Climates and Technological Advance in the Middle Ages," *Viator* 2 (1971): 171–201 (in *Medieval Religion and Technology*, pp. 217– 53).

10. Provocative questions about the meaning of "progress" are raised by Arnold Pacey, *The Culture of Technology* (Cambridge, Mass., 1983), pp. 13–34; and by Eric Wolf, *Europe and the People without History* (Berkeley, Calif., 1982), p. 5 and passim. Though his examples are modern, David F. Noble's *Forces of Production: A Social History of Industrial Automation* (New York, 1984) includes a discussion of progress which I have found invaluable.

11. For an overview of these changes, see *The Cambridge Economic History of Europe*, ed. M. Postan and H. J. Habakkuk (Cambridge, 1952-), 2: 419ff.; for a more specialized study of changes in agriculture, see D. Herlihy, "The Agrarian Revolution in Southern France and Italy, 801–1150," *Speculum* 33 (1958): 23–44.

12. For Byzantine technology, see *The Cambridge Medieval History*, 2d ed. (Cambridge, 1966–67), 4:299 ff.; for China, see Joseph Needham, Wang Ling, et al., *Science and Civilisation in China*, 6 vols. (Cambridge, 1954-), esp. vol. 4, pts. 2 and 3, and vol. 5, pts. 3 and 4. For Africa, where technology in some areas advanced considerably during the European Middle Ages, see Jack Goody, *Technology, Tradition, and the State in Africa* (Cambridge, 1971), pp. 21–38; for the interrelations created by "trade diasporas," see Philip D. Curtin, *Cross-Cultural Trade in World History* (Cambridge, 1984). I hope that the emphasis on European technology here does not obscure the profound influences exercised on this culture by the rest of the world during the whole course of the Middle Ages.

13. For the influence of Chinese invention on Western technology, with analysis of the modes of transmission and the "lag" between Western and Chinese technological innovation, see Needham et al., *Science and Civilization in China*, 1:93–112.

14. For this discussion of China's economic and technological history I am indebted to Mark Elvin, *The Pattern of the Chinese Past* (Stanford, Calif., 1973), esp. pp. 203–34; for China's "high-level equilibrium trap," see pp. 314–315. I must note that opinion is divided on Elvin's thesis; for a thorough critique of Elvin's views, see the essay review by Nathan Sivin, "Imperial China: Has Its Present Past a Future?" in the *Harvard Journal of Asiatic Studies* 38 (1978): 440–80.

15. Elvin, pp. 199, 285 ff.

16. Elvin discusses these changes on pp. 225–34.

17. Ernst Benz, "I fondamenti cristiani della tecnica occidentale," in E. Castelli, ed., *Tecnica e casistica* (Rome, 1964), pp. 241–63.

18. See Benz, "I fondamenti," p. 242; also, Ernst Benz, "The Christian Expectation of the End of Time and the Idea of Technical Progress," in *Evolution and Christian Hope: Man's Concept of the Future from the Early Fathers to Teilhard des Chardin* (Garden City, N.Y., 1966), p. 121; Lynn White, Jr., discusses Benz's thesis in "Cultural Climates and Technological Advance," in *Medieval Religion and Technology* (n. 5 above), pp. 236–38 — and, while I have disagreed with his conclusions, I am deeply indebted to White's discussion. Max Weber considered some of the same ideas in his *Wirtschaftsgeschichte* (New York, 1927), trans. as *General Economic History* by Frank H. Knight (New Brunswick, N.J., 1981), and in *The Protestant Ethic and the Spirit of Capitalism*, trans. Talcott Parsons (New York, 1958), esp. pp. 118–19.

19. Benz, "I fondamenti" (n. 17 above), pp. 248–52; and "The Christian Expectation" (n. 18 above), pp. 122–24.

20. Lynn White, Jr., "The Historical Roots of Our Ecological Crisis," in *Science*, March 10, 1967 (rep. in *Dynamo and Virgin Reconsidered* [Cambridge, Mass., 1968], pp. 75–94).

21. White, "The Historical Roots of Our Ecological Crisis." p. 86.

22. John Passmore, *Man's Responsibility for Nature* (London, 1974). pp. 3–40.

23. William Coleman, "Providence, Capitalism, and Environmental Degradation," in *Journal of the History of Ideas* 37 (1976): 41.

24. Robin Attfield, "Christian Attitudes to Nature," in *Journal of the History of Ideas* 44 (1983): 369–71.

25. See Rodolfo Mondolfo, "The Greek Attitude to Manual Labor," in *Past and Present* 6 (1954–55): 1–5; also Albert Rehm, "Zur Rolle der Technik in der griechisch-römischen Antike," in *Archiv für Kulturgeschichte* 28 (1938): 135–62; Mme. de Romilly, "Thucydide et l'idée de progrès," in *Annali di Pisa* (1966), pp. 183–85; Alison Burford, *Craftsmen in Greek and Roman Society* (Ithaca, N.Y., 1972). For the role that slavery played in determining dismissive attitudes toward labor (such as one finds in Xenophon, *Deconomia*, 4:203), see M. I. Finley, "Technical Innovation and Economic Progress in the Ancient World," in *Economic History Review*, 2d ser., 18 (1965): 43–45. A Roman view of the edifying nature of agricultural labor may be found in Columella, *De re rustica*, bk. 1, preface; and a forceful statement of human power over the natural world is in Cicero, *De natura deorum*, bk. 2, sec. 151–54. And also note Virgil's well-known tag "Labor omnia vincit/Improbus et duris urgens in rebus egestas," which provided not only a defense of labor but a rationale for its value as well.

26. Benz, "The Christian Expectation of the End of Time" (n. 18 above), pp. 126–27. For an overview of the Christian view of time, see Oscar Cullman, *Christ und die Zeit* (Zollikon-Zurich, 1946); and Jacques Le Goff, "Merchant's Time and Church's Time in the Middle Ages," in *Time, Work, and Culture* (n. 5 above), pp. 29–42.

27. Aside from works already cited, see Lynn White, Jr., "What Accelerated Technological Progress in the Western Middle Ages?" in *Scientific Change*, ed. A. C. Crombie (New York, 1963), pp. 248–88. White notes that Benz's views do not take into account the fact that Byzantium shared a Christian culture with the West and yet did not develop a comparable technology; one should also note the incorporation of the images of Genesis into the Qur'an (sura 2, vv. 29–39) and the similar lack of a "progressive" Islamic technology — again, as a means of tempering the kind of technological determinism that seems to grow out of Benz's arguments. Saint Augustine undercuts the God-as-artisan analogy in *The City of God*, bk. 12, chap. 24: "For we must not imagine this operation [the creation of Adam] in the physical terms of experience, where we see artisans working up material from the earth into the shape of human limbs, with the ability of skilled craftsmanship" (trans. David Knowles, *The City of God* [Baltimore, 1972]).

28. See White's essay "Natural Science and Naturalistic Art in the Middle Ages," in *American Historical Review* 52 (1947): 421–35, rep. in *Medieval Religion and Technology* (n. 5 above), pp. 23–41.

29. M. D. Chenu, "Tradition and Progress," in *Nature, Man, and Society in the Twelfth Century*, ed. and trans. Jerome Taylor and Lester K. Little (Chicago, 1968), pp. 310–30.

30. Jacques Le Goff, "Trades and Professions as Represented in Confessors' Manuals," in *Time, Work, and Culture* (n. 5 above), pp. 114 and 121.

31. Jacques Le Goff, "Trades and Professions," p. 115; see also Le Goff's essay "Labor, Techniques, and Craftmen in the Value System of the Early Middle Ages (Fifth to Tenth Centuries)," also in *Time, Work, and Culture*, p. 86, where the date of the revaluation of agricultural labor is pushed back to the eighth century: "There can be little doubt that this valuation [of labor] was also the result of worker pressure on medieval ideology and mentality." See also M. David, "Les *Laboratores* jusqu' au renouveau économique des XIe-XIIe siècles," in *Études d'histoire du droit privé offertes à P. Petot* (Paris, 1959), pp. 107–20.

32. See Arthur T. Geoghegan, *The Attitude towards Labor in Early Christianity and*

Ancient Culture (Washington, D.C., 1945) for a well-documented account of the differences in attitude between Greco-Roman and Judeo-Christian accounts of the role of manual labor in social life.

33. For a few of the points of contact between ancient and medieval technology, see Charles Singer et al., eds., *A History of Technology* (Oxford, 1956), 2:382–96, 423–26 and passim.

34. See Gerhart B. Ladner, *The Idea of Reform*, rev. ed. (New York, 1967), pp. 1–5, 39ff.

35. See *Hexaemeron* in *Sancti Ambrosii opera*, ed. C. Schenkl, in *Corpus scriptorum ecclesiasticorum latinorum* (hereafter *CSEL*), vol. 32 (Vienna, 1896), bk. 1, chap. 5; Ambrose was responsible for bringing Basil's views to the West. For Bede, see *Hexaemeron* in *Patrologiae cursus completus, series latina* (hereafter *PL*), 221 vols., ed. J.-P. Migne (Paris, 1844–64), vol. 91, cols. 29–30. For general accounts of the role played by manual labor in the Bible, see F. Gryglewicz, "La Valeur morale du travail manuel dans la terminologie grecque de la bible," *Biblica* 37 (1956): 314–37.

36. *De genesi ad litteram*, ed. J. Zycha, in *CSEL* 28, p. 1 (Leipzig, 1894), bk. 4, chap. 13.

37. Origen, *In genesim homiliae*, ed. W. Baehrens, in *Origens Werke: Homilien zum Hexateuch in Rufins Übersetzung*, pt. 1, vol. 29 of *Die griechischen christlichen Schriftsteller der ersten drei Jahrhunderte* (Leipzig, 1920), homily 1, sec. 12.

38. For representations of the consequences of the Fall and discussion of its iconography, see Paul Brandt, *Schaffende Arbeit und bildende Kunst* (Leipzig, 1927), pp. 226–34.

39. Clement of Alexandria, *Cohortatio ad gentes*, cited in George Boas, *Essays on Primitivism and Related Ideas in the Middle Ages* (Baltimore, 1948), p. 24.

40. Lactantius, *Divinae institutiones*, in *PL* 6, cols. 517–18.

41. Ambrose, *Hexaemeron* (n. 35 above), bk. 3, chap. 10.

42. "Did God wish the first man to perform agricultural labor? Would it be believable that God would condemn man to labor before the first sin? We would think so, until we saw some do agricultural labor freely [*cum tanta voluptate animi*] and who would consider it a punishment to be called to other labor. Thus the pleasures of agriculture were much greater when nothing adverse occurred, either from the earth or heaven. It was not, therefore, the affliction of labor, but the exhilaration of the will [*sed exhilaratio voluntatis*] when those things which God has created grew with the aid of human labor; thus God should be praised more fully, who gave to the soul in an animal body the ability to reason and the faculty to labor insofar as was enough for the willing soul and not so much for the need of the body [*non quantum invitum indigentia corporis cogeret*]" (Augustine, *De genesi ad litteram* [n. 36 above], bk. 8, chap. 8).

43. Ambrose, *Hexaemeron* (n. 35 above), bk. 6, chap. 4: "Wild animals know what things are good for them, whereas you, man, have no idea what is good for you." Ambrose expands the discussion of Basil, *In Hexaemeron homilae*, in *Patrologiae cursus completus, series graeca*, ed. J.-P. Migne, 162 vols., with Latin trans. (Paris, 1857–66) (hereafter *PG*). For this text see *PG* 29, homily 8, chap. 4.

44. Basil, *In Hexaemeron homiliae*, in *PG* 29, col. 1053.

45. Tertullian, *De testimonia animae*, in *CSEL* 20, ed. G. Wissowa (Vienna, 1890), pp. 135–36; "Therefore it is clear that the Church is for everyone who works with his hands. . . ." For the social history of the early Christian church, see Wayne A. Meeks, *The First Urban Christians: The Social World of the Apostle Paul* (New Haven, Conn., 1983). Minucius Felix, *Octavius*, ed. H. A. Holden (Cambridge, 1853), pp. 54–56.

46. "You must labor all of the time; the lazy are forever disgraced. . . . Thus the sluggards are hateful to God for they are not able to be faithful." *Didascalia et constitutiones apostolarum*, ed. F. X. Funk (Paderborn, 1905), 1:90.

47. Basil, *Regulae fusius tractatae*, in *PG* 31, col. 1013.

48. Gregory of Nazianus, *Orationes*, in *PG* 35, cols. 936, 957; see also Rosemary Radford Ruether, *Gregory of Nazianus* (Oxford, 1969), pp. 141–42.

49. For Jerome, see *Epistulae*, in *CSEL* 56, ed. I. Hilberg (Vienna, 1918), epistle 125, p. 130; also epistle 130, p. 195. For Hilary of Poitiers, see *Tractatus super psalmos*, in *PL* 9, col. 246.

50. Cassian, *De institutis coenobiorum*, ed. Michael Petschenig, *CSEL* 17 (Vienna, 1888), bk. 2, chap. 14; also bk. 10, chap. 21.

51. Cassian, ibid., bk. 2, chap. 14; see also bk. 10, chap. 23 for the consequences to the West of not having a materially productive monasticism.

52. On Cassian's notion of what constituted manual labor, see Owen Chadwick, *John Cassian* (Cambridge, 1950), p. 62; also *De institutis* (n. 50 above), bk. 10, chap. 8–14.

53. Augustine, *De doctrina christiana*, in *Corpus christianorum, series latina* (hereafter *CCSL*) 32 (Turnhout, Belgium, 1962), bk. 1, chap. 3.

54. Augustine, *De opere monachorum*, in *PL* 40, cols. 549–50.

55. Augustine, *De civitate dei*, bk. 22, chap. 24: "Who can adequately describe, or even imagine, the work of the Almighty? And besides this [the virtues given to mankind] there are all the important arts discovered and developed by human genius, some for necessary uses, others simply for pleasure. . . . Think of man's progress in agriculture and navigation; of the variety, in conception and accomplishment, man has shown in pottery, in sculpture, in painting . . . all his ingenious devices for the capturing, killing, or taming of wild animals . . . the weapons against his fellow man . . . all the medical resources for preserving health . . ." (trans. David Knowles [n. 27 above], p. 1072.

56. Ladner (n. 34 above), pp. 27–33, 63–82, 153ff.

57. A survey of medieval Christian attitudes toward nature may be found in Clarence J. Glacken, *Traces on the Rhodian Shore: Nature and Culture in Western Thought* (Berkeley, Calif., 1967), pp. 176– 253.

58. Augustine, *De doctrina christiana*, in *PL* 40, bk. 1, chap. 30.

59. For the "three orders" and their interlocking social functions, see Georges Duby, *Les Trois ordres ou l'imaginaire du féodalisme* (Paris, 1978).

60. Ambrose, *Epistolae*, in *PL* 16, col. 1244 (epistle 63).

61. Gregory of Nyssa, *De virginitate*, in *PG* 46, col. 369.

62. Bede, *Opera exegetica, libri quator in principium genesis*, ed. C.W. Jones, in *CCSL* 118 (Turnhout, Belgium, 1960), p. 68.

63. For Saint Basil, see Rufinus's translation of the *Asceticon parvum*, in *PL* 103, cols. 491–92; for Saint Benedict's views, see Adalbert de Vogüé, ed. and comm., *La Règle de saint Benoît*, 7 vols., in *Sources chrétiennes*, 181–86 (Paris, 1971–72), chap. 48 ("Otiositas inimica est animae . . .") for the balancing of manual labor, divine reading, and prayer. For the place of manual labor in the various monastic rules generally, see E. Delaruelle, "Le Travail dans les règles monastiques occidentales du IVe au IXe siècle," in *Journal de psychologie normale et pathologique* 41 (1948): 51–62; Émile Levasseur, "Le Travail des moines dans les monastères," *Séances et travaux de l'Académie des sciences morales et politiques* 154, n.s. 60 (1900): 449–70.

64. For Saint Anthony, see the *Vita Antonii*, in *PG* 26, col. 835; a Latin translation (by Rufinus?) is in *PL* 73, col. 127ff. For the life of Pachomius, see F. Halkin, *Sancti Pachomii vitae graecae* (Brussels, 1932) trans. as *The Life of Pachomius* by A. N. Athanassakis (Missoula, Mont., 1975). For the roles of both in the early history of monasticism, see H. Bacht, "Antonius und Pachomius: von der Anachorese zum Cönobitentum," in *Antonius Magnus, eremita (356–1956), Studia Anselmiana* 38 (Rome, 1956). A recent treatment of the early history of monasticism is in the introduction to *RB — 1980: The Rule of St. Benedict*, ed. Timothy Fry (Collegeville, Minn., 1981), pp. 3–64.

65. For manual labor at Tabennesi, see Saint Jerome's preface to the Pachomian rule,

in A. Boon, ed. *Pachomina Latina, bibliothèque de la revue d'histoire ecclésiastique* 7 (1932): 3–5; D. J. Chitty, *The Desert a City* (Oxford, 1966), p. 40, n. 45, provides additional texts on manual labor in the early monastic establishments.

66. I have considered the relationship between manual labor and the eremitical and cenobitic traditions in "Manual Labor in Early Monastic Rules," *Viator* 17 (1986): 1–18.

67. For the relations of these early rules — collected by Benedict of Aniane during the ninth century — see Adalbert de Vogüé, "The Cenobitic Rules of the West," *Cistercian Studies* 12 (1977): 177–83. The rules of the *Codex regularum* are collected in *PL* 103; note of critical editions is made below.

68. Critical text is in Jean Neufville, "Règle des IV pères et second règle des pères," *Revue bénédictine* 77 (1967): 47–95; for this passage, see pp. 83, 85 (recension "E").

69. See, for example, chap. 59, "The Offering of Sons by Nobles or the Poor," in the Rule of Saint Benedict, ed. de Vogüé (n. 63 above).

70. Edited in Adalbert de Vogüé, *Les Règles des saintes pères*, 2 vols. (Paris, 1982), 1:374. Additional material in Helga Styblo, "Die Regula Macharii," in *Wiener Studien* 76 (1963): 124–60.

71. *Les Règles des saintes pères*, 1:389: "Illud etiam addendum fuit, ut intra monasterium artificium non faciat ullus, nisi ille cuius fides probata fuerit, quid ad utilitatem et necessitatem monasterii faciat, quid poterit facere."

72. Adalbert de Vogüé, ed., *Le Règle du Maitre*. In *Sources chrétiennes*, no. 106 (Paris, 1964–65), chap. 86, pp. 351–54.

73. Ibid., chap. 50, pp. 229–30.

74. See F. Prinz, *Frühes Mönchtum im Frankenreich* (Munich and Vienna, 1965), pp. 532–40.

75. Later medieval commentaries on earlier monastic rules, like St. Benedict's, tended to qualify the injunction to daily labor and to recognize varying functions for individual religious duties; see, for example, the twelfth-century *Libellus de diversis ordinibus et professionibus qui sunt in aecclesia*, ed. and trans. Giles Constable and B. Smith (Oxford, 1972), pp. 95–97.

76. See B. Jaspert, "*Regula magistri, Regula Benedicti*: Bibliographie ihrer Historisch-Kritischen Erforschung 1938–1970," in *Studia Monastica* 13 (1971): 129–71.

77. De Vogüé (n. 63 above), chap. 48.

78. See Adalbert de Vogüé, "Travail et alimentation dans les règles de saint Benoît et du Maître," *Revue bénédictine* 74 (1964): 242–51.

79. De Vogüé (n. 63 above), chap. 4, "Quae sunt instrumenta bonorum operum," which concludes: "Ecce haec [the monastic virtues] sunt instrumenta artis spiritalis. Quae cum fuerint a nobis die noctuque incessabiliter adimpeta et in die iudicii reconsignata, illa merces nobis a Domino recompensabitur quam ipse promisit [cites 1 Cor. 2:9]. Officina vero ubi haec omnia diligenter operemur claustra sunt monasterii et stabilitas in congregatione." ("These, then, are the tools of the spiritual craft. When we have used them ceaselessly day and night and on the day of judgement returned them, we shall receive the reward God has promised. . . . The workshop where we labor at all these tasks is the enclosure of the monastery and the stability of the community of believers.")

80. *Sancti Columbani opera*, ed. G. S. M. Walker, in *Scriptores Latini Hiberniae*, vol. 2 (Dublin, 1957), chap. 9, p. 138.

81. Ibid., pp. 78–80, instructio 4; see also Delaruelle, "Le Travail dans les règles monastiques" (n. 63 above), p. 61.

6

THE END OF EARLY MEDIEVAL SLAVERY

Ross Samson

Slaves were an integral and numerically important part of English society in the Anglo-Saxon period, yet they do not seem to have excited much attention from scholars.[1]
— David Pelteret

Masterfully understated, for Pelteret then reveals that in Stenton's huge survey of Anglo-Saxon England there are only four references to them! Dependent labor and especially slavery is little studied by medievalists; one cannot assume widespread acquaintance with the evidence. Published work on slavery in Anglo-Saxon England has till recently been restricted to a number of articles by Pelteret. For the serious scholar there has been his unpublished thesis, soon to be joined by the publication of his monograph on the subject.[2]

For scholars of medieval slavery, two massive volumes by Charles Verlinden have long been available, covering the Iberian peninsula, France, and Italy.[3] Emphasis is on early medieval slavery, but there are small sections on the later Middle Ages. The works steer clear of the nature of dependency; emphasis is on "real" slavery, hence the odd chronological concentrations. The works tend not to synthesize; they are accumulated details, largely from laws and formularies, and are most useful to scholars of medieval slavery as the first step, the collation of evidence. For Visigothic slavery in particular there is also an excellent chapter in King's book on Visigothic law and society.[4]

For an introduction to the institution, and symptomatic of how little there is written about medieval slavery, there is Ruth Mazo Karras's book on Scandinavia, with a chapter on European slavery.[5]

A number of articles by Pierre Bonnassie have recently been brought together and translated into English. His theories on rural peasant dependency have been important to social historians interested in the ninth and tenth centuries particularly. English-speaking scholars will have to take more account of him in the future.[6]

A translation of Pierre Dockès's book has been around for a decade now, although it appears to have had little impact on English-speaking historians. Despite its name, much of the contents deals with slavery in antiquity rather than the Middle Ages. Although aimed as a critique of both "bourgeois" and Marxist historians, the very use of the word "bourgeois" reveals that Dockès is writing from a Marxist, albeit slightly revisionist, perspective.[7] The higher than usual visibility of Marxism in this aspect of medieval history, while it should be due to the fact that it is the sort of topic that Marxists grasp to their bosom, is primarily the result of the general apathy or antipathy of Western medievalists to this part of Europe's social history. It most surely does not represent any outrage or moral indignation on the part of medievalists in general, far less any radicalization of their intellectual thought on the nature of society. So far from this being the case, hostility towards Marxism has left many American and Western European scholars almost denying the existence of slavery to disprove Marxist interpretations of a "slave mode of production."[8]

What little else has been written tends, like this paper or perhaps the most famous, that of Marc Bloch, to concentrate on explaining the demise of slavery, not discussing its nature.[9] However, it is not just ignorance of early medieval slavery that makes me balk at suggesting why it ended. Rather it is the nature of the underlying assumptions, the general givens, the theoretical perspectives, and philosophical beliefs that surround, underpin, and actually structure the arguments found throughout the scholarly literature on early medieval slavery that so worry me. The subject is dominated by unsympathetic free-market capitalist mentalities or Christian apologies. The latter is to be found lurking even in explicit condemnations of the Church: Christianity, not in the powerful, organized, institutionalized religious form as "the Church," but as teachings and precepts for a moral life is endowed by apologists with transformitory powers.[10]

Although my ultimate goal is to suggest why slavery came to end, and I place it around A.D. 800–1100, the bulk of this paper is devoted to the investigation of how others have explained the end of slavery. Explanation is perhaps not the best word, for slavery is often made to disappear almost by slight of hand by some scholars. Thus the first two "reasons" for the end of slavery have to be teased out of academic writings. These are what I call semantics and natural demography. In distinction there are three explanations explicitly put forward by historians as contributing causes to the end of slavery: economics, class struggle, and the influence of the Church. Each is discussed in turn. Of these five, the first three I dismiss as quite wrong, the latter two I accept as having played an important role. The sting in the tail is that the role of the Church was incidental, accidental, and unintentional.

SEMANTICS

Pierre Bonnassie begins his arguments on the end of slavery with a section entitled "What is a slave?" Ruth Mazo Karras offers, as the first section heading in her book, "definitions of slavery." Moses Finley suggests seven criteria for distinguishing slavery. [11]

In a sense there is a battle between present-day scholars and the medieval speakers and writers. Karras notes that "classifications created by the community of scholars . . . would [not] have been meaningful to those involved."[12] Well, perhaps Piers the Plowman *might not* have understood our distinction between forms of dependent labor (but I bet he would have); he most surely would *not* have understood why we were defining labor, writing about it, and teaching it today! Let us not be overly sensitive to the liberties we take with the mental structures of medieval people.

We must at least distance ourselves intellectually from the terms of medieval people for the simple reason that the meanings of those terms changed over time, changed from region to region, changed from situation to situation, and changed from social group to social group. Only the Franks used *litus*, only the Lombards used *aldius*, only the Anglo-Saxons used *wealh*. How often did the Franks (and who among them, and under what circumstances) use the terms *meotheus*, *theotexaca*, and *horgauus* that are found in Lex Salica? In legal texts and estate records classifications are serious: they dictate fines and exemptions and rights and duties. In Domesday Book, profession was more informative than legal status: "plowman" listed among "appurtenances" spoke volumes, regardless of legal niceties. *Rustici, villani, agricultores, servi*: such terms may have been used interchangeably by the great of medieval society for social inferiors. However important to his case in court, however passionately felt by the peasant herself, to the noble, free and unfree, slave and serf and tenant farmer might all be lumped into a single class of toiler.

Medieval lawyers and law code compilers have often led modern historians astray. Alas, too often the fault lies squarely on the modern historians' shoulders. "In the eyes of the laws, three duties, when brought together, essentially characterised the servile condition," said Bloch.[13] These were *chevage, formariage,* and *mortmain.* But Bloch is mistaken. These were never seen as characterizing serfdom, these were seen as signs, as *proof* of the condition. What does a law court want but proof? Hypothetically a servile family might, over three generations, successfully find wives for sons from among the lord's tenants, and thus have no *formariage* to pay. If the family produced healthy long-lived sons there was no death without inheritors and no *mainmorte.* Three generations on one plot of land may have seen a century elapse and have only rendered to their lord the annual symbolic *chevage* of fourpence. Fourpence a year was not "the profound essence of serfdom," but it was *proof* of servitude to medieval lawyers.

Historians have been overly concerned with the terms of freedom, especially in terms of recourse to public law. In a fine work, Paul Hyams argues that the classification of English villeins as unfree was the result of an increase in actions taken to royal courts at the end of the twelfth, beginning of the thirteenth century. Villeins became "unfree" in the sense that they had no access to royal justice.[14] Regardless of legal, social, economic, and political consequences of the legal developments of English law in the twelfth century, this "unfreedom" had nothing really to do with slavery. When legally "unfree" was almost synonymous with servitude of slave nature, in sixth-century Gaul, there were many members of society who were "free" but had no right to represent themselves legally (women and children).

As long ago as 1895, Round noted that the numbers of *servi* recorded in Domesday Book for 1066 had decreased considerably by 1087.[15] Their decrease was mirrored by the increase in *bordarii.* Was this a change of name or status? One must incline towards the latter, given the consistency of the source: the questions were asked of the same people at the same time.

In France *servus* remained in common use. In 1919 Bernard employed a simple rule for translation: before the year 1000 *servi* and *mancipia* were translated as "slaves," after 1000 as "serfs."[16] Bonnassie has, in essence, defended the practice. He traces the increasing rarity of the terms *mancipia, servi,* and *ancillae* in documents until they all but disappear by the year 1000, at which time the documents are full of *liti, coloni,* and *liberti.* His simple chart demonstrating the percentage of charters in which the terms appear is taken to reflect "the process of the extinction of slavery."[17] But the word *servus* did not die out at all. Far from it. By the thirteenth century it was the single most common written term for servile rural laborers, for serfs. But what of the spoken language? Are we to believe that between vulgar Latin and modern French the word was continuously used, except during the eleventh century, when it was forgotten?

There is a real danger of writing the history of words, charting changes of nuances, documenting linguistic fashions, without really understanding the social history behind them. That can only be avoided by analyzing more than etymologies and legal distinctions, by looking at the forms of labor performed, whether it was forced or not, how it was controlled, the amount of labor or renders obliged, and by studying the amount of freedom these dependants had to organize and control their own personal lives.

DEMOGRAPHY

I have effectively invented the term "demographic explanation" for much of what is written without an explicit title. The arguments tend to rest on the assumption that slave populations were not self-sustaining. Bloch came out and said this most explicitly, "of all livestock breeding, that of man is the most delicate."[18] Doehard gives examples of how prolific slaves could be, including the example of Erembold, vassal of the church of Verdun, who dontated two properties along with their slaves to the archbishopric of Trier. Most of the slave couples had, 3, 4, 5, and 7 children.[19] The antebellum American South shows modern self-perpetuating slave populations, and ancient Rome gives us the example of conscious concern on the part of masters to encourage such reproduction. Columella claimed that he rewarded a slave mother who produced three viable children with exemption from work and her freedom if she produced more.[20] There is evidence, I might add, that Columella was familiar to some early medieval manorial managers.

The strength of the assumption is revealed by the tendency of historians to concentrate on sources of new slaves as a way of arguing for the continuation of slavery. Verlinden begins each new section of his great opus with evidence of slave trade. Duby stresses the importance of the punishment of crime and the prevalence of warfare in reducing free people to slaves.[21] He, like Bloch before him, essentially argues that the disappearance of such sources of new slaves was partially responsible for the demise of slavery.

Now there is one especial problem with these suggestions. The endemic warfare of the petty kingdoms of pagan England and Merovingian Gaul is seen as particularly productive in making slaves, whereas later Carolingian wars are seen more as political rivalries; only the Viking incursions are accepted as having slave raiding as one of the goals of the violence. Is there truly a qualitative difference in the nature and reasons for wars and battles? Perhaps, but if so it relates to the nature of the political organization of states. And while the petty wars of petty kingdoms may have produced new slaves by capturing free peasants of a neighboring territory and carrying them off, the state apparatus was poorly developed, struggled to help control slaves or prevent their flight, and of course was powerless to recover runaways if the fleeing slaves made it to the next petty kingdom.[22] In short, warfare and violence may have created more new slaves in 600 than they did in 900, but the differences in political and social organization meant that more slaves escaped their tormentors in 600 than in 900.

A similar argument has been made concerning the collapse of central political authority in the late Carolingian period[23]: in Provence magnates hired labor to fill the places of runaway slaves.[24] Bonnassie, who dates the end of slavery to this period, concludes that early medieval societies always seem to have been able to procure slaves. No difficulty of recruitment could be an answer.[25]

What makes these—perhaps pseudo-demographic would be a better term—explanations even more intellectually impoverished is that they lump together all the ways by which the pool of active slaves was diminished: decreased recruitment in wars, high mortality rates, manumission, and so on. But manumission is no "natural" cause for "natural" wastage of a slave population. Religious, legal, nutritional, social, and economic causes for the death, recruitment, reproduction, escape, and freeing of slaves are mixed into one large argument, resulting in intellectual chaos.

Of course, there is also an element of apology in the pseudo-demographic explanation. It is as if slavery should not have existed, so it is only natural that such an evil aberration disappeared.

ECONOMIC EXPLANATION

There is only one economic reason offered by medievalists for why slavery came to an end. It is presented almost uniformly: slaves were somehow not really productive.

There were sound economic reasons for the change. The new lords would find it more expedient to have dependent peasants who fed themselves than to rely on notoriously fickle slave labour that had to be fed at the lord's expense.[28]

That was H. R. Loyn. But the choice of historian to quote was almost arbitrary; the same core argument underlies almost every medievalist's discussion of the end of slavery.[29] Finn claimed that

the elderly or ailing slave was nothing but a liability, and in many a manor it was probably more profitable to emancipate a certain number of slaves and furnish them with the means of subsistence rather than maintain them.[30]

Loyn and Finn were addressing the English situation. Bloch and Duby said identical things of France.[31] Simply browse a piece on the end of medieval slavery in Sweden by Lind and you find the exact same line of argument: "conditions made it more practical to use self-supporting, rent-paying tenants."[32]

Bloch in fact added the last essential ingredient to the orthodox platitudes about slaves: once freed they work much harder because they work for themselves. The composite picture of the economic explanation is as follows. Before: slaves work badly; produce little for their master; eat a lot, and what they eat costs their masters dearly; and generally live poorly. After: serfs work well; produce plenty of rent for their lords; still eat a lot, but somehow what they eat neither directly nor indirectly costs their lords anything; and generally live better.

There are not a few problems with these arguments and their assumptions. One is an outright logical mistake. Finn suggests that it was "more profitable" to "furnish" freed slaves "with the means of subsistence." But other scholars almost seem to believe that by converting slaves into serfs, lords did not have to give them anything, that they then had to make their own way in the world. Loyn talks of dependent peasants "feeding themselves," but they only managed that by working a parcel of land that had come out of their former master's property. Land formerly worked for the master, who took its produce directly, for personal use, for gift or sale, or for the feeding of slaves, was now tilled by peasants who disposed of the produce as they wished, once rent was paid. Just how this "feeding themselves" was meant to be economically advantageous to the former slave master, who now lost both land and labor in return for a rent, is seldom made clear. Finn almost says the obvious: the land was not sufficient to feed the freed who then starved to death. This is the only logical implication of emancipating the elderly or ailing slave whose work did not even cover the costs of their shelter and nourishment.

Given that lords seldom let their dependent serfs die during famine years, because land was of little value without a work force to make it productive, this line of argumentation about freeing masters from the costs of upkeep must be abandoned as too vague in most cases, and based on outright mistakes in others.

There are, in addition, two enormous paradoxes, most ingenious paradoxes, to the economic explanation as I have outlined it. The first paradox is this: once freed, exploited servile peasants work harder and so much harder that *both* the peasants and the former slave master do better economically from the manumission. No one loses; everyone wins. The second paradox is that despite this economic godsend, despite having an alternative that improves everyone's lot economically and improves the lot of one group socially, it took at least a millennium for slavery to disappear in western Europe.

Is it true that dependent servile peasants worked better than slaves and produced more? Of people like Marc Bloch who said "the slave is a poor worker," Moses Finley responded that theirs is merely "dogma resting on the same moral judgement . . . of Adam Smith." I would go further and say they are pernicious sentiments. And the sentiments are widely shared. MacDonald and Snooks discuss the "lower motivation of slaves compared with that of peasants," although I cannot say for certain whether they create an arithmetic coefficient of fickleness for slave labor in their complex mathematical equations that summarize the evidence of Domesday Book.[33]

It simply is not true that slaves lacked motivation or incentives. They could be rewarded with material goods or improved status. Their work load could be reduced. They could be freed. In many ways the incentives open to a slave were far greater than those offered a free but dependent peasant, whose only real reward was more produce. Secondly, slaves were motivated by the desire to avoid a flogging. Both the carrot and the stick were available to increase a slave's labor. The serf was not driven by the rod.

Thirdly, the driving force behind slaves' toil was a lordly desire for produce; and this was closer to a capitalistic endless desire for more than was that of a self-sufficient peasant household. Anthropologists like Marshall Sahlins have built on the work of the great Russian, Chayanov, of the turn of the century.[34] He was probably the first to demonstrate in a scholarly fashion that peasants produce to satisfy their own demands. Those demands changed depending on how hard the work was, how big the family was, how easy or socially acceptable new investment, such as buying or renting new fields, was. But peasant production is unlike the capitalist system which, for example, produces much more of a commodity when its price goes up because it has become more profitable. In a peasant system net production goes down, because household demands are now more easily met; there is little point in producing more than enough. Conversely, when prices slump, instead of decreasing or abandoning production, as happens in a capitalist system, in a peasant system production increases; sufficient food and cash for other obligations, such as taxes, are necessary. The Western colonial experience of these principles in action produced in the minds of capitalists with a Protestant work ethic the stereotype of the "lazy native." Free peasants had the freedom to be "lazy" that slaves lacked. Ælfric's plowman worked so hard, as he said, because he was not free, and lords were insatiable.

Fourthly, we might wonder if the newly freed slaves, with their small households, could have farmed as efficiently as the large lordly demesne farms. Anthropological studies, including Chayanov's of nineteenth-century Russian peasant farming, suggest that it is un-likely. Peasant farming practices vary considerably even within the same village depending on the amount of land available to and the work force and the number of mouths to feed in each household. When circumstances create the most effective balance of labor, land, and demand requirements, peasant households easily produce what is needed and become "lazy"; much that could additionally and effi-ciently be produced is not. Conversely, peasant households (especially those early or late in the household life cycle) with a poor balance of labor, land, and demand requirements often achieve production only by labor intensive and inefficient methods, such as continual weeding or gleaning after harvest, or planting of a second season crop.

The implication is that once turned into free dependent peasants, slaves might easily end up working slightly harder on their small-scale farming enterprises to compensate for the lack of efficiency and still produce no more than when they had been slaves. The assumption that working for themselves they would produce more is much more contentious than Bloch ever dreamed. The possibility that they pro-duced so much more that both former slave/now dependent serf and former slaveowner/now rent-demanding landlord benefited financi-ally or materially is probably fanciful.

Let me move on to the second paradox. It is claimed that there were economic advantages to freeing slaves, and yet it took a millennium for slavery to disappear. Our problem is that we must assume first that there truly were economic advantages to slaveowners in freeing their slaves. This I do not happen to believe. For those who do, we must assume second that slaveowners were able to understand, able to calculate the economic benefits to them reaped from emancipation, and that third they then acted on that knowledge. There is, however, no evidence, no comment from the period to the effect that economic benefits from increased productivity were believed to derive from emancipation. The evidence we do have, from Carolingian capitularies and polyptychs, suggests that powerful and great secular landowners and the Church sought to increase and consolidate their estates, producing larger and more efficient demesnes, precisely where slave labor would be at its most effective. The Visigothic law codes revealed that kings instituted a royal prerogative to buy slaves preemptively. They at least did not see any economic gain from manumission. [35]

There is no evidence that Roman slaveowners ever even thought of an economic benefit deriving from freeing slaves. Such concepts were discussed in the United States before the Civil War, but these arguments for the abolition of slavery were not those most commonly used or most vociferously put forward; they were more in the form of an additional possibility, and then the economic good was on a general level, increasing the prosperity of all, not necessarily the slaveowners in particular. They were put forward by those who opposed slavery mostly on moral grounds. [36] Clearly those who owned slaves in the antebellum South paid no attention to them.

Indeed, even if it were ever accepted by slaveowners that some financial benefit might accrue from emancipating slaves, there was the social loss to consider. Owning fellow human beings was a source of power and a symbol of power; it generated awe and conferred esteem. [37] There is plentiful evidence of people in the Roman world and antebellum America purchasing and maintaining slaves who were of no great economic benefit simply because it was prestigious to do so. Everything we know about medieval European social and economic practices suggests that people were even more likely then to act according to rules of generosity and noblesse oblige, to follow conceptions of fit behavior for one's rank and status in the world, and to deny people rights or rewards if they had been born naturally by the design of God to their circumstance of inferiority.

Finally, the crushing blow, and embarrassingly obvious: how could the Church describe the manumitting of slaves as an act of piety if it not only did not result in material loss to the manumittor, but somehow brought financial gain?

There many still be an economic explanation worth studying in the future; it is related to the rise in the use of coinage. It is possible that lordly greed and desire for silver coins was such that they were persuaded to allow slaves to buy their way out of slavedom and into a closely controlled serfdom. In doing so lords lost out. They lost the malicious joy of owning other human beings, and with it the right to beat them almost whimsically, and similarly lost the financial benefit of being able to possess almost everything they produced. In return they gained the short term benefit of a pocketful of silver, besides which, slave or servile peasant drudge, the fields were still plowed. [27]

CLASS STRUGGLE

That slaves should resent slavery and their treatment and wish to escape their oppression is a generalization I have little fear of making. Abbot William of Æbelholt, Denmark (d. 1203) stated, "it is in the arbitrary power of the master to treat his slave as he likes." West Norwegian law used the phrase "to whip the hide off him completely" in reference to the punishment of a slave who committed an aggravated crime.[38] A slave fled to the sanctuary of Saint Swithun's tomb because her new owner was a "very bad mistress."[39] St. Gerald of Aurillac, despite his sanctity and his "liberal, bleeding-heart" (and not just for the ninth century) attitude towards warfare and bloodshed, threatened his *servi* with mutilation to end their indolence.[40] That was a real threat: King Childebert II had the face of Septimima, an *ancilla*, disfigured with red hot irons and had the ears and hair (perhaps scalp) of the the *servus* Droctulf cut off. [41]

How could slaves help but wish to escape their condition when their masters tended to hate and denigrate them? Pope Leo I (d. 461) wrote, "those who have not been able to obtain their freedom from their owners are raised to the dignity of the priesthood, as if servile vileness could receive this honor . . . the sacred ministry is polluted by such vile company." The supposed conscience of fifth-century Gaul, Salvian, called slaves bad, abominable, and obscene. [42]

Slave resistance is an explanation with much to recommend it and few to expound it. Even Marxist historians like Pierre Dockès make less of class struggle than one might imagine. Orthodox Marxists who wrote in former Socialist European countries, such as Štaerman, were generally content to allow the end of slavery to be the product of a natural crisis in the relations of production. Following severely orthodox Marxist reasoning, the slave mode of production was replaced by the feudal mode of production when the former reached the crisis that theoretically comes to all modes of production: it had developed to its logical conclusion and was incapable of increasing production. [43]

Interest in slave resistance in the late Roman and early medieval period has traditionally been restricted to the *bacaudae* in Gaul. But even now many argue that these were not rebellious slaves, and Van Dam has gone so far as to suggest that these revolts were instigated by people who wanted more leadership and control, not less! [44]

But slave resistance has seldom taken the form of a revolt like that led by Spartacus, alas. Even active individual opposition was and remains rare. All too seldom do we read anecdotes like that of Gregory of Tours in his *History of the Franks* of the slaves of the merchant Christopher, who killed him after he gave them a merciless flogging. Or of the slave of Sichar, who "was exhorting one of his slaves to get on with his work, and had just taken hold of a stick and was belaboring him with it, when the slave dragged Sichar's sword from his belt and had the effrontery to wound his master with it." [45] Murder was an extreme form of struggle and often self-destructive as it proved for some of the slaves who killed Christopher. There are, however, chapters in all the various barbarian law codes dealing with slaves who murdered their masters, revealing that some male slaves might resort to strangulation, while poison was used by female slaves. [46] The Carolingian poem on the siege of Paris by the Vikings, with its depiction of slaves becoming masters, and the masters becoming slaves, I fear, was just employing a literary *topos*, still to be found this century in Harold Pinter's "The Servant." [47]

There were a host of ways slaves might have resisted in daily life, including feigned incompetence, general recalcitrance, subterfuges, and sabotages. But these invited retaliation, punishment, and power was on the side of masters. Moreover, a tactical mixture of incentive and threat could render most resistance ineffective. Slaves might simply be set a task for the day that could take ten hours if one worked well or fifteen if one feigned ignorance and worked badly. Dinner might be in proportion to the bushels harvested. Thus, despite my sympathy for slaves and their struggle, I do not accept that it was sufficiently successful that slaves made "poor workers" or that their labor, in general, was "fickle." Resistance might even have made the slave a particularly good worker. The law code of Wihtræd (695) includes this: "If an *esne*, contrary to his lord's command, perform *þeow-*

weorc work between sunset on Saturday evening and sunset on Sunday evening, he is to compensate his lord eighty *sceattas*."[48] Such a moonlighting slave might well be saving up to purchase freedom.

Slave resistance was most cruicial where slaves sought to escape control completely, and not simply to undermine their masters' enjoyment of the fruit of their toils. Flight and bare-faced lying were powerful weapons available in their attempts to escape their unfreedom.

Flight of slaves was a great problem in the later Roman empire according to late imperial laws.[49] It was the single greatest problem in the Visigothic law codes, given the number of provisions relating to it. The late Roman state itself enlisted many slaves into the army, promising them their freedom. Barbarian law codes complained of lords freeing other people's slaves. Why they should think to do such a thing is never commented on. We must assume that, like the late Roman state, lords were after their able bodies, only in this case as workers rather than as warriors. Lords were effectively poaching the work force of rivals. Slaves were freed illegally to become the serfs of someone else. In this we must assume they readily conspired, perhaps more often than not instigated. Rothair's Edict reveals Lombard masters taking an active part in protecting runaways.

> He who seizes his fleeing slave in the courtyard of another man shall not be blamed because he seized his property in another man's courtyard. If he to whom the court belongs, or any of his men, takes the bondsman from his lord's hand or blocks the way to him . . . he who blocked the way in the interest of the slave or took the bondsman from his lord's hand shall be liable to punishment.[50]

Barbarian law codes enacted against providing runaway slaves with false papers, with wigs, with shelter. *Coloni* and *actores*, themselves probably slaves, were penalized in law codes for aiding and abetting runaways. It is too much to see this as an underground network, a railway for escaping slaves, but sympathetic collusion it surely was.[51]

The fifth century saw a great blow to slaveowning societies in western Europe; masters experienced difficulties trying to recover slaves from neighboring kingdoms. Political fragmentation ended effectual intervention by the state apparatus. But there was always self-help. Rothair's Edict stipulates that anyone who apprehends a runaway slave should "hold him and keep safe the property which he carried with him. The apprehender should immediately send notice to the judge of the place from which the fugitive had fled in order that he may claim him. And this official shall pay two *solidi* for the fugitive in order that he and the properties that he took with him may be returned." Gregory of Tours tells the story of the Frankish masters who ride out after Leo. It can be visualized without much effort in the style of a Western. In the 670s, the saintly bishop, Wilfrid, sent his reeve, Hocca, to wrest the young son from a poor woman who had promised him (but against her will and while in distress) to the Church and had fled the villa Tiddanufri near York where she and her son lived to hide among the British to avoid this unpleasant fate. This was real self-help, a far cry from the Visigothic king's attempt in 702 to set the whole country looking for runaways, when every male was to drag any poorly dressed stranger whom he might meet to a judge, with punishments of excommunication, 300 lashes, and a fine of three pounds of gold for breach of the various provisions.[52]

Slaves were often successful in their flight from unfree servitude by joining the Church, either as monks or priests in the case of men. It is not clear whether *ancillae*, women slaves, were as successful becoming nuns. There is the evidence of Charlemagne's Thionville Capitulary of 806, which prohibited royal *servi* being tonsured or *ancillae* taking the veil except in moderate numbers, and "only where there are enough of them and the estates will not be abandoned."[53] The Church repeatedly pondered the particular problem of ordaining slaves as priests. The general feeling was that slaves polluted the holy office, but equally strong was the feeling that once done, ordination should not be undone. Thus, for instance, the Council of Orléans (c. 8) dealt in 511[54] with the problem of bishops ordaining slaves, unaware of their servile status. Such episcopal ignorance is as good evidence as we have of slaves conniving to escape their slavery, for the slaves in question obviously did not volunteer the information that they were unfree.[55]

Of course, some priests connived with the slaves. In Charlemagne's General Admonition of 789, priests were explicitly ordered not to entice other's *servi* to join orders or become priests without their lord's permission.[56]

THE APPARENT NEGATIVE ROLE OF THE CHURCH

But I strenuously deny that the Church sought in any way to end the pernicious institution of slavery. By an ironic twist, however, as the Church sought to impose some of its petty sexual morals and enforce its varied rituals while imposing its authority on practical daily life, usually in opposition to royal or secular authority, it inadvertently dealt a fatal blow to slaveholding. The irony is heightened by the fact that not only did contemporaries not notice it, but scholars today have overlooked it.

Many apologists have suggested that the Church helped to end slavery.[57] Loyn felt that the "newly vigorous and reformed [Anglo-Norman] church may have had a part in the business."[58] When pressed such apologists often let slip their outrage at the Church's inactivity in combatting the institution, as in the case of Latouche:

> The slave trade affords a typical example of the docility with which the early Carolingians put ecclesiastical precepts into practice. In spite of its immorality, this trade was not forbidden by the Church . . . .[59]

While the slave trade may have been immoral to Latouche, to the Carolingian Church it was not. While the Church condemned things like Gentiles owning Christian slaves, castration of slaves to make eunuchs, and eventually the selling of humans (in the case of Anselm), and while it might on occasion note with a touch of sadness that by the accident of birth it fell to some people to work continuously all their lives and to know precious little joy, it did not condemn slavery.

Rabanus Maurus felt that slaves fled their masters either because of their own pride or their masters' terrible cruelty. In either case he argued they should simply be returned on religious grounds. Agobard, archbishop of Lyon (816–840), actually argued that slavery was *desired* by God. Jonas, bishop of Orléans, argued that it was in human nature to have master and slave, rich and poor, but that God accepted all into heaven.[60] The Carolingian councils were even more "audacious" in their refusal to take the part of slaves than Merovingian councils had been, according to Verlinden.[61] One searches in vain for the moral or theological argument against slavery, but Church thinkers certainly did come up with justifications for its existence.

Apologists often make the mistake of interpreting ecclesiastical praise of manumission as encouragement to abolish slavery. The Church preached the giving up of worldly goods and slaves were simply another aspect of material wealth. Of course there those who did just that, for the good of their souls. Ælfwold, bishop of Crediton (d. 1008), stated in his will that every slave on his estate whom he had purchased himself and all those penally enslaved were to be freed.[62] Those in orders often freed dozens and occasionally hundreds in their wills.[63] St. Caesarius bought so many captives to free that it was a difficult task for his secretary; St. Betharius of Chartres (d. 614) produced a miracle, God sent him 500 *solidi* to ransom prisoners.[64] "One gets the impression that hagiographers considered the virtues of their saint incomplete if they were unable to furnish proof of their merits in the redemption of captives."[65]

To argue that this had a serious effect on decreasing the number of humans in unfree servitude is to argue that the Church had a serious impact on property ownership; but its effect on secular redistribution of wealth was great in only one area. Little was given away to the poor in alms and paupers were rarely granted land from which to feed themselves and few slaves were freed. Instead, the Church had its greatest successes in getting people to divest themselves of wealth in the form of donations to the Church itself.

Slaves were gifted or bequeathed to the Church. In some cases this took the form of freeing slaves who then became the Church's serfs. This special form of manumission/donation perhaps accounted in some small part for the decline of slavery, but in a majority of cases slaves were simply alienated to the Church with the land given in gift.

And the Church had many slaves. When the bishop of Toledo, Elipandus, accused Alcuin of being worldly and too wealthy, Alcuin replied in a letter to three bishops in Gaul in 800:

> The aforesaid father reproached me with having too great wealth and *servi* numbering up to twenty thousand, not knowing in what spirit one may possess the world . . . I have never procured a man to serve me, but rather desired to serve all the servants of Christ my God with devoted love.[66]

Alcuin did not deny having 20,000 *servi*, slaves or serfs, nor did he suggest this was an exaggeration. All he claimed was that he himself had not procured a domestic slave or personal servant. The inference is that he did indeed have 20,000 laborers, but that he had "inherited" them *ex officio* (or rather offices, for Alcuin held a multiplicity of high Church positions). There is a late example as well. "It is often stated that Wulfstan II of Worcester (1062–95) was accustomed to preach against this long-standing habit [of trading in humans]; never has it been demonstrated that in 1086 the combined manorial demesnes of the bishop and monks in the West Midlands harboured 267 male and female slaves, those of the recorded subtenants 205, making a grand total of 472 slaves."[67]

And the Church did not believe in divesting itself of worldly possessions. In 517, for instance, the Council of Yenne forbade abbots from freeing slaves, "for it is not just that slaves should be free while monks are constrained daily by the *opus rurale*."[68] The Visigothic Church tried to make it more difficult for its members to free Church slaves, by making clerics pay compensation, and double the slave's value with *peculium* to free the slave from *obsequium*.[69] Domesday Book shows the sluggishness of the Church in freeing its slaves. The reason: the wealth of the Church was the wealth of God and his saints, not the private wealth of bishops and abbots to dispose of as they saw fit; it was held in perpetuity for the benefit of all and future generations.

THE UNINTENDED CONSEQUENCES OF THE CHURCH'S ROLE

Apologists of the Church have regularly admitted that the Church took no active role in ending, even condemning, slavery. Apologists, however, have always felt that the Church, as the official institutional representation of Christ's teaching, must somehow have been influential in making people believe that it is good to be nice to one another. Thus slavery, a thoroughly unpleasant phenomenon, was slowly undermined by the continuous preaching of pleasantness. If there were any truth in this pious belief, slavery would never have managed to return to such prominence in the New World, settled by people who had been raised in the Christian faith for at least sixty generations. The more cynical and the more radical have simply ignored the Church as largely irrelevant to the end of slavery. Yet it had an important part to play, even if unintended and even if unconscious of the fact.

My argument is this. The Church sought to extend its influence or monopolize regulation of certain spheres of social activity. In some cases this arose from its moral codes of practice, in some cases it was little more than a skirmish with lordly and royal claims to dominate society, to exercise its authority untrammelled. In the establishment of ecclesiastical courts we can see both at work. These courts heard cases pertaining to blasphemy and adultery, but they also sought to exclude royal justice from dealing with the persons of clerics, regardless of the crime committed. And in both of these areas, enforcing Christian moral behavior and competing with secular authority, the Church inadvertently affected master-slave relations.

Two matters arising out of Christian morals and orthodox Christian ritual behavior that had the greatest impact and improved slaves' lives relate to marriage and the Sabbath.

The Church claimed the right to define and even police correct and incorrect sexual relations. It sanctioned marriage, prohibited and punished fornication. A slave "union," *contubernium*, in the Roman empire had not had the legal status of marriage. There were logical reasons for this. The power to contract a legal marriage relied on and imputed freedom to engage in free actions. Slaves were in many ways the legal equivalents of children. Their masters were legally responsible for them. Thus it was difficult if not impossible to see slave pairs as technically married. In practice, however, there was absolutely no desire on the part of slaveowners to recognize such unions, for the threat of separating couples, one from the other, or both from their children, was one of the most forceful powers slaveowners had in maintaining quiescence. Anyone who has read or seen an adaptation of *Uncle Tom's Cabin* will recognize not only the importance of this control, but will realize too that poor slaveowners might have been forced by circumstances beyond their control to sell or give away individual slaves to new masters. It is in the interest of the system of slaveownership that such a threat be real and that slaveownership is spread widely, even to those who could only afford one.

I am unaware of any extant ecclesiastical decisions taken in council concerning the nature of slave union, of *contubernium*.[70] The Church was certainly willing to stand by, well into the Middle Ages, and allow lords to forbid marriage of their serfs to others. The payment of *formariage*, recognition of a lord's consent, even if a formality, was often highly despised and resented by serfs of the central Middle Ages. It seems certain, therefore, that an earlier Church would have had no qualms about slave masters forbidding the marriage of their slaves.

However (and there are two howevers), the Church likewise forbade fornication, and all sexual union outside the sanctity of marriage, *contubernium* included, was fornication. The early Church, in developing its theory of the sacraments, was to conclude that those whom God (the Church) put together no man was to put asunder. Thus, while the Church accepted the right of slaveowners to prevent their slaves from marrying,[71] the Church would have pressed for an end to their union or a legalization of it through marriage. The second however is that, once married, the slave pair stayed married in the eyes of the Church.

Gregory of Tours furnishes us with a horrific anecdote in his *History of the Franks*. Duke Rauching would not give his consent for the marriage of two of his slaves. They nevertheless went off, got married, and then had the bishop promise to help them with the difficult and unreasonable duke. Rauching promised the bishop he would not separate them in life, and promptly had the two buried together, alive. In this instance we see that, despite the absence of lordly consent, slaves might contrive to get themselves married by a priest and that, once married, the Church was willing to intervene between them and their masters to secure the maintenance of the union. The Church was perhaps not the surest guarantor against a homicidal madman like Rauching, but even in this instance one of the two slaves was dug up still alive, and rescued.[72]

There is far more evidence to suggest, however, that slave marriages were left inviolate. The Lombard Edict of Rothair (c. 261) deals with the intricate problem of a slave man of one lord, married to the slave of another lord, who commits a theft.[73] The woman and the children are assumed free of blame, and presumably this is made express because it was the slave's lord who was responsible for paying fines. If the fine were indeed to be paid by the slave himself, the innocence of his children would be irrelevant in the instance of compensation. In short the two different masters are not each partially responsible for payment. The Lombard and Visigothic laws, full of references to crimes involving slaves, repeat this image of slave couples with children, living in nuclear families.

In a letter written to Charlemagne in 776, Pope Hadrian I refers to Charlemagne's "sweet letter" in which he worries about the sale of slaves by the Roman people to Saracens. The pope forcefully denies complicity. "The unspeakable Greeks" it was who bought "families" from the Lombards; "many families were sold by the Lombards at a time when famine was pressing them hard."[74] Perhaps it was just the pope's expression, intended to underline the desperation of the times, but it does sound as if the sanctity of marriage was being observed in the sale of slaves as whole families. This suggestion is one much in need of further research.

The Church's desire to regulate what it considered proper and legitimate sexual unions weakened slaveowners' control of their slaves. Their threat to break up a slave family lost some of its force. In the same way slaveowners found their threat of withdrawing holiday privileges undermined. Within the Roman empire there were institutionalized holidays that slaves enjoyed. These were not numerous, but slaves would have expected to enjoy some of the local, municipal or familial festivities in addition. Roman slave masters used the threat of preventing slaves from having these days off to keep them more docile.[75] But the Church forbade work on the Sabbath and at one stroke produced 52 holidays a year for slaves.

Then too on the next day, Sunday, let them refrain from all manual labor and even from the daily memorizing normally done for three hours a day in both seasons, winter and summer. Instead, after Mass in the church everyone may, according to his preference, read what he wishes or what affords him pleasure as he chooses, and they also have complete freedom to go back to bed. Thus they should rejoice in having Sunday assigned them for resting.[76]

That was the Church regulating the labor of its own. It forbad lay people from working on Sundays in 538 at the Council of Orléans. But in 585 the Church Council at Mâcon felt it had to include *servi* expressly in the general forbiddance of Sabbath labor. Margaret Weidemann argues that it was only in 585 that slaves were "forbidden" to work on Sundays, although "exempted" might be a better word.[77]

Just as with fornication and the sanctity of marriage the Church did its bit, not necessarily with full success, to force people to respect the Sabbath and punish those who did not. And this included slaves made to work on Sunday by their masters. Throughout the works of Gregory of Tours there are many miracles recounted in which divine retribution was manifest against people who sinned, but the punishment fell on their slaves. Perhaps more than from any other stories, from these we get an insight into a prominent ecclesiastic's sympathies, or lack of them, towards slaves.[78] In three cases of breaking the Sabbath, masters suffer a "loss" in the form of physical affliction visited upon the slaves, such as paralysis or blindness, not upon themselves. The righteousness with which such miracles are recounted reveals a perspective on slaves shared with slaveowners, one that held them as "speaking tools." In our eyes these miracles are not the work of a just or merciful God, but of a small-minded, jealous, and terribly bigoted God.

This underlines the argument that the Church did not care to improve the well-being of slaves. It sought to enforce its injunction against working on Sunday, and in typical fashion the Church regaled its contemporaries with tales of how supernatural forces performed the executive function of enforcing those injunctions. The Church itself could use excommunication as well as lesser social pressures to ensure conformity. Moreover, from the Merovingian period on, we have plentiful evidence of kings willing to proclaim laws and use their officers to back the Church. After the Council of Mâcon forbade *servi* from working on Sundays, King Guntramn, on 10 November of the same year (585), announced it in a royal edict. King Childebert later made the same enactment.[79] The Frankfurt Capitulary reflects the ecclesiastical nature, almost synodial, of the assembly at Frankfurt held in 794. Chapter 21 stated "[It was ruled] that the Lord's day should be observed from evening to evening."[80] Other capitularies at other times forbade activities on the Sabbath that might have been less clearly inimical to honoring the Lord. Thus "assembly" was forbidden unless for a clear religious purpose.[81] The Visigothic law codes ordered rest by all on Sunday; Jews who failed to rest were to be penalized by flogging and scalping.[82]

The state was willing to work so closely in connection with the Church that it even enforced the Church's own internal hierarchical authority. Monks were barred, for instance, from leaving their monasteries without the abbot's permission. This was part of most, if not all, monastic rules; the Carolingian state chose to help enforce it. So we should not imagine that the Church simply and piously hoped to keep the Sabbath a holiday and marriages inviolable by the wrath of God. There is every reason to believe that the impact made by the Church in these areas was sufficiently great that there was measurable effect on the nature of master-slave relations.

In a more general way the Church may also have had an effect on that relationship in its worldly desires to expand its authority in society. The Church demanded jurisdiction over the space of its most sacred of buildings, the church structure itself. Lay people were expected to abandon many of their otherwise enforceable rights at the door when they crossed the threshold (such as by disarming). So strong was the claim to absolute authority within the sacred space to become, and remains today, that a church became a sanctuary for those fleeing secular authorities.[83] People without the power to withstand their enemies or persecutors, a group that included slaves, might enlist the power of the Church to aid them. The Church was sought out as a virtual rival. For the Church demanded, under certain circumstances and at certain times, autonomy or exemption from royal or secular authority and demands. It was a position continually under attack and in need of perpetual defense.

Slaves, with the least to lose, could most afford to abandon themselves entirely to the Church. The Church, as already noticed, was full of unsympathetic men, whose world view had more in common with slavemasters than slaves. So we should not expect that the Church, in practice, was often highly motivated to protect slaves as individuals. However, if there was local antagonism between the local churchman and the slave's master, a powerful ally might indeed be to hand.

The Church may also have seen itself as having the role of arbiter. If slaves had a grievance, who was to hear it? Roman law made provision for slave grievance if only because Roman society lived with a latent fear of massive slave uprisings.[84] The fear may have been ill-grounded, but it exercised minds and imaginations all the same. The emperor was meant to act as arbiter, and a slave was theoretically untouchable if he or she could take "refuge" by holding on to a public statue of the emperor. It may have been publicly humiliating to have one's slaves shouting out the details of their mistreatment at the hands, or whatever, of their masters while clutching the neck or leg of the emperor's statue at the local market place, but it offered no real threat to one's dominion over the slave. Revenge would be long and painful for such an act, if not sweet. Powerful as emperors were, they put in little real effort to protecting these poor wretches. The Church, on the other hand, made a concerted effort to do several things. It made a stronger claim and effort to be accepted as a third party than ever the emperor did. It fought for a special sanctity, which extended beyond the inviolate security of its buildings. Many law codes provided that, should a wrong-doer take sanctuary in a church, afterwards their punishment should be less severe than was customary. This was explicitly true for slaves. Before the Church handed slaves back to masters they might demand and expect a promise that punishment would be tempered. The Church Council of Orléans held in 511 proclaimed that a master was to be excommunicated for beating a slave who had taken refuge in a church and was returned to him. [85]

Not surprisingly hagiography reveals the miraculous intervention of saints, punishing masters who insulted the sanctity of the Church.

> The slave of a certain Faretrus, who hated his master, fled into the oratory of this priest. The master, filled with pride and profiting from the absence of the holy man, took his *servus* and slew him. But soon after he was seized by a fever and breathed his last. [86]

Unlucky, unnamed slave! The unnamed slave of Maurus was more lucky. The master, trying to regain his slave, "was transformed and began to dance about the entire church, lowing like an animal and not speaking like a man. When these events were reported to his slaves, they seized him and brought him to his own house." He died and the slave became a free man.[87] Here again the state supported the Church. Charlemagne's Capitulary of Lippespringe, issued in 782, stated that

> if anyone takes refuge in a church, no one is to presume to drive him out by force but he is to have asylum until he is brought to

court; moreover, he is to be granted his life and freedom from mutilation in honor of God and out of reverence for the saints of that church.[88]

Mutilation must be a reference to slaves.

The Visigothic law codes reveal that priests might take further action. If the grounds for complaint were accepted as sufficiently strong, a priest might arrange for the sale of the slave to a new master, passing on the proceeds to the former master. Such action is revealed in the Visigothic law codes when priests acted, or were seen to act by irate and violent slaveowners, overzealously. I suspect that few priests exceeded their powers in this matter, and probably never in a righteous attempt to chastise bad slaveowners for their cruel behavior. Infringements were probably done in collusion with would-be new "generous" masters who were willing to pay priests to put new slaves their way. This personal interpretation is based on other evidence in the Visigothic laws suggesting a general desire for the acquisition of new slaves.

CONCLUSIONS

I have concentrated in this paper on the problems of other scholars' explanations for the end of slavery. In essence they derive from three sources. One is simply a lack of real concern with the issue of slavery and a marked paucity of published academic research on the topic. The second is a tendency to apologize for "our" ancestors and, more particularly, the Christian Church.

The third problem arises from the underlying capitalist assumptions concerning incentives and motivations that are to be found in most of the explanations offered by scholars who have little practical or theoretical knowledge of economic practice in non-industrial, non-capitalist societies. Despite the clarity of the evidence that medieval people did not operate on the strict economic profit calculations that entrepreneurs of today do, medievalists have glibly suggested that such calculations were the direct cause of slavery's demise.

I see the intellectual starting point for an explanation of this historical phenomenon in the struggle by slaves themselves to obtain freedom. It is a constant. The one natural element in the disappearance of slavery was that slaves continually sought to disappear.

Manumission is, in effect, a recognition of that fact. Bradley, in his exceptionally good *Slaves and Masters*, reveals that control of slaves was partially achieved through the promise of freedom.[89] By offering that ultimate reward, by clearly laying out the rules by which it could be achieved, and by liberating others revealing the reality and attainability of the goal, masters achieved control perhaps even more successfully than through threats and punishments. Far from being a "natural" cause of wastage, a drain on the numbers of the slave population, liberation was generally only granted after near life-long good service, and thus after a slave's children had already been born into slavery. In theory, all slaves could eventually be freed without the slave population ever declining.

The key to a fuller understanding of manumission, and ultimately the successful maintenance of slavery as a system or indeed its demise, is in how it functioned in the slave-master relationship. I have offered something by way of an explanation for the end of medieval slavery when suggesting ways that the maintenance of the relationship was weakened. The state regularly sought to maintain the rights of slaveowners rather than of slaves. From the earliest barbarian law codes there were provisions for rewards granted to those who caught runaway slaves and penalties not only for those who harbored or aided them, but for those who simply failed to help in the detection of runaways. In the Capitulary of Mantua we find Charlemagne in 781 forbidding the sale of slaves outside of his kingdom.[90] This was no attempt to improve the lot of slaves. Far from it. In the same chapter, Charlemagne also forbade the selling of arms and stallions abroad. In times of famine he forbade the selling of any food abroad. His concern was not to deprive his subjects of essentials and not to provide enemies with weapons. Precisely where slaves fell is not clear. What is clear is that Charlemagne saw them as important resources for the well-being of his empire.

When the state's ability to support masters weakened, slavery as an institution weakened.[91] But political fragmentation following the fall of the Roman empire did not end slavery in western Europe. The control of slaves, and ultimately the maintenance of slavery, had always been the concern of masters; masters simply had to rely almost exclusively on self-help from the fifth century onwards. From the sixth century, however, masters found that the state apparatus inadvertently made that job of control more difficult. The Church fiercely defended its autonomy, and its authority. Slaves might escape to join a Church that protected its own from secular powers, slaves' marriages were protected by a Church concerned only with regulating sexual mores, and the Church forbade working on the Sabbath, institutionalizing fifty-two compulsory holidays a year.

The end of slavery came about not by lords recognizing a financial benefit from freeing their slaves. Instead slave masters found it ever more difficult to get slaves to work for them like slaves. The worst threats of dividing the family were gone, and for one day a week at least, like that lucky ole sun, they had nuthin to do. They went to church like the free and lived in families like the free. They no doubt continued the same subterfuges as before to escape slavery — denying their position, seeking new lords for whom to work with an improved status. Slave masters cannot have known how much more difficult their position was in the tenth century than it had been five or six hundred years earlier. The lack of total domination over these unfree must have made the position of slave master less impressive in the eyes of contemporaries, who valued and respected power probably even more than people of our society do. When slaves were anxious for manumission in the tenth century, slave masters must have felt they had less to lose than ever a Roman slaveowner had done. When slaves offered to buy their freedom the offer cannot have seemed so unreasonable. There was immediate gain, the long term loss was not so great, and the slaves' threat of running away was removed. Indeed, it may sometimes have appeared as an offer they could not refuse.

NOTES

1. David A. E. Pelteret, "Slave Raiding and Slave Trading in Early England," *Anglo-Saxon England* 9 (1981): 99–114.

2. Pelteret, "Late Anglo-Saxon Slavery: An Interdisciplinary Approach to the Various Forms of Evidence," dissertation, (Centre for Medieval Studies, University of Toronto, 1976); Pelteret, "Slavery in Anglo-Saxon England," in *The Anglo-Saxons: Synthesis and Achievement*, ed. J. Douglas Woods and David A. E. Pelteret (Waterloo, Ont. 1985), pp. 117–33; Pelteret, "Slavery in the Danelaw," in *Social Approaches to Viking Studies*, ed. Ross Samson (Glasgow, 1991), pp. 179–88; his forthcoming book, *Slavery in Early Medieval England from the Reign of Alfred to the Early Twelfth Century*, is to be published by Boydell and Brewer.

3. Charles Verlinden, *L'Esclavage dans l'Europe médiévale*, 2 vols. (Bruges, 1955; Ghent, 1977). Hermann Nehlsen, *Sklavenrecht zwischen Antike und Mittelalter. Germanisches und römisches Recht in den germanischen Rechtsaufzeichnungen*, vol. 1, *Ostgoten, Westgoten, Franken, Langobarden* (Göttingen, 1972), is reputed to be good, but I have never seen it.

4. P. D. King, *Law and Society in the Visigothic Kingdom* (Cambridge, 1972), chapter 6, "Slaves, Freedmen and Nobles," pp. 159–89. All references in this paper to Visigothic slavery as revealed by the laws can be found in King's book.

5. Ruth Mazo Karras, *Slavery and Society in Medieval Scandinavia* (New Haven, 1988). William D. Phillips, Jr.'s *Slavery from Roman Times to the Early Transatlantic Trade* (Minneapolis, 1985) is quite inferior to Karras as an introduction.

6. Pierre Bonnassie, *From Slavery to Feudalism in South-Western Europe* (Cambridge, 1991), which includes his paper most directly concerned with slavery: originally "Survie et extinction du régime esclavagiste dans l'Occident," *Cahiers de civilisation médiévale* 28 (1985): 307–38.

7. As I could be said to write in a revisionistic Marxist vein, I might be expected to have made more of Pierre Dockès's *Medieval Slavery and Liberation* (Chicago, 1982). My own revisionism, however, is far in excess of that of Dockès. His work contains a great deal of orthodox Marxist argument on crises caused by the internal contradictions in modes of production which fail to maintain increased economic production. See pp. 105–106 for slightly more on this. I find this element of Marxist political economic explanation utterly unconvincing. For this reason I have in the past undervalued the work. In returning to Dockès after writing this paper, I discover that some of what I argue in the section "Economic Explanation" in this paper was anticipated by him. For works on Roman slavery that are especially good, I recommend Keith Bradley, *Slaves and Masters in the Roman Empire: A Study in Social Control* (Oxford, 1987) and Keith Hopkins, *Conquerors and Slaves* (Cambridge, 1978).

8. I have tried to show this in a small way for antiquity, Samson, "Rural Slavery, Inscriptions, Archaeology and Marx: a Response to Ramsay MacMullen's 'Late Roman Slavery'," *Historia* 38 (1989): 99–110. For more on the subject there is Moses I. Finley, *Ancient Slavery and Modern Ideology* (London, 1980), whose works, in any case, should be read by anyone serious about studying European slavery.

9. Marc Bloch, "Comment et pourquoi finit l'esclavage antique," *Annales Economies, Sociétés, Civilisations* 2 (1947): 30–44 and 161–70, translated as "How and Why Slavery Came to an End," in *Slavery and Serfdom in the Middle Ages*, trans. William R. Beer (Berkeley, 1975), pp. 1–31; also on the end of slavery, Bonnassie, "Survie et extinction." More importantly, however, is that, should slavery be mentioned in passing in general book-length syntheses of early medieval societies, the topic is almost invariably either the end of slavery or slave trade: Pelteret, "Slave Raiding"; Erik I. Bromberg, "Wales and the Medieval Slave Trade," *Speculum* 17 (1942): 263–69; P. Holm, "The Slave Trade of Dublin, Ninth to Twelfth Centuries," *Peritia* 5 (1986): 317–45; Charles Verlinden, "Wo, wann und warum gab es einen Grosshandel mit Sklaven während des Mittelalters," *Kölner Vorträge zur Sozial- und Wirtschaftsgeschichte* 11 (1970): 26 ff.

10. An obvious exception is Chris J. Wickham, "The Other Transition. From the Ancient World to Feudalism," *Past and Present* 103 (1984): 3–36. The reference to "transition" is the transition from the ancient to feudal mode of production; Marxist theory structures much of what is argued there.

11. Bonnassie, "Survie et extinction;" Karras, *Slavery and Society*; Moses Finley, "Between Slavery and Freedom," *Comparative Studies in Society and History* 6 (1964): 233–49.

12. Karras, *Slavery and Society*, p. 8.

13. Bloch, "Comment et pouquoi," p. 37.

14. Paul Hyams, *King, Lords and Peasants in Mediaeval England: The Common Law of Villeinage in the Twelfth and Thirteenth Centuries* (Oxford, 1980).

15. J. H. Round, *Feudal England* (London, 1895).

16. Verlinden, *L'Esclavage*, vol. 1, p. 635.

17. Bonnassie, "Survie et extinction," pp. 340–41.

18. Bloch, "Comment et pourquoi," p. 34.

19. Renée Doehard, *Le Haut Moyen Age Occidental: Economies et Sociétés* (Paris, 1971), p. 188.

20. Columella, *Re rustica* I.8.9.

21. Georges Duby, *Guerriers et paysan: VII-XIIe siècle, premier essor de l'économie*

européene (Paris, 1973), p. 42.

22. I have argued this in more detail in "Slavery, the Roman Legacy," in *Fifth-Century Gaul: A Crisis of Identity?*, ed. John Drinkwater and Hugh Elton (Cambridge, 1992), pp. 218–27.

23. Dockès, *Medieval Slavery*, p. 235, argues for the final end of slavery following the political fragmentation after the time of Louis the Pious.

24. J.-P. Poly, *La Provence et la société féodale, 879–1166* (Paris, 1976), p. 109.

25. Bonnassie, "Survie et extinction," pp. 326–29.

26. A law of King Alfred decreed that "the four Wednesdays in the four Ember Weeks are to be given to all slaves to sell to whomsoever they please anything of what anyone has given them in God's name, or which they can earn in any of their spare time," *Alfred the Great: Asser's Life of King Alfred and other Contemporary Sources*, trans. Simon Keynes and Michael Lapidge (Harmondsworth, 1983), p. 170.

27. During the twelfth century landlords farmed out manors for cash in England extensively. Karras, *Slavery and Society*, p. 32, notes this in connection with the end of slavery. I am not aware of anyone else who makes this connection. However, she puts it in terms of economics or politics; I submit that it is an example of lordly desire for ready cash, a desire purchased by a decrease in profitability. We can hardly assume that those who farmed the manors failed to make something out of it. Lords, in a sense, mortgaged their future incomes for immediate use.

28. H. R. Loyn, *Anglo-Saxon England and the Norman Conquest* (London, 1962), p. 350.

29. "Demesne slavery in England probably came to an end because it was not as profitable as domiciling the slaves and working the demesne by means of labor dues from free and unfree tenants," Karras, *Slavery and Society*, p. 31, drawing on Pelteret, "Slavery in Anglo-Saxon England," pp. 123–31.

30. R. Welldon Finn, *An Introduction to Domesday Book* (London, 1963).

31. Bloch, "Comment et pourquoi," p. 34; Duby, *Guerriers et paysan*, p. 50.

32. Joan Dyste Lind, "The Ending of Slavery in Sweden: Social Structure and Decision Making," *Scandinavian Studies* 50 (1978): 66.

33. John McDonald and G. D. Snooks, *Domesday Economy* (Oxford, 1986), p. 108.

34. Marshall Sahlins, *Stone Age Economics* (Chicago, 1972); A. V. Chayanov, *The Theory of Peasant Economy*, (Homewood, Ill., 1966).

35. King, *Law and Society*, p. 162 and passim.

36. The Negro University of America has reprinted perhaps a hundred different titles of books originally published on questions of slavery in the early nineteenth century. Having skimmed through a few dozen likely books, I found few economic arguments (moral and religious arguments are almost universal). The exceptions were restricted to fairly general observations such as the decrease in mortality following freedom or the overall increase in exports from sugar producing islands, such as the Antilles. I found no detailed arguments to suggest that individual plantation owners would increase their profits. Dockès compares the complexity of good economic calculations on the profitability of slave labor by A. Conrad and J. R. Meyer and the simplistic and incomplete calculations of Columella (and the even less correct calculations of medieval historians), *Medieval Slavery and Liberation*, pp. 119–32.

37. This comes out strongly in Karras's article in this volume without being explicitly stated.

38. Niels Skyum-Nielsen, "Nordic Slavery in an International Setting," *Mediaeval Scandinavia* 11 (1978–1979): 134–35.

39. *Life of St. Swithun*, quoted in Pelteret, "Slavery in Anglo-Saxon England," p. 125.

40. *Vita Geraldi* 2.11, *P.L.* 133.

41. Gregory of Tours, *History of the Franks* IX.38, trans. L. Thorpe (Harmondsworth, 1974).

42. Leo: *Epistolae* 4.1, *P.L.* 54 (1846), 593, col. 1218 and quoted in A. H. M. Jones, *Decline of the Ancient World* (London, 1966), p. 289; Salvian: *De Gubernatione Dei* 4.3–6, 4.26, in *MGH AA* 1.

43. See Perry Anderson, *Passage from Antiquity to Feudalism* (London, 1974); Charles Parain, "De l'Antiquité esclavagiste au féodalisme," in *Quel avenir attend l'homme?* (Paris, 1961), pp. 36 ff; Elena Michajlovna Štaerman, *La Crise de la société des possesseurs d'esclaves dans les provinces de l'Ouest de l'Empire Romain* (Moscow, 1957); or Elena Michajlovna Štaerman et al., *Die Sklaverei in den westlichen Provinzen des römischen Reiches im 1.–3. Jahrhundert* (Wiesbaden, 1974), for a traditional Marxist version. Wickham's "The Other Transition" is a revisionistic version. In their most orthodox forms, Marxist theories inadvertently leave little room for the efficacy of struggle, for the great wheels of history turn when ready, cannot be stopped, and are seldom hurried.

44. Raymond Van Dam, *Leadership and Community in Late Antique Gaul* (Berkeley, 1985). The older interpretation of slave rebellions is represented by E. A. Thompson, "Peasant Revolts in Late Roman Gaul and Spain," *Past and Present* 2 (1952): 11–23.

45. *History of the Franks* VII.46 and VII.47. The fate of Sichar's slave was cruel and swift in coming: "Sichar fell to the ground. His friends ran up. The slave was seized. He was cruelly beaten. His hands and feet were cut off. And he was hanged from the gallows."

46. Bonnassie, "Survie et extinction," pp. 336–37 gives quite a full list.

47. Abbon, *Le Siège de Paris par les Normands* (Paris, 1942), p. 30.

48. Quoted in *Anglo-Saxon Prose*, ed. Michael Swanton (London, 1974), p. 2.

49. Heinz Bellen, *Studien zur Sklavenflucht im römischen Kaiserreich* (Wiesbaden, 1971). Mutilation of slaves was most frequently a punishment meted out to fugitives, not simply as a penalty, but as a tell-tale sign of their status should they try to flee again. FHE, *Fugitivus hic est*, was sometimes branded on a Roman runaway slave returned to servitude. Alfred's specification of piercing a slave's ear with an awl, mentioned above by Girsch on p. 39, almost certainly "evoked concepts essentially similar to those of contemporary usage," for Merovingian slaveowners regularly slit the nose (less commonly ears) of their runaways.

50. Rothair's Edict c. 273, quoted in *The Lombard Laws*, trans. Katherine Fischer Drew (Philadelphia, 1973), p. 107. King, *Law and Society*, pp. 167–70, offers one of the few thoughtful considerations of the relationship of masters and runaway slaves. Masters clearly hated their own slaves to flee, but were happy to take advantage of those who fled others.

51. For more on flight and abetting in early medieval Gaul and legal references see my "Slavery, the Roman Legacy," pp. 226–27. Anglo-Saxon laws dealing with the man who leaves land without his lord's licence: Ine 39; II Edward 7; II Æthelstan 27; III Æthelstan 4; IV Æthelstan 4–5; V Æthelstan 1.1; II Cnut 28; Alfred and Guthrum 4, 6; the passages are commented upon by C. Stephenson, "Feudalism and its Antecedants in England" in *Medieval Institutions* (1943), pp. 234–60.

52. *The Lombard Laws*, p. 105; *The Life of Bishop Wilfrid by Eddius Stephanus* c. 18, trans. Bertram Colgrave (Cambridge, 1927), pp. 38–41; *History of the Franks* III.15; King, *Law and Society*, p. 167.

53. Thionville Capitulary c. 11, quoted in *The Reign of Charlemagne*, ed. H. R. Loyn and John Percival (London, 1975), p. 87.

54. For the individual councils of the Merovingian and Carolingian Church, see *MGH Conc. Merov.* and *MGH Conc. Karol.* Most decisions made concerning slaves can be found summarized in Verlinden, *L'Esclavage dans l'Europe médiévale*, vol. 1.

55. Church councils in Gaul returned over and over again to the question of what to do in the case of accidental ordination of slaves throughout the sixth century. See Verlinden, *L'Esclavage dans l'Europe médiévale*, vol. 1, pp. 680 ff.

56. Quoted in *Charlemagne: Translated Sources*, ed. P. D. King (Kendal, 1987), p. 205.

57. H. Langenfeld, *Christianisierungspolitik und Sklavengesetzgebung der römischen Kaiser von Konstantin bis Theodosius II* (Bonn, 1977) is good for the earliest period. Also for the early period: Franz Laub, *Die Begegnung des frühen Christentums mit der antiken Sklaverei* (Stuttgart, 1982); Henneke Gülzow, *Christentum und Sklaverei in den ersten drei Jahrhunderten* (Bonn, 1969). See too A. W. Rupprecht "Attitudes on Slavery among the Church Fathers" in *New Dimensions in New Testament Study*, ed. Richard N. Longenecker and Merrill C. Tenney (Grand Rapids, Michigan, 1974), pp. 261–77; Rayford W. Logan, "The Attitude of the Church toward Slavery prior to 1500," *Journal of Negro History* 17 (1932): 466–80; Hartmut Hoffmann, "Kirche und Sklaverei im frühen Mittelalter," *Deutsches Archiv* 42 (1986): 1–24. Bonnassie, "Survie et extinction," summarizes the medieval historians' understanding of the Church's position, pp. 322–26.

58. Loyn, *Anglo-Saxon England*, p. 350.

59. Robert Latouche, *The Birth of Western Economy: Economic Aspects of the Dark Ages* (London, 1961), p. 162. Bloch was equally upset at, or in Bonnassie words "very severe" with, the Church. The apology, however, slips in. "It was, however, no little thing to have said to the 'talking tool' of the ancient Roman agronomists, 'you are a human' 'you are a Christian'," wrote Bloch, "Comment et pourquoi," p. 272. Clémence Dupont, *Les Constitutions de Constantin et le droit privée au début de IVe siècle: les personnes* (Lille, 1937), suggests that Christianity may have been responsible for increasing limitations on a master's power to punish slaves, but this late Roman limitation has been shown by others to be illusory.

60. R. W. and A. J. Carlyle, *A History of Mediaeval Political Theory in the West*, vol. 1, *The Second Century to the Ninth* (London, 1903), esp. pp. 199–203; For Agobard, *MGH Ep. V. ep.* vi.

61. Verlinden, *L'Esclavage dans l'Europe médiévale*, vol. 1, p. 704.

62. Quoted in *Anglo-Saxon Prose*, ed. Michael Swanton (London, 1974), pp. 15–16.

63. St. Yrieiz: 35; St. Cybard: 175; St. Eloi: 100, Bonnassie, "Survie et extinction," p. 324.

64. *MGH SSrrM* 3, p. 493 (Caesarius) and p. 617 (Betharius). More examples of Merovingian saints redeeming captives are found in Wilhelm Levison, *England and the Continent in the Eighth Century* (Oxford, 1946).

65. Verlinden, *L'Esclavage dans l'Europe médiévale*, vol. 1, pp. 665–66. To see this in a non-apologetic Marxist light: František Graus, "Die Gewalt bei den Anfängen des Feudalismus und die 'Gefangenenbefreiungen' der merowingischen Hagiographie," *Jahrbuch für Wirtschaftsgeschichte* 1 (1961): 61–156.

66. Agobard, bishop of Lyon. *MGH Ep. V.*

67. Helen B. Clarke, "Domesday Slavery (Adjusted for Slaves)," *Midland History* 1.4 (1972): 37–46.

68. Council of Yenne (c. 8), *MGH Conc. Mer.* p. 21.

69. King, *Law and Society*, p. 179.

70. It would need the research of an ecclesiastical historian to be categoric, but if there was, *contubernium* would certainly have been condemned as fornication.

71. At the Council of Orléans in 541 (c. 23/4), for example, it was decided that slaves who turn up at a church to be married should be returned to their "parents or masters." See note 54.

72. *History of the Franks* V.3. This has more than a little bearing on Girsch's argument above, pp. 49–50. By the late OE period, the association of sexual servility with the status of slave must have been much weaker than it had been earlier. The Church,

in theory, protected married female slaves from enforced concubinage, by prohibiting masters from committing adultery.

73. *The Lombard Laws*, p. 104.

74. *Codex Carolinus* 37, quoted in *The Reign of Charlemagne*, ed. Loyn and Percival, p. 129.

75. Keith R. Bradley, "Holidays for Slaves," *Symbolae Osloenses* 54 (1979): 111–18.

76. *The Rule of the Master* (c. 75), trans. Luke Eberle (Kalamazoo, Michigan, 1977), p. 239.

77. Margaret Weidemann, *Kulturgeschichte der Merowingerzeit nach den Werken Gregors von Tours* (Mainz, 1982), pp. 289–90.

78. E.g. *History of the Franks* VIII.11.

79. Weidemann, *Kulturgeschichte*, p. 290. For the sanctity of Sunday in early medieval Ireland, see Brady in this volume, p. 131.

80. Quoted in *Charlemagne: Translated Sources*, ed. King, p. 227.

81. Paderborn Capitulary (785) c. 18, quoted in *The Reign of Charlemagne*, ed. Loyn and Percival, p. 53.

82. King, *Law and Society*, p. 135. I have been unable to refer the reader to secondary sources on the Church's attempts to keep the Sabbath free from labor. Ovitt's paper, above, for instance, makes no mention of the phenomenon. Economic and social historians likewise ignore this important topic. Ecclesiastical historians may have much to say about it, but presumably from a religious, liturgical perspective. The omission is all the more remarkable given the popularity of Weber's "Protestant work ethic," and the central position the Church is given by other theorists of European technological and economic supremacy.

83. Many more examples of sanctuary provided by the early medieval Gallic Church can be found in my "A Merovingian Nobleman's Home: Villa or Castle?," *Journal of Medieval History* 13 (1987): 287–315.

84. Alan Watson, *Roman Slave Law* (Baltimore, 1987).

85. Council of Orléans (c. 3), see note 54.

86. Gregory of Tours, *Life of the Fathers* (XVI.3), trans. Edward James (Liverpool, 1985), p. 111. See also (V.1), pp. 48–49 for a similar miracle.

87. Gregory of Tours, *Glory of the Confessors* (c. 66), trans. Raymond van Dam (Liverpool, 1988), p. 72.

88. Capitulary of Lippespringe (c. 2), quoted in *Charlemagne: Translated Sources*, ed. King, p. 205.

89. Bradley, *Slaves and Masters* (see n. 7); and for a wider theoretical generalization see Orlando Patterson, *Slavery and Social Death: A Comparative Study* (Cambridge, Mass., 1982), p. 341.

90. Capitulary of Mantua (c. 7), quoted in *The Reign of Charlemagne*, ed. Loyn and Percival, p. 50.

91. For the Roman state's active role in restoring runaways to their masters see the commentary of Ulpian cited in the *Digest* 11,4.1, quoted in Thomas Wiedemann, *Greek and Roman Slavery* (London, 1981), p. 190. Archaeology may yet contribute something to the study of early medieval slavery; I have suggested that enclosure walls around villas were essential for inferring attempted flight by slaves found outside them, "Knowledge, Constraint, and Power in Inaction: The Defenseless Medieval Wall," *Historical Archaeology* 26:26–44, esp. 32–33.

7

LABOR AND AGRICULTURE IN EARLY MEDIEVAL IRELAND: EVIDENCE FROM THE SOURCES

Niall Brady

Scholars to date have invested little time exploring the dynamics of slavery, servitude, or labor in early medieval Ireland.[1] Issues of rank and status have been dominant. Discussions of work have been concerned with identifying the different types of labor undertaken, and outlining the different classifications of laborers. But we still understand little about work in the daily lives of the people. We are particularly ignorant of the ways in which labor developed during the period, and how this was related to changes in the social and economic system. This paper examines the organization of agricultural labor in early medieval Ireland in an effort to correct the imbalance. It addresses three main questions: who worked? what work was done? and how was it done? The paper focuses on one particular form of labor that was of central importance to the early Irish, plowing.

I begin with a brief critical review of the literature. The sources for the study of labor are plentiful. They describe a very developed structure of work in Ireland between the fifth century and the end of the eleventh, a period known variously by the terms early Christian, early historic, and (increasingly) early medieval. The primary written sources are the secular law tracts, believed to be compiled by the start of the eighth century.[2] They are especially instructive in identifying the categories of worker and how labor was organized. By their nature, the laws are prescriptive. They convey at best an idealized picture of the patterns of life in their day, and must be used with care. The laws were written in Old Irish at a time when only Anglo-Saxon

England elsewhere in Europe could also boast vernacular legal codes. It is unclear whether they were drawn up by professional jurists, or by clerics, but they were certainly not the work of any central legislative authority, such as those associated with kings.

The laws cannot generalize for the whole country. Ireland in this period is noted for the absence of effective high kingship and a single legal system. The laws must have a very local application, but it has proved impossible to identify more than two very broad schools: a northern one and a southern one. They come down to us mostly in fragments, and mostly in manuscripts of the fourteenth to sixteenth centuries. Later scholiasts excerpted segments from the lost exemplars, and enshrined these as "sacred texts," to which they added often confusing and long-winded glosses of the ninth century and later. The work of reconstructing the original texts is aggravated by the fact that segments are sometimes embedded within the glosses themselves. Two main writing styles have been noticed: an alliterative verse one, and a prose style. These have been used as a means of dating the laws internally, but recent work has shown how shallow such an understanding may be.[3] This new work has helped to fuel criticism of the view that the laws embody a reflection of pre-Christian society. In the form that we have them, the laws are those of a heavily Christianised society.[4]

Much of the information contained in the laws is supported and expanded in literary texts.[5] Chief among these are hagiographical accounts.[6] Irish hagiographers used commonplace detail to validate the fanciful events of their heroes. This commonplace detail is often a very fruitful source for learning about daily life. There are two main groups of Irish Lives: a Latin series belonging to the seventh century; and a Latin and Irish series of the eleventh and later.[7] Like the laws, the Lives rarely come down to us in contemporary documents. The seventh-century Lives, however, are particularly attractive as they survive in eighth- and ninth-century codices.[8] Saga literature is another rich source, but again the documents in which the material has survived are late, belonging generally to the twelfth century and afterwards.[9]

The Annals are of less use for our purposes.[10] These chronicles share many features in common with the Anglo-Saxon Chronicle. The earliest traces are found in the later seventh century, and the existing annals began to be compiled in the late ninth and early tenth centuries. They are most useful for reminding us of the external processes that must have been continually affecting the development of society — processes that are perhaps all too readily forgotten when we try to arrive at some understanding of the progression of labor. The eighth century, for instance, was a period of continual famine and pestilence. It seems to have been characterized by adverse weather conditions, which served as a significant check on growth.

Objects are another significant source all too often neglected by historians and literary scholars; they should be recognized as such. Material culture allows us to retrieve actual tools and equipment, often from the very contexts in which they were used.[11] Many of these pieces survive in fragments, because of breakage and damage by weathering. The main limitation is that there is so much of it. One day, the very fields and organization of the landscape will reveal much about the way in which labor was deployed, but as yet attention has focused on the interiors of settlement sites. Outbuildings and field systems have only been chance finds. There are tens of thousands of settlements known, but only a fraction have been examined. The most common type that survives is the ringfort, or *rath* (conservative estimates number them at around 40,000). As the name implies, the bank and ditch fortification encloses a circular courtyard, or *lios*, some 20–30 meters in diameter. The received view sees the ringfort as the typical home of the typical freeman. Souterrains, not surprisingly, are underground chambers and tunnels, and they are often (but not always) found as part of the ringforts. Crannogs — *crannóg* is a derivative of *crann*, "tree, timber," — take their name from the timber palisades that surround artificial islets built on lakes and in marshy and boggy places. They are a greater building challenge than the average ringfort, and are regarded as the residences of more powerful freemen, and some of the nobility. There are fewer than 10,000 examples. The heyday of these kinds of scattered settlements seems to have been between the seventh and ninth centuries. Many have origins that extend back into the early years of our period and even before, though the nature of these earlier forms is still obscure. Ecclesiastical sites are numerous but perhaps the least excavated. Some certainly fulfilled the role of local and regional exchange centers and can be called towns. Whether there were towns before the seventh century remains unclear.

Research into labor during this period has always fallen short of understanding the processes that shaped its development, one of its more important aspects. The fruits of textual study have been sparse indeed. Types of labor and classes of laborer have been identified, but the chronological and contextual shortcomings of these sources have led to little conceptual discussion. Material culture in turn has yielded all too little. The subject of work and labor simply has not attracted sufficient interest to tackle the rapidly increasing numbers of discoveries. A weakness that pervades all the research is that it has progressed without any successful attempt at an interdisciplinary approach. Each source area has tended to be studied in isolation. Given the limitations of each area, it is surprising that interdisciplinary studies have not been more popular. This paper, offered as an introductory contribution in this direction, focuses on the plow, both as an agricultural implement and as a way in which to look at the organization of labor. It was the single most complex piece of equipment needed in preparing the soil for the seed of the future crop, and plowing was a task which required careful management of human and animal resources to operate effectively. The plow is also an artifact that changes in design during our period. Through its development, we can glimpse changes occurring in the working practices that surround it. This in turn tells us about the developing nature of labor. We start, however, by looking at who the laborers in early Ireland were, and what the tasks were to which they were put.

There is a distinction to be made between labor that was undertaken on one's own land, and that which was required by one's lord. The interest of this paper is in the latter, but it should be noted, if only in passing, that there was a strong sense of cooperation in agricultural work throughout society.[12] Irish society was hierarchical in structure, with lords at the top, commoners in the middle, and semi- and unfree at the bottom.[13] Running across these boundaries was a sense of community, and the laws indicate that individuals were brought together in groups which acted for the common good. Individuals contributed equipment and livestock for use in communal operations, such as plowing and herding. Cooperation was also needed between neighbors whose lands provided the necessary sustenance for another's enterprise. The law on conducted water (*Coibnes Uisce Thairidne*), for example, sets out the rules needed to bring water across neighbors' land to power a watermill. The cooperation that existed in Ireland did not extend to sharing the produce collectively. It seems clear that a person's share was directly proportional to the size of their investment.

Most of the labor for the lord was carried out by his non-free dependants. Freemen could owe some labor services to their lords, but these were negligible.[14] The non-free were made up of two groups: those who were neither fully free nor unfree, and the fully unfree. The former consisted of tenants-at-will (the *fuidri*) and cottiers (the *bothach*). The distinction between the two is unclear. The *fuidir* has been called "semi-free" by recent scholars and compared with the Anglo-Saxon

Kentish *laet*.[15] Not all *fuidri* were poor and landless and not all would have labored in the lords' fields. *Fuidirship* seems to have been a transitional rank applied to an individual in the process of changing status, or (more likely) having it changed for them. They had become dependent on their lords, either because they were landless, or as punishment for an offence, or in the commutation of a death penalty. A *fuidir* was not fully free because they did not possess full legal rights and economic independence. They could not enter into contracts on their own. They had to have their lord's consent to do so, and they were obliged to do whatever tasks the lord assigned them. However, barring the lowliest types, they were not unfree either. They were not permanently bound to their lord. Like freemen, *fuidri* entered into agreements with their lords, where they performed certain services in return for material goods and the lord's legal protection. The *fuidri* could, in theory at least, abandon their contracts at any stage without incurring crippling debts, provided they gave two-thirds of their husbandry to the lord and had not committed any crime against him. This was a steep price to pay for abandoning a contract. It is unlikely that *fuidri* were able to do this alone or often.

The unfree were made up of a mixed bag of various impoverished people. They were not all slaves and gallows fodder. Certain *fuidri* eventually became unfree. Should a *fuidir* family remain on their lord's land for three generations, it became *senchléithe*, or "old clients" (literally "ancient dwelling"). *Senchléithe* were apparently hereditary serfs, permanently bound to their lord and wholly dependent on him.[16] They even passed as chattels with the land if it changed hands. An often-quoted episode in the *Tripartite Life of Patrick* (895–901) describes Cinaed son of Congalach offering St. Patrick three *senchléithe* with their land as partial compensation for the then King of Tara's desecration of Patrick's altar.[17] To the jurists, society was hierarchical. If the unfree may be arranged in a hierarchy of their own, then the *senchléithe* were at its pinnacle. Below them came criminals and slaves. *Dóerfhuidri* (base/unfree *fuidir*) were criminals and those otherwise saved from death. To give them their freedom was a sign of poor judgement, a time when the laws tell us that a ". . . lord's produce perishes so that there is a failure of corn and milk and fruit."[18] They share this dubious status with slaves.

Slaves (*mug*) occupied the lowest social rank, possessed few rights of their own and were at the mercy of their lord. They originated as prisoners-of-war, foreigners picked up by slave-traders, and the indebted. They were a valuable labor asset. Literary sources in particular portray them performing many of the menial chores, such as wood-cutting and dairying. St. Patrick's *Confessio* tells how, while a slave in Ireland, Patrick's duty was to herd the livestock.[19] I have not found references to the physical maltreatment of slaves, by means of beatings and disfigurements which have been noted elsewhere in Europe,[20] but the bluntness of the Irish Laws certainly dehumanizes them. Heptad 29 lists slaves alongside criminals, women in marriage, church property, secular forts, and irrestorable land, as those items which are impossible to be given as *rath* (*beneficia*) not because of any respect for human dignity, but rather because their status does not fulfill the usual qualities of the *rath*.[21] If they are given out as *rath*, they have to be returned. In normal circumstances *raths* become the client's property over time provided the proper rent is paid. It is clear that slaves were regarded as a form of property. During our period, slavery becomes more widespread, possibly because of the struggles of Irish overkings for supremacy.[22] The market peaks in the eleventh century.

It is one thing to sketch out a review of who the laborers in early Ireland were; it is quite another to chart the dynamics at work within this labor pool. The limitations of the sources have prevented any penetrating study. The greatest potential could lie in the law tracts but, because the period they represent belongs to the eighth century at the latest, there is very little solid material to work with for the period after this. One approach that could prove useful is to study the glosses of these codes as a source in their own right. Recent scholarship has been concerned with isolating the "sacred texts" from the glosses because considerable confusion and misinterpretation had arisen in the past when text and glosses were read in unison without regard to their chronological differences. The task of sorting through the glosses would be a formidable one. It would be aggravated by the fact that the glossators sometimes misunderstood the cryptic nature of the original codes, and as such their explanations and comments would be irrelevant. However, in the instances where the gloss has captured an accurate understanding of the original text, and the gloss itself can be dated, it could be a useful source for describing the contemporary understanding of the practice that it is commenting on. But this is a task for scholars in the future.

The most satisfactory work on the dynamics within the labor pool to date indicates that the original codes themselves reflect a society which was experiencing change. Research has only looked at freemen. The whole area of the non-free is still a mystery. It appears that freemen were increasingly at risk of becoming impoverished. The law tract on status, *Críth Gablach* (c. 700), asks of the *bóaire*, a comfortable commoner farmer, "[w]hat is it which deprives this man of the status of *bóaire* . . . ," to which it replies, "[b]ecause there may be four or five men who are the heirs of a *bóaire* so that it is not easy for each of them to be a *bóaire*."[23] The implication is that partible inheritance was denying individuals the status they were born into. In Anglo-Saxon England, a similar problem appears to have been resolved by the impoverished freeman (in this case the *ceorl*) losing his land but retaining his status as a freeman.[24] In Ireland, as in Wales, the loss of land was accompanied by the loss of status. To combat this, Irish jurists are believed to have established a new grade of freeman below the *bóaire* with lesser property and wealth, which they called the *ócaire* (literally "young freeman").[25] It is clear, however, that population continued to grow. The seventh to ninth centuries sees the *floruit* of ringfort and crannog occupation. It is still unclear whether the trend was for new areas to be settled or for a greater use of existing land-holdings. At any rate, by the twelfth century, when written sources again show something of the social structure, it is evident that many of the smaller freemen had fallen into semi- and unfree status through indebtedness. [26]

The work to which this growing servile force was put is aptly described in *Cáin Domnaig*, an early eighth-century tract on the Law of Sunday.[27] The *Cáin* permits the following tasks, namely: journeying to a doctor, and to communion, tracking down lawbreakers, herding cattle, tracking after bees or cattle in heat, fetching a midwife for a woman in labor, bulling cows, driving cattle to a cooling pond, and repairing broken field fences. It prohibits others. The sanctity of Sunday, the *Cáin* relates, shall be:

> without riding, without wandering about, without buying, without legal transaction, without suing, without passing judgement, without shaving, without bathing, without sexual union, without aimless running, without grinding, without baking, without churning, without splitting firewood, without cleaning house, without a load on ox or horse or man, without any activity which is proper to servile work. . . .[28]

Elsewhere, spinning, baking, and dairying are described as servile women's chores, while plowing, threshing, woodcutting, and cattle-herding appear to have been men's.[29] Women may also have herded sheep as part of their responsibility for cloth production,[30] while both men and women ground grain at the mill. [31]

Material culture obviously cannot readily reveal the status of the people who carried out the work, but it does have a contribution to make which the written sources are unable to convey. Many of the tasks referred to in the written sources have been corroborated by actual finds on sites,[32] but the unique value of material sources is that they indicate how work was actually done. This allows us to understand the extent to which agriculture was in any way progressive, as well as something about the deployment of labor. In contrast with elsewhere in Europe, illuminations and sculptural reliefs depicting agricultural work do not survive in any number in Ireland. There are no depictions of plowing the land or milling grain. It is even hard to find representations of simpler tasks such as digging with spades. Careful study of the considerable body of material evidence, however, is beginning to yield important results. Much of this work has concentrated on milling.[33]

The application of dendrochronology dating (the technique of dating wood by counting the number of growth rings) has established that watermills were operating in the early seventh century, a period more or less contemporary with the law tract that deals with water rights in relation to mills, *Coibnes Uisce Thairidne*. The mills are sophisticated pieces of engineering and their mechanization of the grinding process reduced the labor requirement considerably. Horizontal wheels and vertical wheels were used. At Little Island, Co. Cork, a complex of two mills (dated c. 630) using three wheels, apparently at the same time, suggests a sizeable market for the grain processed. It is a finding that questions the more traditional view of rural Ireland as a place of non-enterprising, self-sufficient, and subsistent farmers.[34] The point is made more forcibly when the water supply is considered. These were tidal mills. They were carefully situated to avail of the estuarine waters of nearby Lough Mahon so that the mill ponds would have been naturally filled by the flowing tide twice a day, allowing the mill to operate at ease on the ebb tides. In this manner, the owners of the mills would have avoided having to pay a fee to those (according to *Coibnes Uisce Thairidne*) across whose lands the water to power a more land-locked mill runs.

Little Island demonstrates that agriculture was a highly developed economic concern, where investors were keen to improve production levels. Work on milling begs the study of other aspects of the agricultural process. There have been significant inroads made into animal husbandry by examining animal bone assemblages,[35] but scholars have been slow to look at other areas. Some topics have received little or no attention. One that is in need of revision is plowing. It is almost fifty years since anyone carefully scrutinized the material remains. It is timely to look again at the subject because there is now a much more respectable body of information available.[36]

ॐ

The evidence for plowing comes in the form of plow-irons. These are the cutting implements used on plowing devices. There are thirty-five known, and twelve of these come from securely dated archaeological contexts (Figures 1–2). There are two types of plow-iron: shares and coulters. Shares are fixed onto the base of the frame where they serve to undercut the sod horizontally as the plow advances through the soil. Coulters hang vertically above and slightly in front of the share. Their job is to slice the sod on its landward, or unplowed, side in advance of the undercutting action of the share. Examination of the types and sizes of these distinctive parts reveals the type of plowing device that used them. In medieval Europe, there were three main types of device: ards, wheelless plows, and wheeled plows. Ards are simple scratch-plows. They are generally made with light wooden frames and only have shares as cutting tools. Coulters tend to be associated with plows. Plows are able to be used on heavier and wetter soils more effectively than ards, and the dual action of share and coulter facilitates the cutting of a cleaner furrow. They are technologically more sophisticated than ards, and can produce a much better plowed surface.

The Irish irons indicate the existence of a variety of plowing devices and a development in designs during the course of the Early Middle Ages. Ards were used for much of the period, as was the practice in England and most of Europe. We cannot be sure of the type of ard used, but the shares (Figure 1.1–5) could be comfortably fitted onto a simple one-handled type, similar to the prehistoric examples from Donnerupland and Døstrup, Denmark. Such ards were commonly used across Europe into the historic era, and a variation on the types can be seen in the plowing scenes represented on the Utrecht and Harley Psalters.[37] The ards are best suited to lighter soils and can be managed by one person, although two plowmen are not unknown. The plowman would walk on the landward, or unplowed side, and push down on the handle to counter the attempts by the oxen to pull the device out onto the area already plowed.

The earliest coulter from Ireland belongs to the tenth century (Ballinderry, Co. Westmeath, Figure 2.10). Such coulters are characteristically associated with the larger and heavier shares (Figure 1.6–8), and it leads to the conclusion that it is at this period that the Irish first

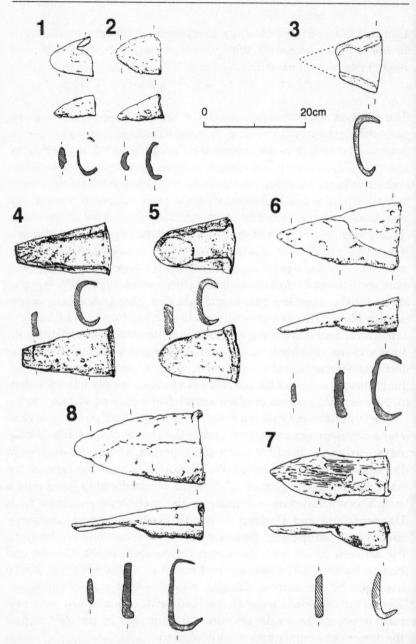

Figure 1: Medieval iron shares from Ireland: 1, Carraig Aille, Co. Limerick (8th century); 2, Whitechurch, Co. Waterford (9th century); 3, Ballyfounder, Co. Down (7th–8th century); 4–5, Fishamble St., Dublin (10th century, courtesy National Museum of Ireland); 6, Dundrum, Co. Down (end of 1st millennium A.D.); 7, Lough Kinale, Co. Longford (12th century); 8, Massereene, Co. Antrim (early 16th century).

used the plow proper. It is of particular interest that the *Dictionary of the Irish Language* cites only late instances of the word *coltar* (coulter), while it has early entries for *soc* (share).[38] It seems that written sources and material sources may for once be in agreement. This pattern of plow development is not unique to Ireland. It is found in Anglo-Saxon England at about the same time, and it points to some basis for comparison.[39] It is tempting to identify the forces that might have helped to produce these developments, but it is sufficient for this paper to note that Ireland, like England, was enjoying considerable commercial contact with the Scandinavian world at this time. This circumstance may well have created the opportunity for development. A metallurgical study of the coulter from Whitefort, Co. Down (Figure 2.9) concluded that it could not have been a particularly effective implement.[40] It is tempting to use this as an explanation for the small numbers of these coulters (2), and to see them as an unsuccessful design. However, since the Whitefort example is the only coulter to have been subjected to an instructive analysis, no conclusions can be drawn until more examples are analyzed.

The most numerous group of coulters, typified by that from Ballinderry (see also Figure 2.11–12), offers the best basis for a reconstruction of the plow type that used them. Their short tang indicates that the coulter must have been situated low down in the plow frame, close to the earth. Otherwise, only the tip of the coulter would have been cutting through the sod. The Ballinderry, Co. Westmeath example (Figure 2.10), preserves its wear scratches from when it was used. Not only do they run two-thirds up the length of the blade, but they also do so at a 45° angle. This indicates that the coulter was set at this angle in the frame, which is a further argument for seeing it placed at a low level. The only comparative coulters that I have found survive on a light wheelless type of plow which was in use in Orkney earlier this century and can be traced back with certainty to the 1760s (Figure 3).[41] The coulters are slightly shorter than the comparable Irish types (c. 38cm in overall length compared with c. 50cm), and while they are set at an angle in the frame, as the Ballinderry example indicates, they are fixed at 30ᶜ. The shares are also similar to the Irish types, although they are not as massive as the largest examples. The overall comparison is nevertheless striking. I believe that this single-handed Orkney plow is a close descendant of the type common in medieval Ireland. We are fortunate that good records survive describing how they were used.

The Orkney plows were used to ridge potatoes, but as the Irish irons

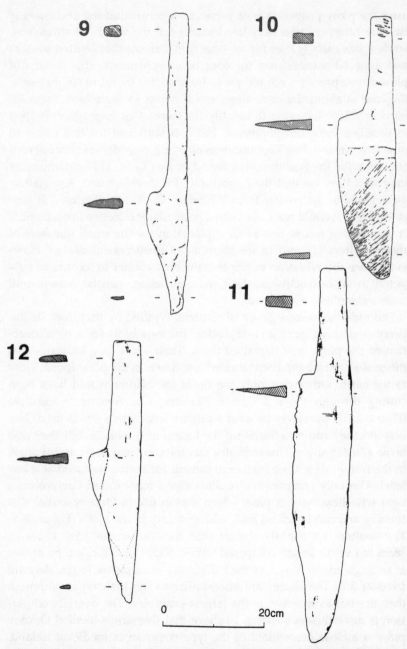

Figure 2: Medieval iron coulters from Ireland: 9, Whitefort, Co. Down (end of 1st millennium A.D.); 10, Ballinderry, Co. Westmeath (late 10th century); 11, Lough Kinale, Co. Longford (12th century); 12, Massereene, Co. Antrim (early 16th century).

are somewhat more massive, it is likely that the versions in medieval Ireland undertook heavier tasks, and that the plows themselves were somewhat heavier. Three people are needed to operate the implement instead of the one or two working the ard. The plowman steers the plow from the rear in the same way as with an ard. A second individual leads the oxen from the front, walking backwards singing to the beasts and striking their faces, while a third person, sometimes a boy, pushes down on the plowbeam either with a forked stick or by actually sitting on it to ensure the plow does not leap out of the earth. The use of such a three-person team has a long tradition in Ireland, and can be traced back with certainty to the early seventeenth century, although such an arrangement of personnel was not special to this type of plow.[42] It may be concluded that the development of plowing devices improved the quality of cultivation. It may also be said that the development increased the labor required to carry out plowing, which contrasts with the mill, where improvement reduced the number of people needed to grind grain.

It is unlikely that the new plows speeded up the process of plowing in any significant way. Plowing with ard or plow is a slow and tedious process. The device has to be continually stopped so that the mud clinging to it can be cleaned off, and the same land might have to be plowed a number of times, depending on the nature of the soil and the type of crop to be sown. It is a labor that attracted considerable attention in medieval literatures. However, as much as it is an essential task for ensuring a good return on the future crop, it is revealing that plowing and the work of the plowman are not listed among those special skills respected in early Irish society, while that of the wright is (and by association the mill wright).[43] In *Cáin Domnaig* plowing is lumped generically with all servile labors that entail plying oxen, horses, and men with loads, and in saints' Lives, plowing is a recurrent topos for the display of saintly *humilitas*.[44] This low status of plowing in Ireland is perhaps support for the literary theme of the plowman as upholder of Adam's sin.

There is a distinction to be made between carrying out the labor of plowing and owning a plow. Ownership was considered a definite sign of status. *Críth Gablach* is very clear on this issue. The *ócaire* has only a quarter share in a plow, while the strong non-noble *mruigfher*, not only possesses his own complete plow, but also has a share in a mill.[45] It is to be noted that only seven of the thirty-five plow-irons known are truly stray finds. All the others were deposited in ways that suggest considerable care was given to preserving them for future use.

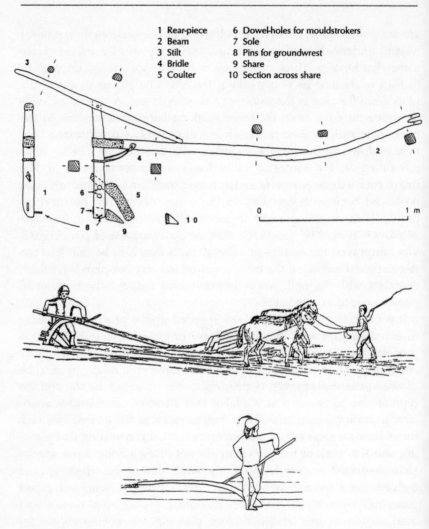

1 Rear-piece   6 Dowel-holes for mouldstrokers
2 Beam   7 Sole
3 Stilt   8 Pins for groundwrest
4 Bridle   9 Share
5 Coulter   10 Section across share

Figure 3: The Orkney plow. Top: Plow A.76 Tankerness House Museum; middle: from a marginal sketch in William Aberdeen's Estate Map E.29 (after Marwick 1924); bottom: from a plowing scene in William Aberdeen's Estate Map E.27, Kirkwall Library.

We may envisage a situation similar to that depicted in Ælfric's *Colloquy* where the plowman fetches the irons from his lord's farmstead in the early morning, and brings them with him into the fields to attach them to the plow.[46] A similar pattern is evident with the mill. Where millstones are not found in the watermills, they occur on ringforts and crannogs.[47] Like the plow-iron, millstones were costly investments, not to be lost. Taking the stones home would also guard against illegal use of the mill by outsiders, an abuse that is noted in the Laws.[48]

ᴁ

It is clear that the effect of technological development on the deployment of agricultural labor is an area that deserves further attention. It will be much more instructive when research extends to other agricultural activities that have not yet been adequately studied. One suggestion would be to consider the other aspects of grain processing.[49] While archaeologists have looked in vain for grain pits on sites, the written sources clearly indicate the use of barns and possibly open stacks for storing the grain.[50] No barn has yet been identified.[51] Until the barns are found, we will be very ignorant about such matters as the size of the harvested crops. This in turn inhibits a fuller understanding of the extent to which manual labor was employed in the various aspects of crop husbandry. Adomnán's *Life of Columba* makes it clear that the barn on Iona was located outside the enclosure. After Columba goes one Sunday to bless the nearest barn, he "left the barn, and returning towards the monastery sat down midway."[52] Similarly, when *Bretha Comaithcesa* defines certain trespasses caused by hens and fowl, it lists those which occur *outside* the enclosure, namely: in the kiln, in the mill, and in the corn stacks.[53] Elsewhere the laws stipulate that threshing occurred within the kiln, or *áith*.[54] Certain dubious features have been excavated within ringforts and posited to be corn-drying kilns, but the evidence is not fully convincing.[55] No flails or winnowing fans have been identified either. Archaeologists could well solve these problems if they would increase their efforts to look outside the immediate household areas. After all, the location of a barn and related structures away from a domestic site is an obvious precaution against the risk of fire.

Historians and literary scholars are also in a unique position to contribute new insights into the question of labor in Ireland. There is a need for a thorough investigation of the development of the servile grades. The limitations of the sources make it a subject that has been difficult to approach, but it is time to scrutinize them once again. If there is evidence for change and impoverishment among freemen, is there any such evidence concerning the non-free? *Senchléithe*, for instance, are the only bound class in Ireland aside from slaves and criminals. They became this way only if they continued as *fuidri* for more than three generations. Were they always regarded as chattels? The laws treat their status as a given, but there is a need for scholars to broaden their own perspectives and begin to think of the dynamics of rural class development. One can see what could happen in the very different situation of later twelfth-century England, where it has been argued that villeinage was initially a legal doctrine developed by lawyers wrestling with the problem of defining status in the emerging common law, but which later came to define the limits of legal juris-diction.[56] It would be comforting to think that at some stage in the future we might be able to understand medieval Ireland a bit better. The attention that agriculture and labor has already attracted has laid a solid foundation for this work, identifying the major activities and the main categories of individuals who undertook them. Research is now in a position to start interpreting this evidence to a far greater degree than has been the case. With this interpretation will come a clearer sense of the dynamics of work in early Irish society and, in turn, a better understanding of the relationship between Ireland and its neighbors.

NOTES

I wish to thank Paul Hyams, Fergus Kelley, and Allen Frantzen for their comments on drafts of this paper.

1. Interest in social history has been mostly concerned with the free element of society: nobles and commoners. Information on these groups is much more readily available than for the unfree, who are usually mentioned only in reference to the free. Ireland's problem is not unique. Much of what is known about servi-tude and work has been brought together by scholars from a range of disciplines, but it is rare to find specialized studies on the non-free, who were the *laborares*. Studies that do consider these matters to varying degrees on the law codes are: R. Thurneyson, ed. and transl., *Irisches Recht*, Abhandlungen der preussichen Akademie der Wissenschaften phil.-hist. Klasse, nr. 2 (Berlin, 1931); D. Binchy, ed., *Críth Gablach*, Mediaeval and Modern Irish Series XI (Dublin, 1941); G. MacNiocaill, ed. and trans., "Tír Cumaile," *Ériu* 22 (1971): 81–86; G. MacNiocaill, "Investment in Early Irish Agriculture," ed. B. Scott, *Studies on Early Ireland: Essays in Honour of M. V. Duignan* (Belfast, 1983), pp. 7–9; and T. Charles-Edwards, *Early Irish and Welsh Kinship* (Oxford, 1993), pp. 307–36. On the written sources there are: C. Doherty, "Some Aspects of Hagiography as a Source for Irish Economic History," *Peritia* 1 (1982): 300–28 and D. Ó Corráin, "Some Legal Re-ferences to Fences and Fencing in Early Historic Ireland," ed. T. Reeves-Smyth and F. Hamond, *Landscape Archaeology in Ireland* (Oxford, 1983), pp. 247–51. On material sources there are: F. McCormick, "Dairying and Beef Production in Early Christian Ireland: the Faunal Evidence," ed. Reeves-Smyth and Hamond, *Land-scape Archaeology*, pp. 253–67; F. McCormick, "Early Faunal Evidence for Dairy-ing," *Oxford Journal of Archaeology* 11 (1992): 201–209; M. Monk, "Evidence from Macroscopic Plant Remains for Crop Husbandry in Prehistoric and Early Historic Ireland: a Review," *Journal of Irish Archaeology* 3 (1986): 31–36; and the life-long work of A. T. Lucas.

2. The laws were poorly edited and translated into English by W. Hancock, et al., *Ancient Laws and Institutes of Ireland*, volumes 1–6 (Dublin, 1865–1901), hereafter cited *AL*, page and line number). For many texts it is still the only edition; for others *AL* has been replaced by D. Binchy, ed., *Corpus Iuris Hibernici*, volumes 1–6 (Dublin, 1978) (hereafter cited *CIH*, page and line number). Binchy provides neither an analytical table of contents, nor a translation. This has made his invaluable corpus inaccessible to many, but F. Kelly, *A Guide to Early Irish Law*, Early Irish Law Series 3 (Dublin, 1988), has done much to rectify this problem. Many of the laws have been reliably edited and translated elsewhere. Of relevance to this paper is Thurneysen, *Irisches Recht*, and sundry papers in the journal *Ériu*. D. Binchy, "The Linguistic and Historical Value of the Irish Law Tracts," *Proceedings of the British Academy* 29 (1943): 195–227, sets out the potentials and limitations of the laws as a tool for historical research. Canon Law and the penitentials must also contain relevant materials, although I am unaware of significant use being made of them; see Kathleen Hughes, *Early Christian Ireland: Introduction to the Sources* (Ithaca, 1972), pp. 67–95.

3. L. Breathnach, "Canon Law and Secular Law in Early Ireland," *Peritia* 3 (1984): 439–459.

4. D. Ó Corráin, L. Breathnach, and A. Breen, "The Laws of the Irish," *Peritia* 3 (1984): 382–438, although F. Kelly, *A Guide*, pp. 232–36, points out certain difficulties with this argument.

5. C. Roth, "Some Observations on the Historical Background of the *Hisperica Famina*," *Ériu* 29 (1978): 112–22, for instance, sees a comparison in the information given on agricultural practices in the *Hisperica Famina* with that stated in the law tract *Bretha Comaithcesa*. A later, more elaborate, and more gustatory source is the eleventh-century *Vision of Mac Con Glinne* which provides a quick guide to diet, K. Jackson, ed., *Aislinge Meic Con Glinne* (Dublin, 1990). The best guides to this material are J. Kenney, *The Sources for the Early History of Ireland: Ecclesiastical* (New York, 1929, reprinted 1966) and M. Lapidge, and R. Sharpe, *A Bibliography of Celtic-Latin Literature 400–1200* (Dublin, 1985).

6. The most concise summary of research into Irish hagiography is R. Sharpe's, *Medieval Irish Saints' Lives: An Introduction to Vitae Sanctorum Hiberniae* (Oxford, 1991), pp. 5–34. A. T. Lucas, "Irish Ploughing Practices," *Tools and Tillage* 2.1 (1972): 52–62, has consistently used *vitae* in his illustrations of agricultural work, although he seems to have ignored their finer chronological limitations. Doherty, "Some Aspects of Hagiography," demonstrates a broader potential, and also explains the relationship between monastic levels of society and secular levels.

7. The intervening period is not without Lives, and lexical work is beginning to show the possibility of redating some of the twelfth-century *vitae* to it, J. Carey, "Review of *Medieval Irish Saints' Lives: An Introduction to Vitae Sanctorum Hiberniae*, by R. Sharpe," *Speculum* 68 (1993): 261–62.

8. Adomnán's Life of Columba survives in the Schauffhausen codex where the colophon identifies the scribe as Dorbbéne (c. 713). The Lives of St. Patrick by Muirchú and Tírechán survive in the *Book of Armagh*, dated 807. Cogitosus' Life of Brigit is found in a significant number of continental manuscripts of the ninth century and later, while a corrupt copy of the *Vita Prima S. Brigitae* was written in southern Germany in the early ninth century, Sharpe, *Medieval Irish Saints' Lives*, pp. 10–15.

9. A comprehensive survey and guide to this literature is still needed.

10. For a general discussion see Hughes, *Early Christian Ireland*, pp. 99–148.

11. M. Duignan's general essay, "Irish Agriculture in Early Historic Times," *Journal of the Royal Society of Antiquaries of Ireland* 74 (1944): 124–45, on early agriculture is still the standard work on the subject. The substantial new material now available that could lead to a total revision has not yet attracted sufficient attention. See

McCormick's "Dairying and Beef Production" and "Early Faunal Evidence" on animal bones and Monk, "Evidence from Macroscopic Plant Remains," on plant remains. On mills see C. Rynne, "The Introduction of the Vertical Watermill into Ireland: Some Recent Archaeological Evidence," *Medieval Archaeology* 33 (1989): 21–31. And on settlement see: J. Bradley, "The Interpretation of Scandinavian Settlement in Ireland," ed. J. Bradley, *Settlement and Society in Medieval Ireland: Studies Presented to F. X. Martin, O.S.A.* (Kilkenny, 1988), pp. 49–78; J. Bradley, "Excavations at Moynagh Lough, County Meath," *Journal of the Royal Society of Antiquaries of Ireland* 121 (1991): 5–26; and V. Proudfoot, "The Economy of the Irish Rath," *Medieval Archaeology* 5 (1961): 94–122. For a general introduction to the archaeology of early Ireland see N. Edwards, *The Archaeology of Early Medieval Ireland* (Philadelphia, 1990).

12. Cooperation was sufficiently important to warrant a number of separate tracts in its own right: *Coibnes Uisce Thairidne*, on the kinship of mill-races (*CIH* 457.11–462.18, D. Binchy, ed. and transl., "*Coibnes Uisce Thairidne*," *Ériu* 17 (1955): 52–85); *Bechbretha*, bee-judgements (*CIH* 444.12–457.10, Thomas Charles-Edwards and F. Kelly ed. and transl., *Bechbretha: An Old Irish Law-Tract on Bee-Keeping*, Early Irish Law Series 1 (Dublin, 1983); *Bretha Comaithcesa*, judgments of neighborhood (*CIH* 64.6–79.12, 191.1–205.21, transl. *AL* 4, 69–159); *Comingaire*, joint-herding (*CIH* 192.1–33, 576.24–577.24, transl. *AL* 4, 101.6–103.26). A useful discussion of joint farming by Thomas Charles-Edwards is found in Hughes's *Early Christian Ireland*, pp. 61–64; see also Charles-Edwards, *Kinship*, pp. 415–30.

13. See D. Ó Corráin, *Ireland Before the Normans* (Dublin, 1972), pp. 42–48, for a readable summary, and Binchy's *Críth Gablach*, pp. 69–109, and Kelly, *A Guide*, esp. pp. 11–12, 26–36, for further details on the particular grades of person identified in the laws and for explanations of legal terms.

14. This was contingent upon the type of contract, or agreement, they had with their lord. Lords entered into contracts with their dependants. In return for advancing land, livestock, or material goods (*rath*), as well as legal representation and protection to their dependants (or clients, *céili*), the lords were able to count the clients among their followers (to varying degrees) and also receive tribute and certain services from them. The amount of labor service increased with the diminishing status of the client. Wealthier freemen could opt for an contract based on free-clientship (*sóerchéile*). This did not require labor services (although a later gloss on the tract on free clientship, *Cáin Shóerraith*, suggests that some services were required). The other option was base clientship (*céile gíallnae*). This did require labor services, but these amounted to joining the lord's harvest party, helping in the construction of the lord's fort, and digging his gravemound, Kelly, *A Guide*, pp. 29–33.

15. A law tract exists on the *fuidir* (*CIH* 426.1–429.12, transl. *AL* V 513–521, and more thoroughly edited and translated into German by Thurneysen, *Irisches Recht*, pp. 62–67). Thomas Charles-Edwards, "Kinship, Status and the Origins of the Hide," *Past and Present* 56 (1972): 9, made the association with the *laet* and coined the phrase "semi-free" to describe the *fuidir*.

16. Very little work has actually been done on the *senchléithe*. There is some discussion by Thurneysen, *Irisches Recht*, pp. 81–83. Binchy's *Críth Gablach*, p. 105, and Kelly, *A Guide*, pp. 35–36, define the term. For illustration in non-legal sources see Doherty, "Some Aspects of Hagiography," pp. 313–15.

17. *The Tripartite Life of Patrick*, part 1, ed. and trans. W. Stokes (London, 1887), 72.14–74.3.

18. The consequences of releasing *dóerfuidri* are the same as those for revoking grants to churches, abolishing tithes, and freeing slaves, see *AL* v 450.12–15.

19. *St. Patrick His Writings and Muirchu's Life*, ed. and trans. A. Hood (London and Chichester, 1978), p. 25, para. 16. He has more recently discussed *fuidirship* in some depth in *Kinship*, pp. 307–36.

20. Pierre Bonnassie, *From Slavery to Feudalism in South-Western Europe*, trans. J. Birrell (Cambridge, 1991), pp. 19-22.

21. Atait secht n-ecmachta ratha la Feine: mug, cumal, cimid, ben a lanamnus, cell co n-a hincrod, dun co n-a tochus, tir di-aithgina. Is e claoidem im-faebur in sin: oro suiet, do suiet. "There are with the Feine seven [things] impossible as stock [i.e. impossible to give to a client as stock]: a slave, a slave woman, criminals, a woman in marriage, a church with its internal property, a *dun* [fort] with its appurtenances; irrestorable land. This is the two-edged sword: when they are given out, they have to be returned" (Heptad 29, *AL* v 222.1-4).

22. P. Holm, "The Slave Trade of Dublin, Ninth to Twelfth Centuries," *Peritia* 5 (1986): 317-345. His is the only recent study of slavery in Ireland, and he is most concerned with understanding the political and economic factors behind Irish slavery from the ninth to the twelfth centuries, rather than looking at the place of slaves in daily life. Such a study has yet to be made, but the material exists, albeit obtusely, in the laws, saints' Lives, and contemporary literatures. There is also the possibility of information in Icelandic sources, such as *Njal's Saga*.

23. Cid nodmbrisi in fer so a bóairechas? Ar bés bid cethrar nó chóicer bíte hi comarbus bóaireach co[n]ách assa[e] bóaire do cach áe (Binchy's *Críth Gablach*, l.145-148; E. MacNeill, "Ancient Irish Law: the Law of Status or Franchise," *Proceedings of the Royal Irish Academy* 36c (1923): 290.1-3). See Charles-Edwards, "Kinship, Status and the Origins of the Hide," pp. 9-14, for comments.

24. Charles-Edwards, "Kinship, Status and the Origins of the Hide," pp. 10-11.

25. Binchy's *Críth Gablach*, pp. 101-102.

26. On this phenomenon see Doherty, "Some Aspects of Hagiography," pp. 320-321 and F. Byrne, "The Trembling Sod: Ireland in 1169," ed. A. Cosgrove, *A New History of Ireland, II: Medieval Ireland 1169-1534* (Oxford, 1987), pp. 11-12.

27. The tract is edited and translated by V. Hull, "*Cáin Domnaig*," *Ériu* 20 (1966): 151-177.

28. ". . . cen imrim, cen imthecht, cen creic cen cundrad, cen acrae, cen brethemnas, cen berrath, cen folcuth, cen fothrucud, cen gním cloíne, cen rith n-espai, cen mbleith, cen fuini, cen maistriud, cen scoltad conduid, cen glanad tige, cen eire for dam na ech na duine, cen nach ngním is dír mugsaine. . . ." Hull, "*Cáin Domnaig*," pp. 160-161.

29. On spinning: (*AL* i 148-151), the tract describes in great detail the equipment of cloth-making and associates it closely with women. On baking: (*AL* iii 275-277). On plowing: (*AL* iii 266-273). On threshing: (*AL* iii, 222-225). On wood-cutting: (*CIH* 285.23-32, trans. *AL* iii 272.23-24). On cattle-herding: (*CIH* 192.1-33, 576.24-577.24, trans. *AL* iv, 101.6-103.26).

30. In Adomnán's Life of Columba, the saint prophesies that Báitán will be buried in that place in which a woman will drive sheep across his grave, and so it later happened that a woman was observed driving her sheep through the burial place, (1.20), *Adomnán's Life of Columba*, revised edition, ed. and trans. A. Anderson and M. Anderson (Oxford, 1991), p. 47.

31. Such work at the mill is colorfully recorded in the late *Life of St. Berach* when the saint is sent to a neighboring lord's mill to grind grain of his monastery. On arrival at the mill, the saint finds a woman of the lord's household grinding her lord's grain. When she refuses to allow Berach to proceed ahead of her, a fight breaks out between the two with both the woman and Berach pouring their grains into the millstone at the same time. Divine intervention separates their respective flours, but in a cruel twist of fate the lord's son, who had accompanied the woman, drowns in the mill-pond and she dies of a sudden illness. Their household rises up against the saint but are all stricken with child-labor pains. When the boy's father hears of the events, he prostrates himself before Berach and surrenders to him unconditionally. Berach cures the household and brings his son

and the woman back to life. The lord then gives the mill and its site to the saint, *Bethada Náem nÉrenn: Lives of Irish Saints*, volumes 1-2, ed. and trans. C. Plummer (Oxford, 1922), i, 26-27, translated ii, 25-26. So much for Irish saintly *humilitas*!

32. A particularly useful (if now somewhat dated) tabulation of the finds from ringforts was drawn up by Proudfoot, "The Economy of the Irish Rath," p. 106. He charted the grain types and animal bones found in the course of archaeological excavation, and there is a close correlation with those described in the laws (principal cereals and legumes *CIH* 2305.6-15, D. Binchy, ed. and trans., *"Bretha Déin Chécht,"* Ériu 20 (1966): 1-66; vegetables *CIH* 1599.34-35, trans. *AL* v 41; livestock and fowl *CIH* 573.23-25, trans. *AL* iv 115-121). The results of excavations since 1961, as well as the finds from other settlement types, can add significantly to this chart and further endorse the evidence from written sources. A general synopsis is found in Edwards, *The Archaeology of Early Medieval Ireland*, pp. 52-67.

33. A. T. Lucas, "The Horizontal Mill in Ireland," *Journal of the Royal Society of Antiquaries of Ireland* 83 (1953): 1-37; Binchy, *"Coibnes Uisce Thairidne;"* M. Baillie, *Tree-Ring Dating and Archaeology* (London, 1982), pp. 180-92; Rynne, "The Introduction of the Vertical Watermill" and "Milling in the 7th Century – Europe's Earliest Tide Mills," *Archaeology Ireland* 20 (1992): 22-24.

34. It is a view that is largely discarded today, but some individuals still support it. For instance, see Nerys Patterson, *Cattle-Lords and Clansmen: Kinship and Rank in Early Ireland* (New York, 1991), pp. 67-68.

35. McCormick, "Dairying and Beef Production" and "Early Faunal Evidence."

36. Duignan's "Irish Agriculture in Early Historic Times," pp. 135-40, was the first to work on the material remains. He was dealing with a total of twelve plow pieces, and only one of these came from a secure dating context. Yet his hypotheses were accepted without argument and they have come to be regarded as fact. Lucas, "Irish Ploughing Practices," dismissed material remains in his study of plowing practices because he felt they offered no scope. Elsewhere, I present a detailed analysis of the evidence for plows and plowing in medieval Ireland: Niall Brady, "Reconstructing a Medieval Irish Plough," ed. Direccin Gral. de Bellas Artes y Archivos, *Primeras Jornadas Sobre Tecnologia Agraria Tradicional* (Madrid, 1993). What follows here is a summary of part of that work.

37. Utrecht, University Library, MS. Script eccl. 484, fols. 21r, 49v, 62v; London, British Library Harley MS 603 fols. 21r, 51v, 54v, 66r.

38. E. Quin, *Dictionary of the Irish Language,* compact edition (Dublin, 1983).

39. See Peter Fowler's, "Farming in the Anglo-Saxon Landscape: an Archaeologist's Review," *Anglo-Saxon England* 9 (1981): 268-70, n. 27-31, on the development of plowing in England, although the types of plow were quite different from those used in Ireland.

40. B. Scott, *Early Irish Ironworking* (Belfast, 1990), pp. 136-38.

41. A. Fenton, "Early and Traditional Cultivating Implements in Scotland," *Proceedings of the Society of Antiquaries of Scotland* 96 (1963): 293-302.

42. A. T. Lucas, "Irish Ploughing Practices," *Tools and Tillage* 2.3 (1974): 155. Illustration of Orkney plow taken from H. Marwick, " 'A Description of Orkney' (1773): an Account of an Unpublished Manuscript of Rev. George Low, Minister of Birsay, 1774-1795," *Proceedings of the Orkney Antiquarian Society* 2 (1924): 49-58.

43. These are listed in the short eighth-century tract on status, the *Uraicecht Becc*, and they comprise: wrights, blacksmiths, brasiers, whitesmiths (?silver-smiths), physicians, jurists and druids, and every art and craft besides (*CIH* 1590-1618, 634-655, 2318-2335, trans. MacNeill, "Ancient Irish Law," p. 277.7-10).

44. Many such scenes are cited by Lucas, "Irish Ploughing Practices."

45. Binchy's *Críth Gablach* 1. 95, 181-182, MacNeill, "Ancient Irish Law," p. 287.1-3 and 291.10-11.

46. *Ælfric's Colloquy*, ed. G. Garmonsway (London, 1939; rev., 1983), l. 22–35.

47. M. Baillie, "A Horizontal Mill of the 8th Century A.D. at Drumard, Co. Derry," *Ulster Journal of Archaeology* 38 (1975): 25–32. E. P. Kelly of the National Museum of Ireland informs me that they are consistently occurring on crannogs (pers. comm. 1992).

48. *CIH* 383.32–33, transl. *AL* i 162.23–24.

49. Monk, "Evidence from Macroscopic Plant Remains," p. 34, is undertaking pollen analysis within a ringfort in search of the chaff and weed seeds that threshing leaves behind, but the results have yet to reveal anything significant.

50. See below notes 52–53.

51. A possible barn was excavated at Ballywee, Co. Down: C. Lynn, "Ballywee," *Excavations* 5 (1974): 4–6. The site is an unenclosed settlement and the rectangular building suggested to be a barn lies outside the main focus of settlement. Unfortunately the definitive site report has yet to be published.

52. Post haec horreum egreditur ad monasterium revertans media resedet via (3.23, *Adomnán's Life of Columba*, ed. and trans. Anderson and Anderson, p. 220).

53. . . . a tri fogladh a vii.ar lis .i. re hathaib — muillib — re daisib arba . . . ". . . and these three trespasses outside the enclosure, namely in kilns and mills and on corn-stacks . . ." (*CIH* 74.9–10, trans. *AL* iv 116–117).

54. Bla susta aith, "exemptions [in case of injury] by a flail [*súst*] in a kiln" (*CIH* 273.29, trans. *AL* iii 220.15). The glosses enumerate the various conditions. It is clear that the threshing is occurring in the *áith*.

55. Edwards, *The Archaeology of Early Medieval Ireland*, pp. 62–63, n. 59. Results are more promising on monastic sites wehere kilns appear to be situated some distance from the central area.

56. Paul Hyams, *Kings, Lords, and Peasants in Medieval England* (Oxford, 1980), pp. 221–65.

8

SIN, CONQUEST, SERVITUDE: ENGLISH SELF-IMAGE IN THE CHRONICLES OF THE EARLY FOURTEENTH CENTURY

Douglas Moffat

In this essay I intend to further the examination of racial disharmony in medieval England that has recently been reintroduced into historical discussion by literary scholars.[1] I agree with the claim made by Thorlac Turville-Petre, that "received opinion about the happy state of racial harmony in late medieval England must be reassessed . . . ."[2] However, I believe the evidence he usefully brings to the issue needs careful reconsideration for at least three reasons. First of all, this evidence is more complicated than Turville-Petre allows, and it does no good to minimize these complications. In fact, they can enrich our appreciation of the complexity of medieval English society. Secondly, the ramifications of this evidence are more far-reaching than Turville-Petre suggests. Specifically, the social and linguistic impact of racial disharmony in late medieval England is neither negligible nor trivial. Thirdly, a more forthright effort is needed to allay the suspicion, and even hostility, of historians who are accustomed to favor analysis of class over that of race and discussion of an emerging national identity over that of submerging racial ones.[3] My aim is not to deny the obvious importance of class and national identity in medieval or subsequent English history but to promote the consideration of racial disharmony as another factor that contributed significantly to the dynamics of medieval English society.

Turville-Petre's evidence consists of a collection of statements, which occur in chronicles written in English around 1300, that, on the face of it, give voice to feelings of racial resentment harbored by the

"English" against the "French." By "English" I mean those of Anglo-Saxon descent who occupied the lower reaches of society — "lower" being used with deliberate ambiguity at his point — and by "French" I mean those of non-Anglo-Saxon descent who held positions of relative power and prestige. These passages all associate low social standing with servitude, with Anglo-Saxon ancestry, and with the defeat and conquest of the Anglo-Saxons by the Normans in 1066. The most explicit expressions of these feelings are located Part 2 of Robert Mannyng's *Chronicle*, which was completed sometime before 1338: [4]

> Siþen he [William] & his haf had þe lond in heritage
> Þat þe Inglis haf so lad þat þei lyue in seruage;
> He sette þe Inglis to be þralle, þat or was so fre;
> He þat bigan it alle in þe geste may ȝe se.   (p. 8)

> [William] sette vs in seruage, of fredom felle þe floure;
> Þe Inglis orgh taliage lyue ȝit in sorow fulle soure.   (p. 66)

> Now ere þei in seruage fulle fele þat or was fre.
> Our fredom þat day for euer toke þe leue.   (p. 71)

> For alle þis þraldam þat now on Inglond es
> Þorgh Normanz it cam, bondage & destres.   (p. 261)

Similar passages occur in the chronicle of Thomas of Castleford, dated c. 1327:[5]

> Fra Englisse blode Englande he [William] refte,
> Na maner soile wiȝ þam he lefte . . .
> Duelle þai salle alls bondes and thralles
> And do alle þat to thraldum falles,
> Lif forth and trauaile in bondage,
> Þai and þar blode euer in seruage.
> Englissemen þat wer noȝ bousum
> Als for to lif in slik thraldum,
> Voide þe regne and go qware þai walde,
> Duel langre in Englande þai ne salde.   (31925–6, 31935–42)

and in the chronicle of Robert of Gloucester, which was completed around 1300:[6]

> & þus was in normannes hond þat lond ibroȝt iwis
> Þat anaunter ȝif euermo keueringe þer of is.
> Of þe normans beþ heyemen þat beþ of engelonde,
> & þe lowemen of saxons, as ich vnderstonde.   (ll.7498–501)

[147]

Robert of Gloucester's assessment of his society is more detached than his fellow chroniclers'. He says that the "lond" has passed into the possession of the Normans and then remarks, without apparent concern, that it is doubtful that it will ever be recovered. Interestingly, he transfers the racial differences of the 1066 combatants to his own age: the "low men" in contemporary England descend from the Saxons, the "high men" from the Normans. It will be argued below that Robert's moral view of history requires that he prolong into the present this racial distinction between "Saxon" and "Norman," but we would be wrong to conclude that he was inventing this way of dividing up his society. The other two chroniclers not only share his idea of an "English"/"French" polarization at the turn of the fourteenth century, but show as well that, for those who identified with the "English," this idea could be infused with feelings of loss, resentment, and perhaps anger.

Where Robert of Gloucester flatly states that "was in Normannes hond þat lond ibroȝt," Thomas of Castleford stresses the unity of "blood" and "land" and the utter alienation of the Anglo-Saxons after 1066: "Fra Englisse blode Englande he refte, Na maner soile wiȝ þam he lefte." After the Conquest there were two choices for the "English." Leave the land and live in exile or accept "thraldum," which displaces land as the inheritance one passes on through one's "blood." Like Robert of Gloucester Thomas offers no prospect of amelioration in the future, at least in this world, and no middle ground between the racially-determined extremes of society. But whereas Robert speaks colorlessly of "high" and "low," Thomas dwells on the "thraldum," "bondage," and "seruage" of the "English" in contradistinction to the unmentioned but implicit freedom of those above them. By emphasizing this extreme Thomas forces us to consider that the words he chooses to characterize the "English" condition convey a meaning much closer to "slavery" than the historical reality would countenance. The "English" were not enslaved by the Normans, and these terms of servitude need not denote slavery in Middle English. But within the polarized context of this passage, focussed as it is on irretrievable loss, this vocabulary all but requires a reader, particularly an "English" reader, to judge the servitude of the "English" not in the light of feudal relations but in the light of slave and master.

Robert Mannyng goes a step further than Thomas of Castleford. He does not emphasize the relationship of blood and land as Thomas does but concentrates instead on loss of freedom, a loss still felt at a personal level by the "English." Mannyng collapses the historical frame: William the Conqueror "set vs in seruage, of fredom felle þe floure," that is, he not only bound the Anglo-Saxons of some 250 years ago but, in effect, he continues to bind "vs" as well. The line that follows this, "þe Inglis þorgh taliage lyue ȝit in sorow fulle soure," forces "vs" to connect one of the primary marks of contemporary servitude, tallage, with the loss of freedom and the enforced bondage in 1066. Like Thomas of Castleford Mannyng rhetorically constrains the reader to understand the terms of servitude in the light of slavery rather than some less onerous kind. Unlike Thomas, who describes primarily the impact of the Conquest on the defeated Anglo-Saxons, Mannyng speaks to those who have inherited through the blood the servitude imposed generations earlier. The emphasis falls less on the tangible loss of land in 1066 than on the perpetual loss of freedom experienced anew by everyone who is "English." Mannyng makes immediate the consequences of history.

On the face of it, the evidence seems fairly clear in its presentation of one important fact: even as late as the 1330s some were willing to write about the ongoing servitude of the "English," a servitude imposed in 1066. One can argue, as one always can, about tone. Robert of Gloucester seems rather matter-of-fact about the situation; Mannyng and Thomas of Castleford, on the other hand, could be read as outraged, embittered, or merely rueful. But before arguing about aesthetics, more fundamental questions must be addressed. Why did these three chroniclers, who were certainly not unfree themselves, give voice to these sentiments? Do their motivations allow them to be accurate informants of "English" feelings? And most important of all, who are the "English" to whom they refer?

Of the three chroniclers, Robert Mannyng provides us with the best opportunity to answer these questions, and this is fortunate, since he is also the chronicler who most closely identifies with and characterizes the feelings of those whom he calls the "English." Turville-Petre devotes much of his essay, in fact, to examining Mannyng's possible motivation for writing the *Chronicle* and how this motivation relates to his statements on the "English." Turville-Petre claims that for Mannyng, as a Gilbertine, the writing of such a massive work as the *Chronicle* could not have been a trivial undertaking, a leisure-time activity or hobby. There must have been a purpose for it sanctioned by his house.[7] His stated purpose is to offer solace and pleasure to those who cannot read Latin or French:

Not for þe lerid bot for þe lewed,
ffor þo þat in þis land wone
Þat þe Latyn no Frankys cone,
ffor to haf solace & gamen
In felawschip when þai sitt samen.[8]

Ideally Mannyng's readership would have excluded the clergy, although in reality perhaps not the lower levels thereof; it also undoubtedly would have excluded some of the laity as well, especially those in the higher reaches where administrative duties and cultural pressure encouraged an understanding of French and Latin.[9] It could be said, then, that Mannyng was writing for an "English" audience, that is, an audience that could read, or more likely understand, a long narrative account in English only. Turville-Petre suggests that the Gilbertines, who were not faring especially well in attracting aristocratic patronage, may have been trying at this time to appeal for financial support to richer members of the peasantry. Mannyng's *Chronicle*, he reasons, would have fit well into such a campaign and was probably composed for this audience.[10] The sympathetic expressions of racial solidarity in the work would follow naturally from its purpose.

This argument raises a number of problems. If Turville-Petre's hypothesis about Mannyng's motivation for writing the *Chronicle* is correct, it is not difficult to respond rather more cynically than he does to Mannyng's expressions of racial solidarity with those in a state of servitude. Obviously some sort of effort would have been made to render the work attractive to potential donors. Hatred of the Scots, rife in Mannyng's source, Peter Langtoft's *Chronicle*, would have struck a responsive chord in Lincolnshire.[11] Clearly another potential strategy could have been to emphasize the racial solidarity between the peasants and the Gilbertine clerics of English descent. The fact that those in orders could not themselves be in "servage" and were, in fact, capable of having their own bondsmen would not have proved useful selling points in such an appeal, if in fact the unfree formed part of the perceived audience. Still, when Mannyng laments the loss of "our freedom" his legally baseless assertion of identity with those who are truly unfree must have rung hollow. If the defining characteristic of being "English" is to be in a state of servitude, which seems a reasonable conclusion to draw from the chronicle evidence, then neither Mannyng nor his fellow chroniclers are "English" themselves, nor is anyone else who is free and of Anglo-Saxon descent.

The general economic situation in the late thirteenth and early fourteenth centuries also presents difficulties for Turville-Petre's hypothesis that the work was directed in some part toward the unfree peasantry. Christopher Dyer concludes that these were "hard times, especially for smallholders."[12] He demonstrates that this period was characterized by famines, cattle plagues, wet weather, and increasing taxes and rents concurrent with little economic growth. Peasants with larger holdings may have weathered this "concentration of problems,"[13] but the hard times must have hurt many of them economically, and not a few of the lower gentry, as well. Although it is scarcely credible that even those who prospered during this period would have been in much of a giving mood, surely it is more likely that Mannyng targeted the survivors of these groups rather than unfree peasants as potential contributors. But if the well-off peasants, many of whom would be free, along with the lower gentry formed Mannyng's audience — if they, in fact, are the "English" — then it strikes one as odd that Mannyng would describe them as being in servage or thraldom, because they certainly were not in such a state in a strictly legal sense. It would seem that if one insists on finding in Mannyng an accurate reflection of the legal reality of servitude at the time he wrote, then his apparently clear statements on the servitude of the "English" are not, in fact, clear at all. Equally unclear from this perspective is his understanding of who constitutes the "English."

Nevertheless, the fact remains that not only Mannyng but Thomas of Castleford and Robert of Gloucester as well must have thought that their audiences would have appreciated the "English"/"French" distinction they drew in their chronicles, not to mention the stark terms with which they characterized it. If no such distinction were being made in late thirteenth- and early-fourteenth century England, and if it were not being made by those who formed these audiences, then it seems unlikely we would find evidence for it in three different chroniclers. The chronicle passages do not reflect the strict legalities of historical servitude, but I suggest that they were not composed with that intention. To force this sort of interpretation onto a text such as Mannyng's is the way *not* to discover what he is telling us about the racial identity of the "English" and its connection with servitude. I believe that Mannyng, Thomas of Castleford, and, mutedly, Robert of Gloucester are revealing to us in these passages not the legal reality of servitude in the England they knew but rather an idea of racial servitude that effectively bound those of Anglo-Saxon descent together whether they had achieved personal freedom or not. An array of shared customs and beliefs and the knowledge that English was "their" language must also have helped to maintain a distinct racial identity for this group. But the idea of racial servitude — neither "myth" nor "memory" can be the right word because of the enduring reality of servitude for so many — would have fostered and sustained racial feelings, especially feelings of resentment, that could ultimately be traced back to the defeat of 1066.

Armed with the understanding that the chroniclers are appealing to an idea of English racial servitude and not to a specific state of unfreedom being suffered by any particular group of Anglo-Saxon descent, we can make sense of the apparent anomalies in the chronicle evidence. The existence of such an idea explains not only how the free Mannyng might claim identity with the unfree "English" but also allows a wider audience of freemen to participate in this claim as well. Moreover, that an idea of racial servitude lies behind the statements of Mannyng and his fellow chroniclers clarifies their particular use of the vocabulary of servitude. All the chronicle passages, even that of Robert of Gloucester, are characterized by a reliance on extremes that creates an oversimplified and even false impression of the legal reality of servitude. Mannyng and Thomas of Castleford, moreover, use the polysemous vocabulary associated with servitude to widen further the distance between freedom and servitude so that the latter is situated much closer to slavery than the actual historical situation. The goal is to accentuate rhetorically the gulf between the free "French" and the unfree "English" in order to engage more deeply the emotions of the latter; the goal is not to give an accurate picture of states of servitude in contemporary England and to appeal only to those who are unfree.

It may seem improbable at first glance that freemen, even of low standing, would give assent to an idea that would have them bound even metaphorically in some sort of debasing servitude akin to slavery. I think, in fact, it is not that improbable. The idea of racial servitude imposed in 1066 and still widespread 250 years later would have provided for free and unfree alike a ready and general explanation for their need to struggle constantly against hardship. It could be invoked as the underlying cause of any social or economic disadvantage one was suffering. Moreover, it is an idea that could be easily aligned with feelings of antipathy toward the upper levels of society, feelings which must have been intense during the late thirteenth and early fourteenth centuries, because of the hard economic conditions. These feelings, most obviously associable with the lowest levels of the peasantry, could well have been felt with equal intensity by those somewhat higher up on the social scale — not only free peasants but the lower gentry and clergy as well — who witnessed the hard times of this period and realized the precariousness of their own economic well-being. To find such feelings couched in convenient racial terms is surely unsurprising. Race provided the bond to unite the miserable and the apprehensive from different strata of society, each man, of course, being the arbiter of his own misery. Race also simplified the complexities of society into a bipolarity, "English" and "French," and provided thereby a clear rationale and focus for the feelings of discontent.

This ethnic division between "English" and "French" is probably not best understood as a medieval precursor of the idea of the "Norman Yoke" so carefully analyzed by Christopher Hill.[14] Hill demonstrates that this idea, which persisted among English political reformers from the seventeenth to the nineteenth centuries, is only apparently a racial argument; its real use was to sharpen and promote divisions according to class, not race.[15] He does suggest that the theory "may well have had a continuous history since 1066,"[16] but he offers little in the way of support for this statement. The chronicle evidence does not supply this lack unless we are willing to make some considerable adjustments in Hill's formulation. It is true that loss of the freedom enjoyed in Anglo-Saxon times is both the cornerstone of the "Norman Yoke" idea and certainly evident in the chronicle passages, especially the excerpts from Mannyng. However, one does not find in the chronicles the idealizing of Anglo-Saxon institutions or the perception of pre-Conquest England as a perfect society, both of which are central features in the theory as documented by Hill. Further, those who articulated and supported the idea of the "Norman Yoke" could only point to vestigial remnants of the Conquest as it affected their everyday existence. This was emphatically not the case for those of Anglo-Saxon descent at the turn of the fourteenth century. The linguistic consequences of 1066, which will be briefly discussed below, were still clear to all, but even more obvious was the on-going condition of servitude for thousands of people of Anglo-Saxon ancestry. I have already suggested that economic and social disadvantage should not be divorced from a consideration of racial disharmony in medieval England, but to dismiss racial disharmony as merely displaced anxiety about socio-economic inequities is simply to turn a blind eye to the evidence.

In what follows I will briefly explore the impact of racial disharmony in the late thirteenth and early fourteenth century on two different historical developments in the later fourteenth century, the increasing use of the English language and the formation of a peasant class. In both cases more questions will be raised than answers given. Finally, I wish to look in more detail at the evidence in Robert of Gloucester and particularly in Mannyng to discover the peculiarities of each.

All three chroniclers draw attention to the linguistic division between English and French. In Mannyng one finds only the fairly commonplace introductory explanation for composition in English (as opposed to French or Latin), which has been quoted above. Similar statements occur in other works of the period.[17] Thomas of Castleford remarks that the ignorance of French presented a legal disability for the English in the post-Conquest period:

> Schirefes he sette and ek iustise
> On alle þas walde agains him rise,
> Þe domes to saie in Frankisse toung,
> Þe folk to deme, ba3 aelde and yong,
> For þe bondes of Englisse linage
> Salde noght witte, bi þe langage,
> How þai þam dampnede, wele oþer ille,
> Bot als bestes stande to þar wille.   (31943–50)

It is unclear from the text whether or not Thomas of Castleford sees inability to speak French as a contemporary liability, although it obviously was.

Robert of Gloucester speaks of the post-Conquest linguistic division along racial lines as still prevalent in the England of his time:

> Þus com, lo, engelond in to normandies hond,
> & þe normans ne couþe speke þo bote hor owe speche
> & speke french as hii dude atom, & hor children dude also teche
> So þat heiemen of þis lond, þat of hor blod come
> Holdeþ alle þulke speche þat hii of hom nome;
> Vor, bote a man conne frenss, me telþ of him lute,
> Ac lowe men holdeþ to engliss, & to hor owe speche 3ute.
> (ll.7537–43)

Careful reading of this passage yields a picture of the linguistic situation that accords with what many modern commentators believe to have been the case. Clanchy stresses that in early thirteenth-century England Latin, French, English, and even Hebrew all came into play.[18] While knowledge of Hebrew was very restricted, ability to operate in the other three tongues was necessary for the administration of the land at all but the lowest levels as well as for the acquisition of cultural status. Robert of Gloucester does not mention Latin, but he is certainly correct when he says that at the end of the thirteenth century a man without French is of little account. It may be that his claim that the Normans and their descendents taught their children French points to the generally accepted idea that by the thirteenth century those born in England, regardless of descent, probably had English as their native tongue and had to acquire French as a second language.[19] Finally, his statement that the low men "hold to English yet" is also accurate. Bi- or trilingualism among the aristocracy and clergy was either necessary or desired, and was certainly achieved by many. Among the peasants, memorially acquired knowledge of some French and Latin phrases, and some Latin prayers, is likely to have been achieved, and some rudimentary education may have been more widely available than has previously been supposed. There are many instances of peasants moving into and even rising through the ranks of the clergy. The "great majority" of people in England at the time, however, were monolingual speakers of English, and they were, as Robert of Glou- cester says, the "low men."[20]

The emphasis on aristocratic speech habits in the study of language usage in medieval England has obscured the impact of monolingual- ism on the vast majority of the population. Because English has come to be regarded as the probable native language of almost everyone born in England in the thirteenth century, and perhaps earlier, the be- lief has become established that mono-, bi-, and trilingualism in this period simply marked one's social status. However, it seems reason- able that, if a degree of racial disharmony still existed at the end of the thirteenth century between monolingual speakers of English on the one side and the "French" on the other, then language difference surely played a fundamental role in maintaining it. That is, it is incon- ceivable that if the "English" perceived themselves as distinct from the "French," that language difference did not play a major part in shar- pening and maintaining the distinction.[21] However, such an analysis contradicts the traditional view of the relationship between the two languages found in the standard treatments. Baugh, for example, offers the following assessment:

> For two hundred years after the Norman Conquest, French remained the language of ordinary intercourse among the upper classes in England. At first those who spoke French were those of Norman origin, but soon through intermarriage

and association with the ruling class numerous people of English extraction must have found it to their advantage to learn the new language, and before long the distinction between those who spoke French and those who spoke English was not ethnic but largely social.[22]

This perception of the primarily social importance of bilingualism may accurately represent the attitudes of those in the upper classes who were bi- or trilingual. As Clanchy points out, on the one hand they could regard themselves as Englishmen, but on the other they were not thereby establishing a basis of equality between themselves and the lower classes.[23] But what was the linguistic perception of the monolingual English speakers in positions of social and economic disadvantage that clearly had more than a little to do with their inability to function in French, let alone Latin? Linguistic incapacity would have functioned for them not only as a cause of social and economic disadvantage but also as a constant reminder of an underlying reason for this disadvantage. That is, the English/French linguistic division would have served as a natural focus of racial resentment. It would have mattered little what the actual impact of 1066 was on the ancestors of any particular family; it would have mattered not at all whether the French was of Stratford-atte-Bowe or of Paris. To Chaucer, and to modern analysts, such dialectal distinctions are highly significant, but it is difficult to imagine that monolingual speakers of English in 1300 would have noticed any such difference, assuming their experience afforded them the opportunity to compare. That linguistic irritants could be interpreted as a cause of socioeconomic disadvantage, and could spark memories of a distant national defeat and fuel feelings of racial resentment, is far from unthinkable at the best of times.[24] When times are not the best, as in the late thirteenth and early fourteenth centuries, it is difficult to believe that such thoughts and feelings were not inevitable.

Turville-Petre does argue that language served as a marker of racial division in early fourteenth-century England. Unfortunately, however, in his brief presentation of subsequent linguistic history he adopts the traditional point of view from which that history has usually been told, albeit with a political twist. The traditional argument is that the abandonment of French was greatly accelerated by the Black Death, which increased the economic power of the English-speaking peasants, and by the Hundred Years War:

> At one time the knowledge and use of French had served to maintain the distinctiveness and superiority of the ruling class

over the governed, for whom it was a foreign language that most of them could not even understand. Now that the rulers needed the forces of a resentful people to fight against the French, the pressure was in the other direction. In every sphere of their activities þe gentils hastily abandoned French and stopped reminding everybody that their families had come over with the Conquest.[25]

In the course of the fourteenth century, English, which had been "the language of a subject people, regarded as crude and inelegant and un-suitable for the expression of fine feeling," gradually "eclipsed French in virtually every sphere of life and literature at every social level."[26]

That English rose toward a position of dominance through the fourteenth century and achieved that position in the fifteenth and sixteenth is certainly true. But what, one wonders, were the thoughts and feelings of the "English" to this adoption of their language by their social and economic superiors? Perhaps more to the point, what was the impact of this linguistic homogenization on the relations of the monolingual lower classes to those above them? The standard treatments reflected in Turville-Petre's assessment regard this movement as one of amelioration. If one is interested primarily in the "glorious history of English," in the language as a vehicle of cultural refinement and as an "expression of the genius of the English people," and so forth, then of course this ascendancy of English over French, whether the Anglo-Norman or the Central French varieties, must be viewed as a triumph. (It should be added that the scholarly writers of histories of the language, who are usually medievalists, do not portray the ascendancy of English over Latin in learned circles quite so triumphantly.)

However, finding one's own language coming increasingly out of the mouths of those who are socially and economically one's superior, where before that was not the case, would not, I submit, be an unambiguous source of pride and satisfaction, especially when not accompanied by any significant change in socio-economic status. For the unfree, to be now a "thrall," a "bondman," or a "churl" would carry with it no obvious advantage over being a "servus" or a "villein." For the higher freeman of Anglo-Saxon descent, however, an easing of linguistic boundaries could be turned to economic and social advantage. I suggest that the increasing use of English by the social and economic elites would have contributed to a new and a radical change in the relations of the various social and economic groups in England. For the monolingual peasant, free or unfree, what used to be his own language, a distinctive marker of his racial identity, could be turned by this adoption, by the "triumph of English," into a tool of oppression. In an ironic twist, the triumph of English marks the end of the "English." By the end of the Middle Ages one of the primary markers of racial distinctiveness, of "English" ethnicity, had been removed. And with its removal the way is cleared for the creation of the myth of English unity, "Merrie Olde England," already apparent in the opening lines of *The Canterbury Tales*, but more famously portrayed in *Henry V* and especially in John of Gaunt's speech near the beginning of *Richard II*. And of necessity, those in the lower socio-economic strata of England, upon losing this mark of their distinctiveness, would have been forced to think of their position vis-à-vis those above them in a different way. The obvious difference of language that reinforced the easy distinction of race gradually disappeared. It would stand to reason that the beginning of class consciousness among the lower levels of English society would be located in the fourteenth century accompanying the process of linguistic homogenization.

What is being proposed is that, before the elimination of linguistic difference as a persisting boundary between the "English" and the "French," the opposition between these groups, while clearly social and economic as well, would have been perceived by both, but especially by the monolingual "English," as fundamentally an ethnic division resulting from military conquest. A traditional Marxist view of this situation might regard this ethnic consciousness as a peripheral feature of medieval English society, a mere mask concealing the reality of class struggle. More recent Marxist analysts, such as Christopher McAll, seem more willing to take race seriously. Although he speaks specifically about advanced capitalist societies, McAll might agree that in early fourteenth-century England as well "ethnicity is not the mask that conceals class, nor an alternative to class as the basic explanatory concept, but an integral part of class: the luxuriant tangled foliage that both conceals and reveals, nourishes and is nourished by its roots, and is thus part and parcel of the plant."[27] The argument here is not that analysis of race should have priority over that of class but that in the examination of the lower levels of medieval English society both race and class must be considered.

Consideration of the racial consciousness amongst the English peasantry may reveal an important source for ideas that survived the slackening of ethnic division in the fourteenth century and came eventually to play a significant role in the rising of 1381. One of the distinguishing features of the English peasant class that R. H. Hilton frequently brings to our attention is "the constant demand for freedom of status sustained until 1381 and reiterated then when the actual economic advantages of free tenure were by no means as obvious as they had been a century earlier."[28] He claims that this desire is "already found in the thirteenth century, often enveloped by the technicalities of pleadings for the privileges of ancient demense."[29] But surely this desire for freedom is not unconnected to the same lost freedom lamented in the passages given at the beginning of this essay. We see in these lines expressions of racial servitude rhetorically linked to slavery and imposed on a people formerly free: not imposed on this one whose ancestors were "ceorls" and therefore free in Anglo-Saxon times, but not on that one whose ancestors were "theows," and were never free, but rather on all of the "English." While there is no space to explore the connections here, it seems possible, if not indeed likely, that this shared sense of lost freedom lies behind "the constant demand for the freedom of status" and the right to own land and pass it rather than servitude along to one's heirs. Other remarkable features of the 1381 rising, specifically that it was not geographically isolated or confined to the lowest social classes,[30] may also be related to the now submerged sense of "English" unity.

The evidence of the chronicles of Robert Mannyng, Robert of Gloucester, and Thomas of Castleford, when taken together, reveals the existence of an "English" historical self-consciousness in the late thirteenth and early fourteenth century, a racial self-consciousness that was on brink of being subsumed into a larger national identity. Moreover, this evidence also shows that substantial feelings of racial discontentment were present in England at this time among those whose social and economic status was low and whose only language defined them as "English." By examining Robert Mannyng's and Robert of Gloucester's treatment of the idea of racial servitude, we can also begin to differentiate between the responses of the "English" to their situation. Robert of Gloucester provides a traditional interpretation of English history in which racial sin requires the divine punishment of racial servitude. Robert Mannyng, on the other hand, presents a strikingly original interpretation of history in which a particular individual Englishman from the past is condemned so that the race as a whole might be free from sin and from servitude.

As much as the descendants of the Anglo-Saxons might have felt resentment at their position of servitude, the "historical" explanation for it could have struck no one, or at least no one of any learning, as surprising or improbable. The servitude of the "English" resulted from defeat in battle, which from time immemorial had been understood to include disadvantage, subjugation, and loss of freedom, if not exactly slavery in the case of the English in 1066. Acknowledging servitude as a consequence of military defeat is a commonplace in medieval considerations of unfreedom. The Latin word *servus* was traditionally derived, as Augustine points out in of *The City of God* (19.16), from *servare* ("to conserve") since slaves were those who were "conserved" from the slaughter of the battlefield. This etymology is ubiquitous, occurring, for example, in Isidore (5.27.32) — "Apud antiquos enim qui in bello a morte servabantur servi vocabantur" — in Bartholomeus Anglicus, and in Trevisa's English translation of the latter.[31] In the codifiers of law one finds the view expressed that lack of freedom was not a natural state of man but a situation which naturally arose as a consequence of war.[32] This is not to suggest that resignation to servitude would necessarily follow from this commonplace understanding, only that there would have been a widespread recognition, probably not confined to the learned, that, unfair as it might be, servitude is a consequence of war. In fact, it is possible to interpret even Mannyng's statements about "English" servitude as expressions of frustrated resignation rather than anger and resentment, a tonal shift that would not negate the racial basis of the feelings involved.

At the level of morality there is another commonplace explanation for the fall into unfreedom of individuals or races in ancient or medieval or modern times: the belief that servitude is somehow the result of sin. David Brion Davis calls this relationship the "Ancient Legacy" of slavery.[33] Among the biblical examples of whole races falling into slavery, familiar, one imagines, to every medieval, two are prominent. The descendents of Ham are condemned to slavery for the transgression of their progenitor, the mockery of his father Noah's nakedness; the Jews suffer the Babylonian exile where military defeat and loss of freedom are explicitly connected with the sinful nature of the people. References to these biblical stories yoking sin and servitude would have been frequent in the homilies heard by peasant congregants, not to mention the equally frequent mention of the enslavement of individual souls to sin or the Devil.

The connection of military success with God's election, and of military defeat with racial sinfulness, had been hallmarks of medieval historiography since Eusebius. Robert Hanning has demonstrated that for medieval historians of British as well as English history, from Gildas to Bede, the connection was standard. The interpretation of the Normans as the agents of God's retribution on the sinful English seems to have been present almost from the beginning in the minds of some. In the annal for 1066 in the Worcester or D version of the Anglo-Saxon Chronicle the *folces synnon, urum synnum,* are mentioned as a reason for William's victory.[34] In Henry of Huntingdon's *Historia Anglorum,* one of the primary sources for the later English chronicles, an overriding structure is the five *plagas,* the five invasions of the island that were divinely ordained as punishments for the sinfulness of the inhabitants. The last of these *plagas* is the Norman Conquest, the effects of which, Henry points out, are still being felt.[35] This moral overview of the history of the island also appears at the beginning of Peter of Langtoft's French chronicle, which heavily influenced Mannyng, and it is in Mannyng as well.[36]

The five *plagas* may have been only a framework for Henry of Huntingdon, as Nancy Partner argues,[37] but he does persist with it as a structural device. While Mannyng regards the Norman Conquest at the outset of his work as one of the five wounds or sorrows of England, he apparently follows Langtoft in dropping this organizational structure later in the work. Langtoft and Mannyng have nothing comparable to Henry's preface to Book 5 in which he reiterates the view that the Conquest was God's punishment for the English.[38] But whereas Langtoft almost completely leaves the question of sin out of his account, Mannyng departs from his French source to reintroduce sin as a cause of national disaster by means of the deathbed vision of Edward The Confessor:

> Who so lokes his life, & redis his vision,
> What vengeance ordeynd was on Inglond to be don
> Of princes of þe lond, it sais of þam þis sawe,
> Þat þei dred no þing God, no ȝemed euenhed of lawe,
> Bot felawes vnto þefes, to robbours of ilk cuntre,
> Þar wekednes was fulfilled, venged behoued it be.
> Prelates ne no prestes, non of þam lyued wele,
> Þe did not Goddes hestes, bot brak þam ilk a dele.
> Licheros lif þei led, & þouht it in þar breste
> Holynes did away, of þe kirke gaf þei leste.
> Edward God bisouht, þat it suld be forgyuen,
> & amendid with penance, & þerof clene be scryuen
> Of þat þat þei had don, & þat þat suld betide
> To warne þam þerfro, & fle it on ilk side
> Bot þis was ansuere ageyn, "a day þer in salle falle,
> Þare wiknes is fulfilled, þer in ere waxen hard.

God has sette þat ȝere, a day þer in salle falle,
Þe Inglis salle go to suerd, to pyne þar soules alle.
Dede & fire salle fede þe scheperdes & þare schepe." (pp. 65–6)

And Mannyng adds "þis vision ȝis it to drede, þink & gif Gode kepe./ I trowe it is ouergone þorgh William conqueroure." (p. 66) The sinfulness of the English is clearly connected by means of this vision with the Conquest that is soon to occur, but the working out of the connection is not as straightforward and traditional as one might expect.

Mannyng's account of the deathbed vision of Edward the Confessor is actually a précis of a much fuller vision which is found in William of Malmesbury.[39] It appears as well in Robert of Gloucester's *Chronicle*, and it is clear, not only from the fuller account of the vision itself but also from the explicit comments that follow the defeat at Hastings, that Robert of Gloucester understands the Conquest in the manner of the traditional moral historians, as a harsh, but just, retribution for the sins of his countrymen:

Ac ich vunderstonde þat it [the Conquest] was þoru godes wille ydo
Vor þe wule þe men of þis lond pur heþene were
No lond ne no folc aȝen hom in armes nere
Ac nou suþþe þat þet folc auenge cristendom
& wel lute wule hulde þe biheste þat he nom
& turnde to sleuþe & to prute & to lecherie
To glotonie & heyemen muche to robberie
As þe gostes in auision to seint edward sede
Wu þer ssolde in engelond come such wrecchede
Vor robberie of heiemen vor clerken hordom
Hou god wolde sorwe sende in þis kinedom. (ll. 7503–513)

The possibility must be entertained that even among the peasantry there likely were some who viewed their Englishness, as Robert of Gloucester apparently did, as a misfortune and the defeat of 1066 as divinely ordained punishment for sin. It would be surprising, morality aside, if there had not been a great many who regarded their position with stoic resignation.

There is a clear connection between the sins of the English and their conquest by the Normans in Henry of Huntingdon and in Robert of Gloucester, and it is certainly echoed by Mannyng in the vision of Edward The Confessor, a passage not in his immediate source, Langtoft. Nevertheless, a crucial distinction must be made between Man-

nyng, on the one hand, and Robert of Gloucester and Henry of Huntingdon, on the other. The vision in Mannyng speaks clearly of "the
English going to the sword and their souls to pain or torment"; it
seems a blanket prophecy opening the way for the traditional interpretation of racial sin and divine punishment found in the other chroniclers. But the following passage of explication seems to narrow the
focus. William came and slew *ilkone þo wikked men* and then set *us* in
servage, us being the "English." I think what is being implied here is
that while "English" servitude does result from sin and wickedness, it
is not a racial or general sin that has led to this servitude but rather the
actions of some particular sinful persons, primarily lords and clerics. A
similar allotment of sin is also in Robert of Gloucester, even though
punishment is to be meted out generally. However, what becomes
quickly apparent is that Mannyng wants to narrow the focus even further: the fact is that *we,* the "English," find ourselves in servitude because of one sin of one particular man, namely, Edward the Confessor's successor, Harold Godwinson.

Mannyng is not alone in making an explicit connection between
English servitude and Harold's falsehood, that is, his forswearing of
his oath to facilitate William's accession to the English throne. However, in Thomas of Castleford at least equal emphasis for William's
military action is interestingly placed on Harold's untruthfulness to
his Norman wife, William's sister. In Robert of Gloucester the general
sinfulness of the people is the cause of the Conquest, even though
Harold, the false king, plays his role. In Mannyng there is no such dif-
fusion of blame. Harold's oathbreaking is portrayed as the primary
cause of the Conquest and, therefore, of all the misery that follows.[40]
This shift in focus from general racial sinfulness to the sin of one man
is crucial to the revision of history Mannyng proposes, and to the justification of the "English" desire for freedom especially evident in his
chronicle.

For the historian of the Conquest and the events preceding it, the
accounts in the early fourteenth-century English chronicles are almost
wholly without value, since they derive by and large from other
known sources. The assessment of Harold as oathbreaker, and of his
forswearing as the cause of military invasion, as opposed to something
more peaceful, is a staple of the propaganda from early in William's
reign, when his own legitimacy may still have been in question. The
most thorough-going attack on Harold is in William of Poitiers where
Harold is consistently portrayed playing the devil to Duke William's
saint. This wholly negative view of the last Anglo-Saxon king as a

fraudulent tyrant is not restricted to Norman histories of the Conquest; it became the official view expressed in passing in royal documents, like Domesday Book and the Charter of Battle Abbey. [41]

In the following centuries some revisionist assessments of Harold did appear. Some English twelfth-century chroniclers, for example, William of Malmesbury, invented excuses for Harold's falling into the power of Duke William, probably to give the impression that the oath eventually broken was extracted under duress. The most well-known of these excuses is that Harold had no intention of going to France but was blown off course in a storm while boating in the channel.[42] In one late English metrical chronicle, and in its French original, the defeat of Harold is described as a "villainy."[43] Perhaps the most remarkable example of a revision of Harold's character is the *Vita Haraldi*, in which Harold escapes from the battlefield at Hastings, repents his past deeds, and becomes a holy hermit.[44]

One might expect works giving voice to feelings of resentment amongst the "English" to lean toward some kind of revisionist assessment of the last English king. However, while there may be a hint of sympathy for Harold, Mannyng makes no effort to change Harold's role from what it was in the "official" version of history. In fact, because of the medieval attachment of sin to servitude mentioned earlier, the maintenance and magnification of Harold's sin is crucial, not irrelevant, to Mannyng's perception of the "English" situation in the early fourteenth century.

After the vision of Edward, Harold is chosen king by the barons who *held him trewe*; that is, contrary to Norman propaganda, the election is described here as just to all appearances. As usual for this portion of his chronicle, Mannyng follows Langtoft, except he adds one line:

> Après la mort Eduarde, Harald est elu
> Ray par la commune, la coroune ad resceu,
> En drayture et ley leaus est[-il] tenu. (l. 398)

> After Saynt Edward, Harald kyng þei ches
> Þorgh conseile of þam alle, & he þe scheld les
> Right & in lawe, þe barons held him trewe
> Neuerles his falshed brouht vs sorwe alle newe. (p. 66)

The falsehood whose consequences remain is, of course, Harold's forswearing. Mannyng follows Langtoft in placing the story of Harold in Normandy and the oath between the accounts of the battles at Stamford Bridge and Hastings. He differs, once again, from his source in emphasizing Harold's perfidy. At the close of the Normandy episode Langtoft remarks that "La chose, kaunt tens vent, est mys en oblay" [the thing, when time comes, is put into oblivion] (l. 404). Mannyng is a touch more direct: "þe oþe þat he suld hold, it is forgeten clene" (p. 69). The forswearing is mentioned again in an anecdote not in Langtoft. William trips and goes head over heels upon landing at Pevensey. When he stands up his helmet is *fulle of mire*. One of his knight's remarks: "þat þe lond is þin, þi helm schewes it þe,/ Forsuorn is Haraldyn, he salle no dure" (p. 70). Finally there is the long passage, only hinted at in Langtoft, where Harold's loss of land because of his forswearing seems linked by the telescoped syntax to the English loss that persists:

> Allas for Sir Harald, for him was mikelle reuth,
> Fulle wele his awen suld hald, if he had kept his treuth.
> Bot þat he was forsuorn, mishappyng þerfor he fond,
> Suld he neuer els haf lorn for William no lond,
> Ne bien in þat bondage, þat brouht was ouer þe se,
> Now ere þei in seruage fulle fele þat or was fre.
> Our fredom þat day for euer toke þe leue,
> For Harald it went away, his falshed did vs greue.   (p. 71)

By focusing on the sin of Harold and accepting the Norman party line, Mannyng and any of his persuasion effectively remove the stain of sin from the "English" in servitude. Those who regard themselves as English are not being punished because of English sinfulness in the past, which, as Englishmen would stain them as well, but because of the freely acknowledged sin of a single Englishman. The only reason they were on the losing side in 1066, the only reason, in fact, there was a war at all, was this same man's faithlessness. As a result, Harold, the last English king, becomes in Mannyng a scapegoat for the "English," bearing for them any sinfulness that may attach to the idea of racial servitude, and bearing moreover the responsibility for that servitude. The purpose of the scapegoat is to relieve the burdens of others, and that is how the figure of Harold could function for those of English descent under Norman rule. With full connivance in the Norman interpretation of events, Harold could be used to exonerate the English from responsibility for causing their own downfall and therefore could allow them to feel more strongly and more justly aggrieved at their state of servitude It is a remarkably economic revision of English history that throws off the fatalistic series of racial lapses and divine punishments while retaining the crucial element of sinfulness situated

[165]

in the individual who can damage the race through his actions but who should not be allowed to condemn it. While he couches his re-counting of the consequences of 1066 in racial terms, Mannyng seems to point the way, by means of the intensification of Harold's sin, to a possible integration of the "English" and the "French." How wide-spread such a sophisticated interpretation would have been is difficult to gauge, but even if unique it is worthy of consideration. It may have been a factor in the establishment of the new, inclusive English identity that would begin to take hold in the decades that followed. [45]

NOTES

1. Of particular importance is Thorlac Turville-Petre's "Politics and Poetry in the Early Fourteenth Century," *The Review of English Studies* n.s. 39 (1988): 1–28. See also Daniel Donoghue's "Laȝamon's Ambivalence," *Speculum* 65 (1990): 537–63, especially pp. 554–63.

2. Turville-Petre, p. 17.

3. For a particularly dismissive statement on importance of race in medieval Eng-land, see Rodney Hilton, "Were the English English?," in *Patriotism: The Making and Unmaking of the British National Identity*, ed. Raphael Samuel vol. 1, pp. 39–43, especially p. 40. On the development of an English national identity, see M. T. Clanchy, *England and its Rulers, 1066–1272: Foreign Lordship and National Identity* (Oxford, 1983), particularly chpt. 10, and by the same author, *From Memory to Written Record: England, 1066–1307*, 2nd ed. (Oxford, 1993), chpts. 6 and 7.

4. Robert Mannyng, *Peter Langtoft's Chronicle*, ed. T. Hearne, 2 vols. (Oxford, 1725; rpt. London, 1810). Part 1 is edited in *The Chronicle of Robert Manning of Brunne*, ed. F. J. Furnivall, 2 vols., Rolls Series 87 (London, 1887). As Turville-Petre points out, little attention has been paid to Mannyng's *Chronicle*. For a recent, concise appraisal, see Edward Donald Kennedy, *Chronicles, and Other Historical Writings*, A Manual of the Writings in Middle English 8, gen. ed. Albert E. Hartung (New Haven, 1989), pp. 2625–28.

5. Thomas Castleford, *Chronicle*, in *Medieval English: An Old and Middle English Anthology*, ed. Rolf Kaiser, 3rd ed. (Berlin, 1958), pp. 364–65. The first complete edition of this chronicle, by Caroline D. Eckhardt, is forthcoming. I am very grateful for the assistance she has given me with the Castleford material. For a brief assessment of the work, see Kennedy, pp. 2624–25.

6. *The Metrical Chronicle of Robert of Gloucester*, ed. W. A. Wright, 2 vols., Rolls Series 86 (London, 1887). See Kennedy, pp. 2617–21.

7. Turville-Petre, p. 4. Turville-Petre discusses what little is known of Mannyng's life on pp. 2–3.

8. Mannyng, *Chronicle*, part 1, ll. 6–10.

9. Clanchy, *Written Record*, pp. 200–206 (pp. 154–59 in the 1st ed.).

10. Turville-Petre, pp. 19–20.

11. Ibid., pp. 7–10. See fn. 36 for bibliographical details on Langtoft.

12. Christopher Dyer, *Standards of Living in the Later Middle Ages: Social Change in England c 1200–1520*, Cambridge Medieval Textbooks (Cambridge, 1989), p. 184.

13. Ibid., p. 264.

14. Christopher Hill, "The Norman Yoke," in *Puritanism and Revolution: Studies in*

Interpretation of the English Revolution of the 17th Century (New York, 1964), pp. 50–122.

15. Ibid., p. 57.

16. Ibid., p. 58.

17. Four such statements are conveniently gathered together by Albert C. Baugh and Thomas Cable in *A History of the English Language*, 3rd ed. (Englewood Cliffs, 1978), pp. 137–38 and 143–45. They are from *Cursor Mundi*, ll. 232–50; *English Metrical Homilies* (Northern Homilies), pp. 3–4; William of Nassynton's *Speculum Vitae*, ll. 61–78; *Arthur and Merlin*, ll. 19–30.

18. *Memory to Written Record*, p. 202.

19. Ibid., p. 198 ff.

20. Ibid., p. 206.

21. It seems to have played a part during the hostilities in 1263. D. A. Carpenter in "English Peasants in Politics: 1258–1267," *Past and Present* 136 (1992): 3–42, quotes the St. Alban's Chronicler who remarks that "whoever did not know the English tongue was despised by the masses and held in contempt" (p. 32). The Latin is in *Flores Historiarum*, ed. Henry Richards Luard, Rolls Series 95, pt. 2, p. 481: Nam quicunque Anglicum idioma loqui nesciret, vilipenderetur a vulgo et despectui haberetur. Carpenter demonstrates that political alliances involving peasants and their socio-economic betters could certainly occur.

22. Baugh and Cable, p. 113. The other major treatments of the history of the English language pay surprisingly little attention to this question. Exceptional in this regard are Williams, who offers much evidence but no conclusions, and Bolton, whose rhetoric is less naive than Baugh's but whose views are not substantively different. Joseph M. Williams, *Origins of the English Language: A Social and Linguistic History* (New York, 1975); W. F. Bolton, *A Living Language: The History and Structure of English* (New York, 1972). In a very recent treatment by Jeremy Smith the traditional view is accepted: "The Use of English: Language Contact, Dialect Variation, and Written Standardization During the Middle English Period," in *English in its Social Contexts: Essays in Historical Sociolinguistics*, ed. Tim William Machan and Charles T. Scott, Oxford Studies in Sociolinguistics (Oxford, 1992), pp. 47–68. The question is ignored in the massive *Cambridge History of the English Language*, vol. 2, ed. N. F. Blake (Cambridge, 1992).

23. See Clanchy, *England and Its Rulers*, pp. 241–42.

24. On the long memory of peasants see Rosamund Faith, "The 'Great Rumour' of 1377 and Peasant Ideology," in *The English Rising of 1381*, eds. R. H. Hilton and T. H. Aston, Past and Present Publications (Cambridge, 1984), pp. 50, 54–55. She demonstrates that the ancestral memory of the peasants in regard to the status of land as royal demesne was long, stretching not only 300 years back to Domesday Book but in some cases even as far back as the seventh century, 700 years earlier.

25. Turville-Petre, p. 28. For a less glib assessment, see Dick Leith, *A Social History of English*, Language and Society Series (London, 1983), pp. 30–31.

26. Turville-Petre, p. 25.

27. Christopher McAll, *Class, Ethnicity, and Social Inequality*, McGill-Queen's Studies in Ethnic History 6 (Montreal & Kingston, 1990), p. 222. McAll's book contains many references to other Marxist approaches to the problem of ethnicity.

28. R. H. Hilton, *The Decline of Serfdom in Medieval England*, Studies in Economic History (London, 1969), pp. 25–26. Also see Christopher Dyer, "Social and Economic Background of the Revolt of 1381," in *English Rising*, pp. 9–42, especially pp. 40–41.

29. "The Peasantry as a Class," in R. H. Hilton, *The English Peasantry in the Later Middle Ages: The Ford Lectures for 1973 and Related Studies* (Oxford, 1975), pp. 14–15.

30. See Rodney Hilton, *Bond Men Made Free: Medieval Peasant Movements and the English Rising of 1381* (New York, 1973), especially pp. 164–85, and Dyer, "Social and Economic Background," pp. 14–19.

31. *On the Properties of Things: John Trevisa's Translation of Bartholomus Anglicus, De Proprietatibus Rerum*, eds. M. C. Seymour et al., vol. 1 (Oxford, 1974), pp. 311–12.

32. *Britton*, ed. Francis Morgan Nichols, vol. 1 (Oxford, 1865), pp. 194–95 (chpt. 32); de Bracton, Henry, *De Legibus et Consuetudines Anglicae*, ed. George E. Woodbine, vol. 2 (New Haven, 1922), pp. 29–31 (fols. 4b-5a).

33. David Brion Davis, *The Problem of Slavery in Western Culture*, (Oxford, 1966), pp. 62 ff.

34. *Two of the Anglo-Saxon Chronicles, Parallel*, ed. John Earle, rev. Charles Plummer, vol. 1 (Oxford, 1892), pp. 199–200.

35. Henry of Huntingdon, *Historia Anglorum*, ed. T. Arnold, Rolls Series 74 (London, 1879), p. 8.

36. *The Chronicle of Pierre de Langtoft*, ed. T. Wright, 2 vols., Rolls Series 47 (1866-68).

37. *Serious Entertainments: The Writing of History in Twelfth-Century England* (Chicago, 1977), pp. 22–24, 202.

38. Huntingdon, p. 138.

39. *De Gestis Regum Anglorum*, ed. William Stubbs, Rolls Series 90, vol. 1, p. 277.

40. Turville-Petre, p. 14, sees the connection but pays it little attention.

41. For an assessment of the Norman propaganda against Harold, see Sten Körner, *The Battle of Hastings, England, and Europe: 1035–1066*, Bibliotheca Historica Lundensis 14 (Lund, 1964); a summary of Körner's views appears on pp. 136–37.

42. Malmesbury, vol. 1, p. 279. Körner analyses some of these revisionist versions of Harold's journey to Normandy on p. 137.

43. *An Anonymous Short Metrical Chronicle*, ed. Ewald Zettl EETS OS 196 (London, 1935), p. 37, l. 865: William bastarde of Normandy/Hym [Harold] cant [disposes of], þat was vilanye. In an earlier version this reference does not appear: Tho com with gret chevalrie/ William bastard of Normundie . . . Kyng Harald he ouercom,/Ant lette him to dethe don. *Ancient English Metrical Romances*, ed. Joseph Ritson (London, 1802), vol. 2, p. 308, ll. 903–4, 907–8.

44. *Vita Haraldi: The Romance of the Life of Harold, King of England*, ed. Walter De Gray Birch (London, 1885). A new translation of this work (Birch's edition also has one) can be found in *Three Lives of The Last Englishmen*, tr. and introd. Michael Swanton Garland, Library of Medieval Literature Series B vol. 10 (New York, 1984).

45. I have benefitted greatly from the questions and comments of Allen J. Frantzen, Paul Hyams, and Ruth Mazo Karras in writing this paper.

9

JUSTICE AND WAGE-LABOR AFTER THE BLACK DEATH: SOME PERPLEXITIES FOR WILLIAM LANGLAND

David Aers

But þow lyue by loore of *Spiritus Iusticie*
The chief seed þat Piers sew, ysaued worstow neuere.

(*Piers Plowman*, XIX.405–406)[1]

In the epigraph to this essay Conscience is the speaker, and the seed invoked was sown under the divine guidance of Grace (XIX. 274–318). It is a fitting comment on an author for whom individual salvation is inextricably bound up with the attempt to live a life that embodies the virtue of justice. Furthermore, the poet saw that such an attempt is inseparable from the forms of relationship encouraged by particular communities. His thinking here was shaped by Christian-Aristotelian tradition, and like its founder he sees repentance as allied to justice, a moral virtue without which sin cannot be forgiven.[2]

St. Thomas Aquinas argued that it is natural for human beings to live in association with each other.[3] Only in relationship with others can we learn what Will so desperately searches for, "Dowel," what will make us become good human beings. To lead a good life, St. Thomas maintained, we need both to act in accordance with virtue, in a community fostering virtuous peace, and to have "a sufficiency of the material goods that are necessary for virtuous action."[4] Since we are all necessarily part of some political community, it is impossible to be good unless we act in accord with the common good (*ST* I-II. 92.1). So if a community is organized in a manner opposed to the pursuit of the virtues, it would foster "good" citizens (that is, ones obedient to its laws) whose goodness would actually foster, even demand, wickedness — take the example of a "good" Nazi citizen in Germany during the 1930s and 1940s.

Justice, the *Summa Theologica* tells us, regulates human action according to a standard of right reason rendering it good and directing us to our final good (God). It is a disposition to render to each what is due, a virtue which leads the will towards perfection.[5] Religion itself is understood as part of the cardinal virtue of justice, directing us to render what we owe to God.[6] From within this tradition Langland decided to make *redde quod debes* one of the most prominent refrains throughout his poem.[7] The risen Christ himself stresses that the powers of forgiveness and mercy he bestows on Piers are conditional upon *redde quod debes* (XIX. 182–87), a condition confirmed, not surprisingly, by Grace (XIX. 258–61). The point is that justice is actually constitutive of the good life under the new dispensation. Not that St. Thomas suggests that justice can lead to beatitude uninformed by the supernatural virtue of Charity, a gift he treats before addressing justice and the other cardinal virtues.[8] Nevertheless, it would make no sense, in this tradition, to make a move that has become familiar in Langland scholarship. This move involves identifying the demands of justice with a punitive legalism, allegedly the mark of an "Old Testament" totally superseded in the Christian dispensation, a supersession allegedly figured forth from the sixteenth passus of *Piers Plowman*.[9] But Langland does not align the virtue of justice and its demands with an un-Christian or unacceptably "pelagian" ethos superseded in the Christian dispensation. On the contrary, his own commitment to this virtue and its place in human salvation is affirmed at all stages of the poem and through a wide range of speakers including, as we have just noted, Christ and the Holy Spirit. I see no reason to think that Langland dissented from St. Thomas's view that the order of justice is not superseded in the Christian dispensation but is in fact strengthened.[10] Even the power of the Eucharist, we are shown, is conditional upon the recipient having "ypaied/To Piers pardon þe Plowman *redde quod debes*" (XIX. 389–90). Even the Holy Spirit's own commands include the establishment of an agency for enforcing the demands of justice on those who reject justice: "*Spiritus Iusticie* spareþ noȝt to spille þe gilty" (XIX.302). This may well involve the use of force, even of "Foluyles lawes" (XIX.245–47).[11] If individuals are to lead the life of the virtues, they need communities committed to enabling and safeguarding such a life.

If a tradition is to survive, it will not be as a closed, static system serenely transcending economic, political, demographic and military changes, serenely ignoring new challenges. The maker of *Piers Plowman* grasped this clearly, and part of his poem's greatness is its tenacious engagement with contemporary circumstances which were posing some new and perplexing challenges to the tradition I have so crudely outlined above. As James Simpson has recently written, *Piers Plowman* is committed to a spirituality which "can be realized only through 'true' social relationships of interdependent labour," a poem "concerned to examine the institutions which nourish the individual."[12]

The problems addressed in the present essay are those posed around the practices of wage-labor after the Black Death. Here Langland's moral tradition was confronting a major challenge. The poet shows us how the option he had initially favored would not be compatible with that tradition, even if it could have solved the current economic and political conflicts he was considering. This option is the one chosen by the ruling elites. They passed the first *national* legislation on wages and their own control of laborers; they sought to enforce it through the existing coercive apparatus; and they evolved a rhetoric of abuse in which those who resisted this self-interested legislation were identified as able-bodied mendicants, dangerous vagrants, idle parasites with endless sums of money to spend in the ale-houses of England, and, in the language of the poet's contribution to this assault, wasters, embodiments of injustice and lawlessness. I have recently analyzed the ideological moves made by the poet here and their relations to contemporary conflicts between employers and the "laborers" who struggled "ayeins þe statut" (VI.313–20).[13] I have no wish to rehearse that account of the complex and shifting ideological strategies in Langland's construction of "wasters" and the work ethic in Passus VI, nor of the basic texts such as the Statute of Labourers (1351) and the commons' petition against vagrants (1376). Although these are points of reference in the present essay, the main question here is how and why the sale of labor-power after the Black Death could bring the poet's powerful tradition of moral inquiry under severe pressure. A related question is the consequences of such pressure for that tradition.

That slavery is in no sense "natural" to human beings, but the product of human contrivance, was a commonplace of Christian doctrine.[14] And there were certainly masses of women and men in Langland's England who were convinced that serfdom was not compatible with natural reason or a just society. For them the time had come to sweep it away, however clerics might gloss the story of Ham or preach that God "made man soget & þral to man for þe synne of Adam, as seyth Sent Austyn."[15] The events and explicit demands of June 1381 were only the most concentrated, forceful and dramatic manifestations of these convictions.[16] Yet it is neither the long-term decline of serfdom nor the conflict over villein tenure and status that draws the poet's attention. He seems to take its continuation for granted — and to approve of this continuation. For him bondage represents a world where workers' mobility is completely dependent on the will of the lord, where they have no right to make a charter and where they not only have no right to sell land but no right even to dispose of what they saw as their own personal goods — without permission of the lord (XI.127–30: C XII.60–63).[17] The poet took for granted this mode of production, its forms of dominion and its extremely heavy exploitation of villeins' resources.[18] These extractions are allegedly sanctioned by "lawe," "reson," and "conscience" (XI.127, 131, 132). Similarly, he assumes that if the social order is as it should be, then the lord will be free to fine his tenants at will — a mark of villein tenure and the state of serfdom. That is why the lord can only be exhorted to exercise this franchise with whatever he counts as "mercy," even as he is exhorted not to oppress or torment these people unless "truþe" assents (VI.37–40). The poet occludes the fact that villeins themselves lived in communities which were self-regulating, self-policing and the repositories of their own versions of tradition and custom. Their own understanding of "truþe," as 1381 showed with especial clarity, might not coincide with their lords'. In reality, the terms of "mercy" and "truþe" in these relationships were negotiated within a complex web of forces and decisions, including the major demographic changes caused by the Black Death and succeeding plagues. Despite this, the customary appearance of servile forms of tenure and status, the family formations they determined and their embeddedness in the culture's learned languages, enabled the poet to perceive them as somehow static, securely trans-historical. This was, as already observed, not a universally "medieval" perception but a class-determined one demonstrably not shared by masses of contemporaries, those who fought covertly and openly against villeinage and persuaded King Richard, on that memorable day in June 1381, to abolish serfdom.[19] Nevertheless, Langland himself seems unperturbed by what strikes many observers as the core of the conflicts leading into the great rising and the demands made at Mile End.[20] Nor do the poet's revisions to a poem which had been used by some of those involved in the rising show any significant changes to his assumptions in *this* area. The fact is contemporary villeins, bondmen and bondwomen, are marginal, shadowy but striking absences in *Piers Plowman*. What takes their place in the poet's representation of productive labor, and why?

My answer to this question is that in *Piers Plowman* the villeins of England are displaced by wage-laborers, craftspeople and small scale traders. What kind of presence did such people have in the late medieval system of production and exchange? All attempts to quantify forms of work in this period, even the attempt to make the classifications on which calculations must be based, are fraught with methodological and empirical difficulties. Granting this, recent studies of different regions have used a wide range of evidence and controls to come up with some rough figures that can, at least, serve as indicators of the scale of wage-labor one might find in various areas of England. Here are a few very rough examples: in Suffolk and Essex between 50% and 63%, while *not more* than a quarter of families in central and northern Essex "derived their livelihood from agriculture or their own properties" and half or more "were substantially dependent upon wages"; in Cuxham (Oxfordshire), a small village, the proportion of wage-laborers was in excess of 50% of the male population; in south Staffordshire the proportion of wage-earners was in excess of 30%, in Gloucestershire in excess of 40%. In a town such as Coventry, even when the city was in decline, wage-laborers would make up over half the working population.[21] We need also to recall that precise definitions of forms of most working people's livelihood are hazardous because of the fluidity of forms of work, the changing forms appropriate to different phases of peoples' life-cycles and the decisive role of gender. Nevertheless, the research of recent years has demonstrated that despite sharp regional differences, despite crucial gender differences, and despite the fact that one person's life-cycle was very likely to include a multiplicity of forms of work, "wage earning was widely diffused in English society," both rural and urban, in Langland's lifetime.[22]

Were this not the case, there would not have been the national legislation on wages and the mobility of laborers after the Black Death, nor would there have been the sustained attempt to enforce this legislation with all the means of state and local power. True enough, in the long run this coercion failed. However, people do not live "in the long run," nor are their struggles conducted "in the long run." We need to remember that the elites' coercive activity seems to have succeeded up to the second great plague of 1361, which killed a further 10% of the population. It was this, together with the sharp fall in grain prices from 1376, which seems to have provided the determining factor in this particular struggle between wage-laborers and employers.[23] Since those who were prosecuted and fined in the 1350s, 1360s and 1370s could see no end to any "long run," we should not use the "long run" to obscure either the intensity of the employers' coercive efforts in the forty years after the Black Death or its significant role in the network of factors leading to the rising of 1381.

The few examples of indictments I shall now offer were utterly commonplace during the period in which Langland wrote and re-wrote *Piers Plowman*. They were so commonplace that in 1352 there are surviving records of 7,556 people being fined in Essex alone under the terms of the Statute of Labourers.[24] In his outstanding study of north and central Essex, L. R. Poos calculated that, "roughly one in seven Essex people older than their mid-teens, or nearly one in four Essex males in the same age-range, were fined for violating the labour legislation in a single year."[25] Elizabeth Furber earlier had found that in 1377–1379 "two hundred of the two hundred and eighty extant indictments before the justices of the peace [in Essex] involved labour offences," while in 1389 Poos found, in one series of Essex indictments, 791 fines against the Statutes of Labourers.[26] His comment is especially relevant to the concerns of the present essay:

> The sheer numerical weight of Statute enforcement in the county . . . makes much more vividly comprehensible the ferocity directed towards the county-level agents of law enforcement (like Bampton, Gildesburgh and Sewale) by a rural society so heavily infused with wage labour and rural industry.[27]

The standard charge, experienced by many thousands of English workers acting "ayeins þe statut" (VI.320), went along lines such as these:

> they present that Alicia Gylot (from the same place) takes excessive wage in autumn, that is 4d., and also moves from place to place . . . they present that Emma Shepherd (from the same place) does the same . . . they present that John Mory of Castle Hedingham moves from place to place in autumn for excess wages . . . they present that Henry atte Watere (ploughman) takes 20s. a year from William Andrew, 4 days use of a plough, one new tunic and grain, namely a quarter of corn every twelve weeks, against the statute . . . they present that Richard

Waterford is a good ploughman and refused that work [we can see how Langland's Piers would have seemed to his local Justice in Passus VII!] . . . they present that John Loue of High Easter is a common reaper and moves from place to place for excessive wages, and gets others to act in the same way against the statute . . . they present that Robert Craddok (of Thaxted), labourer, takes 2d. a day and food.[28]

In her still indispensable study of the enforcement of the Statute of Labourers, Bertha Putnam observed that, "The constables report long lists of labourers who are rebellious and refuse to take oaths of obedience to the statutes."[29]

On top of this an important factor to which I will return when considering Langland's treatment of the Church, was the clergy's involvement in the nexus of wage-labor and legislation. In her study of proceedings before the Justices of the Peace, Bertha Putnam produced evidence of the King's Bench removing a case from Hertfordshire against a vicar and a hermit for "preaching that the statutes of labour are wicked and that there is nothing to prevent labourers from taking what wages they please."[30] Such a vicar and such a hermit, it needs recalling, are as much part of late medieval mentalities, as "representative," as are prescriptive texts composed by orthodox preachers or by John Gower. Furthermore, the clerisy included not only employers of wage-labor but also those whose situation was precisely analogous to wage-laborers'. We find an Essex jury presenting a vicar for charging excessive prices for his labor-power in administering the sacraments.[31] Similarly in Wiltshire we find John Bryan, clerk, being presented for taking excessive wages for his labor.[32] In 1362 the commons' petitions include complaints about the costs of priests: "les Chapelleins sont devenuz si chers q'ils ne voillent demurrer ove nuly meins que dys marcz ou dusze, a grant grevance & oppression du poeple."[33] The king's response agrees to fix wages of such priests and to restrain their mobility, to stop them "passant d'une Diocise a autre."[34] Langland himself joined in with this complaint too, one levied against himself in the C version by Reason and Conscience.[35] Such complaints and resolutions are a good reminder of how integrated were the lower clergy in standard practices and relations of wage-labor. On this topic too Bertha Putnam made yet another indispensable study. There she traces the "growing demand for stipendiary priests at just the time when the supply was being diminished both by the plague and by promotion of many of them to fill the gaps in the

ranks of rectors and vicars." She described the social and economic
"gulf" between a mass of unbeneficed clergy and "the beneficed
clergy, whose employees they normally were," a gulf she found close
to that "between the labourers and the governing classes." The
changes in supply and demand led to substantial increases in the
wages these unbeneficed men could claim. The response of the *ecclesiastical* establishment was to pass "clerical statutes of labourers," ones
whose working Putnam investigated.[36] This legislation fixed rates,
giving penalties for charges classified as excessive, forbad priests to
leave the diocese without a bishop's letter, and chose the same rhetorical strategies as the parliamentary legislators used against secular
wage-laborers. In 1354 Bishop Grandisson complained about the "ex-
orbitant salaries" demanded by his priests — they too, like Langland's
"wasters," seem to inhabit taverns more than churches.[37] But the unbeneficed clerical wage-laborers did not necessarily accept their
masters' legislation. For example, in 1364 a royal commission of oyer
and terminer was directed against chaplains in the archdeaconry of
Leicester. The commission was:

> to investigate the assault made by chaplains on the parsons
> [i.e. rectors] who had been deputed to act as the bishop's
> commissaries in enforcing the second *effranata*. The chaplains,
> bound together by oaths, had broken up the parsons' sessions
> by horrible words, almost killing them and even lying in wait
> for the bishop himself.[38]

Stirring times indeed, ones in which we can never assume that a classification such as "clerical" entails a predictably conservative, consistently orthodox and obedient set of attitudes in a homogeneous
social and ideological group.

What we are now in a position to see is how wage-labor after the
Black Death carried an extremely rich and troubling range of meanings for Langland, ones that were ethical and political in the broadest
sense. Wage-labor suggested to the poet a culture of independence, as-
sertiveness and anti-authoritarianism. Nor were his impressions un-
warranted. It seems no coincidence that the region with probably the
highest level of wage-labor in England was found by L. R. Poos to be
"the centre of a deeply rooted strain of anti-authoritarianism during
the later fourteenth and fifteenth centuries, which manifested itself
both in rural revolts and uprisings and in a persistent subculture of
religious nonconformity."[39] No wonder, then, that Langland was so
interested in wage-labor and found it more disturbing than the tradi-

tional forms of conflict between rural villeins and the seigneurial classes. His vision shares something with Bertha Putnam's closing comment to her study of the enforcement of the Statute of Labourers: "the statutes of labourers must not be regarded as having created a new system or a new set of economic relations, but as affording proof that radical changes had occurred, ushering in a new era."[40] The grounds for such a strong claim were not only that the Statutes were the first attempt of "the central authorities to apply to the country as a whole, uniform legislation on wages and prices." More important still, in the contexts of the present essay, was the fact that in the past, "wages of agricultural labourers were apparently regulated by custom."[41] That is, relations around wage-labor now presented an exceptionally sharp challenge to a nexus of traditional practices, understandings and negotiations. Langland was acutely conscious of the implications this carried for his tradition's version of the cardinal virtue of justice.[42]

An important part of Mede's prominent role in the first vision of *Piers Plowman* is to dramatize some of these implications. From Passus II to Passus IV Mede symbolizes a culture in which not only production but all human relations become exchanges in a market for commodities. The figure's gender is given in accord with conventional stereotypes of received misogynistic discourses. These identified the letter, carnality, instability, insatiability and supplementarity with "femininity," the "other" against which "masculine" identity could be defined but which, simultaneously, and always, threatened to subvert this identity from without and from within.[43] Mede is both powerful courtly lady and ubiquitous common prostitute, a "baude," a "hore," as "commune as þe Cartwey to knaue and to alle," totally uninterested in social status.[44] The "female" figure thus becomes the symbol for Langland's vision of communities in which, as the Wife of Bath observed, "al is for to selle."[45] She figures forth a culture determined by the kind of exchange St. Thomas had viewed with such grave misgivings, one shaped not by what he considered the quest for the "necessities of life" but for "profit." Such motivation deserves blame, he maintained, because it fosters "the greed for gain," and this "knows no limit and tends to infinity" (*ST* II-II.71.4). This is the economy and culture symbolized by Mede. Not surprisingly then, Mede is presented as the dissolvent of just relations in all domains.[46] "Mede ouermaistreþ lawe," observes the reforming king (IV.176), and neither Reason nor Conscience dissents from this view.

Where Mede is everywhere, the poet evokes a community with no boundaries, with no cogent moral principles, with no criteria other than pragmatic responses to profit and loss in the market. Here there can be no common project to foster institutions, relations and laws which could help people to cultivate the virtues in pursuit of their final good, as understood by the tradition to which the poet belonged. In a community driven by what Mede symbolizes, it is not at all clear that we would even understand what *redde quod debes* could mean, let alone act on it as a decisive imperative. And it is to just this version of society that the poet returns in the courageous and devastating final vision of *Piers Plowman*. There, quite explicitly, "þe comune" rejects the cardinal virtues and the demands of Conscience to pursue them: what does not contribute to financial profit, to "wynnyng" is unreal.[47] In such a community, however gradually, however celebrated as a desirable liberation from fetters (as at III.137–39), all ethical discriminations will become incoherent, even impossible. No-one will be able to know, "Wheiþer he wynne wiþ right, wiþ wrong or wiþ vsure" (XIX.350). Once again, we are forced to ask how anyone could know what *redde quod debes* might entail in such a society.

How will we be able to determine, in good conscience, what constitutes a just wage and just conditions of employment? There will never be problems in offering rationalizations of self-interest, no problem in developing rhetoric to demonize those whose interests conflict with one's own. Nor will there be much problem for those in command of the legal and coercive apparatus to pass "laws" in their own interests and to set about enforcing them as best they can, classifying all opponents as people hostile to God, Reason and Justice (see VI.312–18). This, however, has nothing to do with the understanding of justice in the Christian-Aristotelian tradition from which the poet came. As St. Thomas argued, and as not all commentators on Chaucer's *Clerk's Tale* have remembered, legislators that make tyrannical laws have no legitimate claim to obedience. Tyrannical law, he insists, is not truly law because it only serves private interests and harms the people, setting up forms of life at odds with their true end — the life of the virtues in accord with reason. Most pertinently for the present context, he argues that to rebel against a tyrannical government is *not* illicit, since such a government denies the ends of government and impedes the citizens' pursuit of the good.[48] If the employers' legislation was narrowly self-interested, as it was, what did it have to do with justice and what moral force could it have? What good moral reasons could be offered against the vicar and the hermit of Hertfordshire who were charged with telling laborers that the legislation in question had no moral force? The relevant questions had indeed become extremely difficult to answer. As *Dives* says to his instructor in *Dives and Pauper*, "It is hard to knowyn what is þe ryȝte value of a þing."[49] It was especially hard when that "þing" was a peculiar commodity capable of turning over the tables on which it was displayed for sale. In *Dives and Pauper* the instructor gives the answer taught by St. Thomas and others, one that was standard enough:

> Þe ryȝte value & þe iust prys of a þing is aftir þat þe comoun
> merket goth þat tyme, & so a þing is as mychil worþ as it may
> ben sold so be [*sic*] comoun merket — tanti valet quanti vendi
> potest . . .[50]

The issue here is central to the present essay. As St. Thomas argued, "it is an act of justice to give a just price for anything received . . . an act of justice to make a return for work or toil" (*ST* I-II.114.1, resp). In relation to wages and labor-power, however, the definition of the just price given in *Dives and Pauper* held unwelcome consequences for employers and legislators after the Black Death. This is so because its definition assumes a *free market*. The "just prys" is the price a commodity fetches on an open market, "þe comoun market," a market free from manipulation by monopolizers, forestallers or any other self-interested person or groups. Along these lines, fixing prices by a small minority in their own interests could not be defended, and those who resisted their attempts to rig the market in this way could reasonably claim to be acting rationally and justly. Perhaps it was an attempt to think coherently along the lines of this tradition that led the vicar and hermit in Hertfordshire to tell local people the Statutes of Labourers "are wicked."[51] Perhaps John Ball, first recorded as in trouble with the authorities in 1366, had been a Christian-Aristotelian who had no need to hear Wyclif before challenging the justice of current ruling class policies of legislation and taxation.

Be that as it may, Langland's line is, of course, hardly that of the vicar from Hertfordshire. In a much-discussed passage, greatly elaborated in the C version, he had Conscience address the problems of labor and the just wage.[52] In relation to earthly relations, Conscience seeks to distinguish the culture of Mede from what is here called "measurable hire." This, he emphasizes, is "no manere Mede." Because our world knows the disasters consequent upon the long-term pursuit of Mede in a society where Mede rules, because we can now see its catastrophic teleology, this reader has great sympathy with Langland's ethical intentions in trying to address the complex prob-

lems of limits and justice in this domain. But sympathy should not oc-
clude the unresolved difficulties concealed in the "solution" he attributes to Conscience. It sounds fine to attack priests who "taken Mede
and moneie for masses þat þei syngeþ" (III.253). After all, this certainly looks like simony, what Chaucer's Parson describes as, "Espiri-
tueel marchandise."[53] But the situation was actually not so simple, and
attacking priests who sang masses for money was not necessarily fine.
As we have already noticed, this was a period of increasing demand
for unbeneficed clergy, for chantry priests, for the service of priests
without the security of a regular living or independent funds—priests,
in fact, with nothing to live on but the "mede" they obtained for the
religious services they performed. As we also noted, these priests were
subject to ecclesiastical legislation and prosecution similar to that imposed on their brothers and sisters who were secular laborers. But
how does the poet expect unbeneficed priests to go on singing masses
and offering other spiritual services if not by taking "moneie for
masses"? If he concedes that such wages are not, after all, simony,
how then should the just price be fixed? Through an open market for
priests and their performances? That sounds bad, for it suggests profoundly unspiritual market negotiations over the means of grace. But
if not that, then, once more, by what principle should the just wage
here be reached? The problems were stark and fresh, bound up with
the massive demographic collapse of the Black Death and the plague
of 1361, and bound up too with corresponding shifts in expectations
and aspirations which could not necessarily be answered by appeals to
customary rates in a web of contexts that were now far from customary. There *is* one answer here which the poet, given his commitment to
orthodox traditions, could not consider, although it was clearly articulated by Lollards in the later fourteenth century and thereafter —
namely, declare the priesthood of all believers and cure both the shortage of priests and the "sale" of spiritual gifts at a stroke![54]

A similar set of problems emerges in the poet's treatment of secular
wage-labor at this point. Conscience teaches that what "labourers"
take "is no more manere Mede but a mesurable hire."[55] This sounds
both traditional and reasonable. Yet in Passus VI the poet supports the
employers' labor legislation with such vehemence that he even suggests, deploying his own prophetic idiom, that "werkmen" who resist
the Statute of Labourers are leading England to some divinely sent
chastisement in which the plague of famine will be "Iustice" (VI.312–
31).[56] Now the many people prosecuted under the new legislation
hardly saw their wages as "Mede mesureless," especially when they

looked at the worldly consumption of those judging and taxing them. This is plain enough both from their sustained resistance and from their demands for a fully free market in labor and wages made at Mile End in June 1381.[57] So the question returns: by what principles are we to resolve the competing versions of a just wage, of "mesurable hire" in the circumstances after the Black Death? Why should we now abandon the guidelines for establishing the just price so lucidly articulated by St. Thomas and reproduced in texts such as *Dives and Pauper*, quoted above? The only answer can be that those who abandon the received framework at this juncture do so to defend the employers' material interests in a context where the market in labor, and after 1376 in grain prices, is unfavorable to them. But this takes us, or should take us, back to the Thomistic account of a tyrannical legislation, already outlined, an account which teaches us that our own material self-interests may not actually be identical with the common good and the virtue of justice. This is not a comfortable lesson for anyone. One could pursue the difficulties here further, but we have reached one of those moments where the poet turns out to have explored a major moral and political issue to a point where the force of the questions he has raised and dramatized is in excess of any solution he can find — probably in excess of any solution anyone could find. The employers' legislation was a pragmatic self-interested response which failed. It also failed to meet the demands of justice and the terms of the just price in the tradition to which Langland belonged. But the laborers' demands for a free market in labor-power and wages, understandable as they are, did not offer a satisfactory solution either. Although they were in fact grounded in a pragmatic opportunism similar to their opponents', they may in theory seem closer to the traditional idea of how the just price should be established. However, when the commodity is human labor-power and human lives there are massive moral problems at stake. One only has to look forward to the appalling situation of wage-laborers in the very different demographic and market situation of the sixteenth century to begin unpacking the grave inadequacies of their ancestors' solutions in the later fourteenth century. It seems to me that *Piers Plowman* here dramatizes a genuine aporia for the poet's tradition in the new circumstances with which the poem engages so admirably. The problems he was exploring have turned out to be quite as recalcitrant to the paradigms dominant in our own liberal, unprecedently secular and capitalistic societies.[58]

Langland himself emphasized how intractable he found the cluster of problems I have been addressing. He did so not only returning to the issues they raise but in the haunting self-representations he weaves into his own poem. Having launched attacks on mobile clerics and on mobile wage-laborers who resist the employers' work ethos and legislation, he shows himself as lacking land, lacking traditional occupation, always on the move, a vagrant whom we encounter as he goes "by þe wey" (XX.1), a wanderer who confesses, "forþ gan I walke / In manere of a mendynaunt many yer" (XIII.2–3), one who "romed aboute" (VIII.1), "In habite as an heremite, vnholy of werkes, / Wente wide in þis world wondres to here" (Pr. 3–4).[59] The dazzling new self-referential passage in the C version (V.1–108) elaborates these passing depictions to bring out the ways in which his form of life cannot be understood in terms of any traditional version of the just life in which one renders to others their due in a web of reciprocal obligations. Reason sees him as "an ydel man . . . a spille tyme," and to stress the implications of a life led in defiance of traditional versions of justice, the poet invokes Christ's words of warning: "*Reddet unicuique iuxta opera sua*" (He will render to each one according to his works, Matthew 16.27). Although we and our communities may reject the terms of *redde quod debes*, making them virtually incomprehensible, the warning is that we will nevertheless be held responsible and answerable within its framework. The projected self of the poet represents precisely what he cannot assimilate to his own tradition. It is no wonder that he was more gripped by the problems of wage-labor and market exchanges in relation to traditional accounts of justice than he was by current struggles between villeins and lords over services and status. His own identity, elusive and mobile, is convicted, in his own eyes, by God's umpires, Reason and Conscience (C V. 92–93, 102–104). That is, he himself, a kind of clerical laborer, represents his own understanding of the dissolution of the good and just community, both effect and cause. In this he is another Haukyn.[60] Like that figure, Will is painfully struggling towards a conversion but, again like that figure, it remains quite unclear what form of life he would, or could, pursue. Converted in a community under the domination of Mede, what will his options be? At one point in the B version he claims that if he knew what the virtues were he would "neuere do werk" — precisely what Reason and Conscience attack him for in C V — "but wende to holi chirche / And þere gidde my bedes" (XII.25–28). In the end, he remains an isolated man, immobilized by age (XX.183–98), on the verge of death (XX.199–202), with a disintegrating Church under the rule of Antichrist's forces and still asking *how* to combine the evangelical commands to love with a licit way of obtaining the necessities of embodied life in this community (XX.204-11: cf XX.322-86). It is worth stressing that the collapse of the Christian communities founded by the Holy Spirit and Piers in the poem's final Passus is directly related to the pressures addressed in this essay. In conclusion I will discuss some aspects of this founding activity and its catastrophic reversal.

The Holy Spirit gives a diversity of graces in the originary foundation of Christian communities (XIX.225-61: I Corinthians 12.4-31).[61] James Simpson is certainly right to see this passage as an attempt to incorporate, "Labour, or works . . . in the scheme of salvation," to see how "labour can find a place in the scheme of salvation."[62] For the final time the poet returns to one of the issues that most perplexed him, only now he tries to imagine an originary, utopian moment which could serve as a corrective model for his own intractable present. In an interesting reading of this passage, James Simpson has argued that Langland keeps his attention on "the fundamental questions of social hierarchy and labour that he had confronted in Passus VI," while he finally displaces the "hierarchical or coercive . . . feudal structure" assumed earlier in the poem.[63] In response to this claim, the first question to ask is the following: if by "feudal" Simpson means a social formation in which the dominant and basic form of production is carried out by "agriculturists"[64] holding land (much of it in villein tenure) from lords in a political regime legitimizing a massive extraction of services and money from these tenants, while excluding the vast majority of people from any political voice, then what form of labor is envisaged as replacing the traditional agriculturist in her/his web of obligations, fines, taxes and suit at the lord's court? Simpson's answer is that we now see "Langland's renewed vision of society as modelled on urban horizontal structures, despite the manorial and hierarchical images which are also employed."[65] By "urban horizontal structures" Simpson, explicitly, means "trade guilds, craft guilds." Indeed, he claims that now "the bourgeois model of the 'crafte' (XIX. 236, 242) or guild is invoked as a model of brotherly love."[66] This seems a little surprising, for at least two reasons. Firstly, Grace is offering a prophetic admonition to the future craft guilds of Langland's own world:

> And alle he lered to be lele, and ech a craft loue ooþer,
> Ne no boost ne debat be among hem alle. (XIX.250-51)

As is the way with utopian forms, the negation ("Ne . . . ne") is directed against present norms and practices. It is mistaken to think that here *present* institutions are being used "as a model of brotherly love." Indeed, Simpson himself acknowledges that "the guilds of Langland's London were in fierce rivalry" — and not only, he might well have added, of London.[67] Langland was as well placed as Thomas Usk to see how easily the rhetoric of fraternity turned into the practice of fratricide, and perhaps he would not have been entirely surprised: "For soþest word þat euer god seide was þo he seide *Nemo bonus*" (X.447 [Luke 18.18]). Furthermore, the craft guilds were committedly exclusivist, hierarchical and profoundly authoritarian organizations designed to serve the political and economic interests of a minority of males.[68] *Piers Plowman* gives us no reason to think that "urban" forms of production, competition and exchange were admired by a poet for whom the practices and institutions of the markets, including the crucial markets in labor-power, were profoundly disturbing.

It seems to me that in the passage attributed to the Holy Spirit the poet does not, in fact, really address what Simpson calls "the fundamental questions" about forms of labor. What Pentecost and Grace give us is a utopian vision that sets aside "the fundamental questions" thrown up by economic and social relations in England after the Black Death. In Grace's oration we meet, for example, the following: those who earn their licit livelihood "by labour of tongue" (some hope here for the poet given such a bad time by Ymaginatif in the B version and by Reason and Conscience in C?); licit market exchange; wage-labor — but wage-labor that is "lele" and classifiable as "trewe" (whatever that would mean in the 1370s); tilling, making hay cocks and thatching (whether these are villein services, sale of labor-power or work on a family's free holding is not specified); astrology; asceticism; and a multitude of cooperating, loving crafts (XIX.229–51). The poet has thus *bracketed* the most vexing problems about justice, wages, conditions and work, while, understandably enough, choosing not to go back to the most challenging vision of early Christian community found in the Acts of the Apostles and given such striking application by early fifteenth-century Taborites and by seventeenth-century Diggers. If one sought, in Simpson's manner, to apply the passage to "fundamental questions" about work after the Black Death, its vagueness might seem to sanction everything — as long as it is part of "a lele life and a trewe" (XIX.237). The problem, as we have seen, was that the constitution of "lele," "trewe" forms of labor and wages was in serious dispute. The vision of harmony Holy Spirit offers here is admirable, but it does nothing to address the profound difficulty of ascertaining what constitutes a just price, what constitutes a coherent application of the tradition's understanding of justice in the poet's society. Indeed, and contrary to Simpson's optimistic account, we find that Holy Spirit sanctions, even in this utopian vision, the existence of a mounted (hence elite) law-enforcement agency (XIX.245–47).

Nor does the poet, of course, leave us with this post-Pentecostal utopian vision. In the same Passus he invents a scene in which "al þe comune," showing unusual solidarity, rejects the fundamental imperative of justice, *redde quod debes* (XIX.390–92). Here, alas, is the "horizontal" fraternalism James Simpson was looking for, a solidarity in the rejection of the Christian-Aristotelian tradition the poet wished to bring into contact with new and extremely testing circumstances. It is a solidarity Holy Church herself had already articulated with memorable clarity (I.5–9).[69] But coming towards the end of the poem, *after* the great shewings of Christ, his teachings on *kindness* (XVII.215–64), his living exemplification of love and saving solidarity with humankind (B XVIII), coming after the Pentecostal graces (B XIX), this has a far more disturbing resonance than it could in the poem's opening passus. The poet actually reinforces this with the aggressive and shocking intervention of one of the commodity producers so recently, and so blandly, sanctioned in the poet's utopian vision:

> "Ye? baw!" quod a Brewere, "I wol no ȝt be ruled,
> By Iesu! for al youre Ianglynge, wiþ *Spiritus Iusticie*,
> Ne after Conscience, by crist! while I kan selle
> Boþe dregges and draf and drawe at oon hole
> Thikke ale and þynne ale; þat is my kynde,
> And noȝt hakke after holynesse; hold þi tongue, Conscience!
> Of *Spiritus Iusticie* þow spekest much on ydel." (XIX.396–402)

This brilliantly inventive rhetoric shows us how a fixed and deludedly autonomous individual can be produced by a certain kind of community, one in which the market is god: such individuals are persuaded that the pursuit of profit and self-interest constitute rationality and felicity, even as they are persuaded to deny the roots of creatureliness and the fluid contingency of the self. Unlike the poem's Will, so remorselessly castigated, such a self feels no need to search, to search for the virtues and their end. The passage dramatizes how certain forms of work and community can transform someone's *kynde*, persuading them that the teachings of the Samaritan/Christ, of Grace and of Piers are vapid. In Langland's terms, the collective rejection of justice in Passus XIX and XX displays a terrifying rejection of the final good disclosed by the good Samaritan, by the life of Christ and his orations in the Harrowing of Hell. Probably the worst of all for the poet, the

Church, the ark of salvation, is assimilated to the brewer's community, fulfilling the worst prognostications of Passus XV. Once more, the refusal to meet the demands of justice, of *redde quod debes*, seems to be decisive (XX.306–72). As I observed earlier, the virtue of penitence is allied to justice (*ST* III.85–86), and so with the contemptuous rejection of the tradition in which justice is articulated goes the rejection of penitence, of *redde quod debes*, a practice, for this poet, essential to any serious commitment to the Christian dispensation. Not surprisingly then, when Conscience appreciates, belatedly enough (such is indeed the way of our consciences), what s/he has colluded in, s/he *leaves the Church* to search for Piers and Grace outside the ark. This means that Conscience must become an isolated, wandering, mobile, independent searcher, someone who might well fall on the wrong side of the labor legislation and the commons' petition against the vagrants of 1376. Noone had to wait for the twentieth century and the grace of postmodernism to find an aporia.

Having engaged in some argument here with James Simpson, it is appropriate to conclude with his description of the ending of *Piers Plowman*:

> This is clearly a moment of catastrophic proportions: not only is the ideal of the apostolic Church rendered useless, but the very constitution of selfhood, to which the whole poem from Passus VIII has been directed, is on the point of disintegration. . . . Conscience's departure at the end of the poem is from the Church, in its failure. Langland has exhausted the discourses of both conservative and radical wings of the Church, and it is unclear to me what discourses the poem could possibly adopt, or what institutional form it could imagine.[70]

This is well put, the product of an engaged commentary that grasps admirably the implications, for the poet, of the poem's ending. The poem has shown how, and why, false views are generated and can come to seem not only plausible but natural, *kynde*. Here, according to this poem, the market has a constitutive role. Those of us who live in liberal-market societies, live with the emaciated versions of "justice" propagated in the years of Thatcher-Major and Reagan-Bush, may well find provocation for some serious reflection in this poem and its own perplexities — unless, of course, we have learnt to inhabit the consciousness of the brewer of Passus XIX.

NOTES

1. The edition of *Piers Plowman* cited in the text of this essay, unless otherwise stated, is *Piers Plowman: The B version*, revised ed., G. Kane and E. T. Donaldson (London, 1988). For the C version I use *Piers Plowman*, ed. Derek Pearsall (London, 1978).

2. *ST* III. 85–86: the Latin text used in this essay has been *Summa Theologica* (Taurini, 1952), the English translation by the English Dominican Province (London, 1929). Hereafter the *Summa* is cited as *ST*.

3. *De Regimine Principum*, in *Aquinas: Selected Political Writings*, ed. A. P. D'Entreves, tr. J. G. Dawson (Oxford, 1965), chapter one; the more reliable translation seems to be in Paul E. Sigmund, *St. Thomas Aquinas on Politics and Ethics* (New York, 1988), pp. 14–17.

4. *De Reg*, chapter 15: quoting here from Sigmund's translation, p. 29.

5. See especially *ST* II-II:57; 80; 123. 1; 44. 6; and also *ST* I-II. 90–91. This is congruent with Langland's own approach to the journey of Will in *Piers Plowman*. On Langland and justice, see the following: M. W. Bloomfield, *Piers Plowman as a Fourteenth-century Apocalypse* (New Brunswick, 1961), pp. 127–43; P. M. Kean, "Love, Law and *Lewte* in *Piers Plowman*," *RES*, 15 (1964): 241–61 and "Justice, Kingship and the Good Life in the Second Part of *Piers Plowman*," chapter 3 in *Piers Plowman*, ed. S. S. Hussey (London, 1969); Myra Stokes, *Justice and Mercy in Piers Plowman* (London, 1984).

6. *ST* II-II. 81; II-II. 79. 1.

7. Much has been written about this: especially see Bloomfield in note 5 and R. W. Frank, *Piers Plowman and the Scheme of Salvation* (New Haven, 1957), pp. 100–109; B. J. Harwood, *Piers Plowman* (Toronto, 1992), pp. 43–44, 114–16, 130–32, 151.

8. *ST* II-II. 23–44; II-II. 47–168.

9. This kind of argument tends to make Piers in BV-VI a figure representing the "Old Law," the "Old Testament:" for a typical example, Barbara Raw, "Piers and the Image of God in Man," chapter 6 in *Piers Plowman*, ed. S. S. Hussey (London, 1969), pp. 145–46, 163–65, 168.

10. *ST* II-II. 104. 6.

11. On "Foluyles lawes" see Pearsall's note to C XXI. 247 (p. 351 of his edition of *Piers Plowman*, cited note 1), and A. Baldwin, *The Theme of Government in Piers Plowman* (Cambridge, 1981), pp. 39–40.

12. J. Simpson, *Piers Plowman* (London, 1991), pp. 71, 220; see similarly pp. 88, 165. Important approaches along congruent lines are by Anne Middleton, "William Langland's 'Kynde Name'," chapter 1 in *Literary Practice and Social Change in Britain*, ed. Lee Patterson (Berkeley, 1990), and David Lawton, "The subject of *Piers Plowman*," *Yearbook of Langland Studies*, 1 (1987): 1–30.

13. Aers, *Community, Gender and Individual Identity* (London, 1988), pp. 20–49.

14. See *ST* I-II. 57 and I-II. 94; Augustine, *City of God*, XIX. 15, tr. M. Dods (New York, 1950), pp. 693–94.

15. On Ham see *Dives and Pauper*, ed. P. H. Barnum (E. E. T. S., 275, 1976), IV. 1, vol. 1, pp. 305–306; quoting here from volume 2, pp. 125–26.

16. On the 1381 rising the literature is now immense: especially helpful are the following: R. B. Dobson's superb anthology, *The Peasants' Revolt of 1381* (London, 1970, revised 1986); R. H. Hilton, *Bond Men Made Free* (London, 1973); E. B. Fryde, chapter 8 in *The Agrarian History of England and Wales*, ed. Edward Miller (Cambridge, 1991); Nicholas Brooks, "The organization and achievements of the peasants of Kent and Essex in 1381," in, *Studies in Medieval History*, ed. H. M. Harting and R. I. Moore (London, 1985); Caroline Barron, *Revolt in London* (London, 1981); T. Prescott, "London in the Peasants' Revolt," *London Journal*, 7

(1981): 125–43; L. R. Poos, *A Rural Society after the Black Death* (Cambridge, 1991), chapter 11.

17. On the traditions here and the fourteenth-century situation, R. H. Hilton, *Bond Men* and *The Decline of Serfdom in Medieval England* (Oxford, 1984); L. R. Poos and L. Bonfield, "Law and Individualism in Medieval England," *Social History*, 11 (1986): 287–301.

18. For a good account of this domain, see J. R. Maddicott, *Law and Lordship* (Kendal, 1978); also Richard W. Kaeuper, *War, Justice, and Public Order* (Oxford, 1988), chapter 4 and pp. 104–17.

19. On the abolition of serfdom in 1381, see Hilton, *Decline*, p. 42; Dobson, *Peasant's Revolt*, p. 161.

20. The key attack, however, was on the administrators of current law: see on this topic Alan Harding, "The revolt against the Justices," chapter 7 in *The English Rising of 1381*, ed. R. H. Hilton and T. H. Aston (Cambridge, 1984).

21. Figures here are drawn from the following work: Christopher Dyer in *The Agrarian History of England and Wales*, ed. Edward Miller (Cambridge, 1991), pp. 645–46 and Dyer, *Standards of Living in the Later Middle Ages* (Cambridge, 1989), pp. 211–12, 214 (Coventry); Hilton, *Bond Men*, pp. 171–72; Poos, *A Rural Society* (note 16 above), pp. 18–31, quoting pp. 23–24. On women in this context, Dyer, *Standards*, p. 212, and especially Judith Bennett, *Women in the Medieval English Countryside* (New York, Oxford, 1987), pp. 32–33, 52–57, 82–84.

22. Dyer, *Standards*, p. 214.

23. On the Statutes of Labour and the ensuing struggles see the classic work by Bertha Putnam, *The Enforcement of the Statutes of Labourers* (New York, 1908); Poos, *A Rural Society*, chapter 10 is an important and well documented recent study.

24. Poos, *A Rural Society*, pp. 220–1, 241; 20% were women.

25. Poos, *A Rural Society*, p. 241; see too Elizabeth Furber, *Essex Sessions of the Peace* (Colchester, 1953), pp. 68–69.

26. Furber, *Essex*, p. 69; Poos, *A Rural Society*, p. 241.

27. Poos, *A Rural Society*, p. 241; see too Nora Kenyon, "Labour conditions in Essex in the reign of Richard II," *Economic History Review*, 4 (1934): 429–51.

28. These examples are taken from Furber, *Essex*, pp. 159–60, 164, 168, 170; see too pp. 171, 176–77; she prints the Latin and gives an English version which I have occasionally adapted as I think appropriate. For some Suffolk examples, Aers, *Community*, pp. 28–29.

29. Putnam, *Enforcement*, p. 76.

30. Bertha Putnam, *Proceedings before the Justices of the Peace in the Fourteenth and Fifteenth Centuries* (London, 1938), p. cxxv.

31. A. Harding, "The revolt" (note 20, above), p. 186.

32. "Offenders against the Statute of Labourers in Wiltshire," tr. E. M. Thompson, *Wiltshire and Natural History Magazine*, 33 (1903–1904), 384–409, here p. 387.

33. *Rotuli Parliamentorum*, 6 vols. (London, 1783), 36 Edward II, vol. 2, p. 271.

34. *Rotuli Parliamentorum*, vol. 2, p. 271.

35. On mobile priests seeking better pay, *Piers Plowman*, Prologue, 83–86: see too the friars there, 58–63. His own self-representations are discussed below.

36. Bertha Putnam, "Maximum Wage-Laws for Priests after the Black Death, 1348–1381," *American History Review*, 21 (1915–1916): 12–32: quotes here come from pp. 14 and 15.

37. Ibid., pp. 20–21 and 24.

38. Ibid., p. 25 (*Calendar of Patent Rolls 1364–1367*, 4 September 1364).

39. Poos, *A Rural Society*, p. 229: see chapters 11 and 12; on the incidence of wage-

labor in this part of Essex, chapters 1 and 10; on mobility chapter 8; see too Hilton, *Bond Men*, pp. 171–75, 190–92. This context should highlight the grave inadequacies of modern literary histories which assume that any challenge to "social distinctions" in this period *must* have struck all medieval people as "an impious affront to the ordained order of the universe:" this shows a bizarre ignorance of the number of people actually making such challenges at many different levels of society, rural and urban. The quotation here is from M. Stokes, *Justice and Mercy in Piers Plowman* (London, 1984), p. 211: see too the vehement attack on laborers resisting employers, p. 212, an attack that, presumably, coincided with the attack of the Thatcher government on the sustained strikes in defense of their jobs.

40. Putnam, *Enforcement*, p. 223.

41. Ibid., pp. 3, 156.

42. His vision would have been sharpened by life in one of the greatest North European markets, London: on Langland as "a London poet" see Caroline Barron, chapter 5 in *Chaucer's England*, ed. Barbara A. Hanawalt (Minneapolis, 1992).

43. On this now familiar material, see, for example, Carolyn Dinshaw, *Chaucer's Sexual Politics* (Madison, 1989), Introduction and chapter one; Elaine T. Hansen, *Chaucer and the Fictions of Gender* (Berkeley, 1992); R. H. Bloch, "Medieval Misogyny," *Representations*, 20 (1987): 1–24.

44. Here see, III. 129, IV. 166, III. 131–35. On Mede see especially J. A. Yunck, *The Lineage of Lady Meed* (Notre Dame, 1963).

45. *Wife of Bath's Prologue*, 414, *Riverside Chaucer*, ed. L. D. Benson (Oxford, 1988).

46. See III. 136–69; IV. 47–107; IV. 149–56; IV. 171–76; also Kaeuper, *War*, pp. 334–35.

47. See XIX. 451–53: there is no reason to question the accuracy of the vicar's perceptions here since they accord with what the poet shows us in Passus XIX-XX, XV, VI, II-IV and Prologue; they confirm Holy Church's gloomy observation, I. 5–9.

48. *ST* I-II. 92. 1; II-II. 42. 2; *De Reg*, ch. 3.

49. *Dives and Pauper*, II. 154 (written c. 1405–10: see note 15 for edition used).

50. Ibid., II. 154.

51. Discussed above: Putnam, *Proceedings*, p. cxxv.

52. See B III. 230–58 which is discussed here; the C expansion is substantial and reflects the poet's continuing attempt to deal with the vexed issue, C III. 285–405. On the C version, here much has now been written, but see Janet Coleman, *English Literature in History* (London, 1981), pp. 252–61.

53. *Parson's Tale*, X. 781, 783.

54. Examples of Lollard claims concerning the priesthood of all believers can be found among the East Anglian people rounded up in the persecutions of 1428–31, *Heresy Trials in the Diocese of Norwich, 1428–31*, ed. Norman P. Tanner (London, 1977), pp. 52, 57, 73, 142. On this teaching in Lollardy, see too Anne Hudson, *The Premature Reformation* (Oxford, 1988), pp. 325–27.

55. See III. 255–56: compare Mede at III. 217–18, and Theology at II. 119–23.

56. See Aers, *Community*, pp. 47–49.

57. See *The Anonimalle Chronicle*, ed. V. H. Galbraith (Manchester, 1927), pp. 144–45: at Mile End, he notes, the demands include the following: "et que nulle ne deveroit servire ascune homme mes a sa volunte de mesmes et par covenant taille;" English tr. in Dobson, *Peasants' Revolt*, p. 161.

58. Profound studies of the changes in moral paradigms at issue here are in two books by Alasdair MacIntyre: *After Virtue*, second edition (London, 1985) and *Whose Justice? Which Rationality* (London, 1988).

59. See Middleton, "William Langland's 'Kynde Name' " (cited in note 12) and Lawrence M. Clopper, "Need men and women labor? Langland's wanderer and the labor ordinances," chapter 6 in *Chaucer's England*, ed. Hanawalt.

60. On Haukyn, XIII. 220–XIV. 335.

61. I call it an originary moment to emphasize dissent from James Simpson's view that the poet is here representing "a renewed apostolic Church" in "a renewed society," *Piers Plowman*, p. 223 (similarly, pp. 220, 224). Langland is, however, clear that the passage in question follows immediately on the first pentecost, with Piers now figuring St. Peter, the first and true Pope.

62. Simpson, *Piers Plowman*, p. 224.

63. Ibid., pp. 225 and 224.

64. On this term and its uses in current controversies over the "peasantry" in England, see L. R. Poos, *A Rural Society*, pp. 21 and 43–51.

65. Simpson, *Piers Plowman*, p. 225.

66. Ibid., pp. 225–26.

67. Ibid., pp. 226–27. For examples of the conflicts, see M. James, "Ritual, drama and the social body in the late medieval English town," *Past and Present*, 98 (1983): 3–29; Ruth Bird, *The Turbulent London of Richard II* (London, 1949); R. B. Dobson, "The Risings in York, Beverly and Scarborough," in *The English Rising*, eds. R. Hilton and T. Aston (Cambridge, 1984); on the political force and composition of craft guilds, especially useful is Heather Swanson, *Medieval Artisans* (Oxford, 1989).

68. On this dimension see Swanson (note 67) and Martha Howell, *Women, Production and Patriarchy in Late Medieval Cities* (Chicago, 1986); an excellent introduction here is by Judith Bennett, "Medieval Women, Modern Women: across the great divide," chapter 5 in *Culture and History 1350–1600*, ed. David Aers (Hemel Hempsted, 1992).

69. On this G. Bourquin, *Piers Plowman*, 2 vols. (Lille, 1978), p. 183.

70. Simpson, *Piers Plowman*, pp. 242, 243.

10

Hearing God's Voice: Kind Wit's Call to Labor in Piers Plowman

Louise M. Bishop

When y ȝong was, many ȝer hennes
My fader and my frendes foende me to scole,
Tyl y wyste witterly what holy writ menede
And what is beste for the body, as the boek telleth,
And sykerost for þe soule, by so y wol contenue.
And foend y nere, in fayth, seth my frendes deyede,
Lyf þat me lykede but in this longe clothes.
And yf y be labour sholde lyuen and lyflode deseruen,
That laboure þat y lerned beste þerwith lyuen y sholde.
In eadem vocacione in qua vocati estis. (C.5.35–43)[1]

In this passage, unique to the C-version of *Piers Plowman*, the dreamer, explaining to Reason what work he is best suited to, presents two ways of understanding the propriety of his labor. In one, the dreamer's learning determines what labor he should perform, and thereby earn his living: he has been trained in holy writ and educated to fit the long clothes of the cleric. The biblical citation at the end of the passage, 1 Corinthians 7:20, provides the other explanation: God's call, his "vocation," certifies the dreamer's labor. Langland adds this passage to the C-text to make even clearer through personal example how the voice of God has ordered his narrator's — and his own — clerical labor. Citing one of the two verses in the Vulgate Bible that use the word vocation, the poet grounds his dreamer's training and his labor not only in his understanding of holy writ, but on his apprehension of a divine call to his particular *liflode* ("the means to procure the necessities of life" — *Middle English Dictionary*). God calls the cleric to his livelihood, his vocation.

As this passage indicates, the dreamer's will did not move him towards his clerical vocation. Father and friends provided schooling for the poet-cleric-narrator, who would have entered his vocation early,[2] although not as the result of inheritance, since clerical celibacy precludes hereditary vocations. His ultimate success as a cleric depends on his being educated to hear God's call; and his very nature precludes him from wielding a sickle, as he tells Reason:

> Y am to wayke to worche with sykel or with sythe
> And to long, lef me, lowe to stoupe,
> To wurche as a werkeman eny while to duyren.   (C.5.23–25)

The autobiographical accuracy of this passage is not of primary interest here, but how God's voice constructs clerical labor. The narrator's clerical vocation is the response to a call. The passage's concern with other kinds of labor too, and with determining the propriety of all labor, adds to a far-reaching, multi-leveled metaphor of labor throughout *Piers Plowman*. Does Langland restrict this calling to the clerical vocation? How does he figure or represent God's voice within the poem? Where does God's voice come from, and how does the narrator — and others — hear it?

The Latin *vocatio* originally means "calling," and appears in the Vulgate, 1 Corinthians 7:20, "Unusquique in quo vocatione vocatus est, in ea permaneat," the verse Langland cites in the above passage. English "vouch" and Old French *vocher*, from the same root, approximate the calling used primarily in law, a summons to court.[3] The meaning of vouch as "to call a person to witness" is exemplified by Hoccleve's 1412 *De Regimine Principum*, "God of heuen vouch I to record, þat. . . Thow schalt no cause haue more þus to muse." "Vocation" takes a different route into the language.

"Vocation" first appears in written English in the early fifteenth century, meaning "religious work."[4] At the beginning of the sixteenth century it is used in a completely secularized context to denote any profession.[5] By the end of the fifteenth century, a hundred years after Langland, the role of God's voice in establishing the propriety of clerical labor has disappeared, nor is it used to establish secular work.

Another Middle English word used to translate the Latin *vocatio* is *clepinge*. *Clepen* means "to invite and summon, or to choose," and denotes the multivalent "calling" evident in the Latin *vocatio*.[6] *Clepinge*, unlike the *vocatio*, denotes more than just religious vocation: it implies the voice of God in the ordering of this world and the next. Thus, the *Middle English Dictionary* cites Gower's *Confessio Amantis*: "And tho ben . . . That God of his eleccioun Hath cleped to perfeccioun." The Wyclif Bible provides two examples of "cleping" as "voice of God": 1 Cor. 7:20, "Ech man in what clepyng he is clepid, in that dwelle he"; and Ephesians 4:1, "byseche that ȝe walke worthily in the clepinge in which ȝe ben clepid, with al mekenesse,"[7] both translating the Latin *vocatione*.

Langland uses *clepen* to denote religious calling. Even Christ is *cleped*, as Langland recounts the miracle at the marriage feast at Cana, the beginning of Christ's ministry.

> So at þat feest first as I bifore tolde
> Bigan god of his grace and goodnesse to dowel,
> And þanne was he cleped and called noȝt oonly crist but Iesu,
> A fauntkyn ful of wit, *filius Marie*. (B.19.115–18)[8]

Notice that Christ is *cleped* to his ministry, while he is called (named) Jesus. *Clepen* provides more than an alliterative formula: it reveals God's voice in Christ's vocation, his ministry.

Elsewhere in *Piers Plowman* Langland does not limit God's voice to the religious calling; *clepinge* is not lexically restricted, as *vocatio* is, to religious labor. The larger circle of labors is represented in the poem, as Langland deals with all three estates and the errors within them.[9] The voice of God in *Piers Plowman* calls all labor, designates all *liflodes*, and, in the poem's later dreams, all of creation. The verses from the Wyclif Bible quoted above resound with the measure, order, and range of labors that Langland portrays, noting the fittedness, measure and right running of the universe when creation is attuned to its calling.[10] Langland notes such fittedness when Patience instructs Hawkin the Active Man in the fifth dream; Patience's apostrophe to Creation in Passus 14 connects *liflode* with the life of all creatures, from the worm to the fish and birds:

> For lent neuere was lif but liflode were shapen,
> Wherof or wherfore or wherby to libbe:
> First þe wilde worm vnder weet erþe,
> Fissh to lyue in þe flood and in þe fir þe Criket,
> The Corlew by kynde of þe Eyr, moost clennest flessh of briddes,
> And bestes by gras and by greyn and by grene rootes,

In menynge þat alle men my3te þe same
Lyue þoru3 leel bileue, as our lord witnesseþ:
Quodcumque pecieritis a patre in nomine meo &c; Et alibi, Non in
solo pane viuit homo set in omni verbo quod procedit de ore dei.
(B.14. 39–46)

Thus all creation has a *liflode* to earn the three "necessities," established by Truth in the first dream, and explained to the Dreamer by Lady Holy Church:

And comaunded of his curteisie in commune þree þynges:
Are none nedfulle but þo; and nempne hem I þynke.
And rekene hem by reson: reherce þow hem after.
That oon is vesture from chele þee to saue;
That oþer is mete at meel for mysese of þiselue;
And drynke whan þee drieþ ac do it no3t out of reson
That þow worþe þe wers whan þow werche sholdest. (B.1.20–26)

Labor and *liflode* are divinely ordained through God's voice. How does creation hear that voice? In the first dream of the B-text (Prologue and Passus 1 through 4) Langland describes the pursuit of Truth as an occupation, a *liflode*. He then details the abuse of Truth in subsequent dreams. In the second dream, Hunger, motivator for labor, gives Piers his account of all earthly labor:

Kynde wit wolde þat ech wi3t wro3te,
Or wiþ techynge or tellynge or trauaillynge of hondes,
Contemplatif lif or Actif lif; crist wolde it als. (B.6.247–9)

For Langland, the agent of the call, the voice of God, is Kind Wit. Kind Wit, an amalgam of natural instinct and human reason, negotiates the distance between the heavenly and the earthly by an internal mechanism of "knowing." The distance between the heavenly and the earthly is the operating room of *Piers Plowman*, and of Kind Wit: this formula suits the dream vision genre itself, as dreams operate in an intermediate space between the conscious and unconscious.[11] As such, Kind Wit, identified with the voice of God, establishes through an internal call all occupations, estates and labors. Langland uses God's voice to establish the propriety of not only clerical labor, but of all earthly labors through the agency of Kind Wit.

The three necessities — food, drink, and clothing — are earned through "work," through labor. Yet observation in the fourteenth century, like today, shows that these necessities are not distributed equally. How are these necessities apportioned? Surely not simply through manual labor, or the rector, who does not work with his hands, procures the three necessities as a parasite.[12] Rather, the labor of the clergy must be elevated to a "higher calling" through Kind Wit's agency in establishing the three estates. The tension among the means to procure the necessities of life, the status accorded those who labor in various ways to procure those necessities, and the clergy's special "calling" prompts Langland to focus his poem on the religious *liflode*, the religious calling, with all the uncertainty such a calling involves.

The figure in the poem who listens most attentively to Kind Wit's call is Piers the Plowman. Piers, of course, is as central to the poem as the narrator, and Piers's labor provides the nexus from which all discussions of human labor emanate. Elizabeth Kirk remarks on Langland's invention of a positive, rather than negative, social icon in Piers, and his new valorization of manual labor.[13] Stephen Barney certifies the important metaphoric connection between preaching and plowing in exegesis and sermons:

> In medieval literature the hard heart is likened to an untilled field, the truth to be spread to seed, the virtue which follows from a life of faith to a fruitful tree, the act of spreading the word to sowing, the act of preparing the heart to receive the word to plowing.[14]

In his exploration of the symbolic context of a preacher-plowman, Barney connects plowing and manual labor to preaching, and shows Langland using a metaphor that connects the labor of the hands with the labor of the educated tongue. This metaphor implies that God's voice calls the cleric who labors as He calls the plowman to earn his *liflode*. The preacher uses the word of God, holy writ, to preach with his plowshare; he is called to this labor, as the plowman is called to his. In the figure of Piers, then, we have the naturalization of an ideology of human labor constructed around the voice of God.

Despite Kind Wit's ministrations, the voice of God is sometimes ignored. Subsequent dreams narrate abuses of an idealized vision of labor, from the insincerity of the "faitours" (B.6.121) to the pomposity of the Doctour eating the high-cholesterol diet he hasn't earned (B.13.60–63). The tension Langland explores pits the ideal — figured in God's omnipresent voice delivered by Kind Wit, establishing the estates — against the way God's earthly representatives, the clergy, sometimes abuse the call. The word used to denote order, *clepinge*, can also denote the earthly abuse of Kind Wit. In the third dream, once Dame Study has upbraided Wit for throwing pearls before swine (B.10.9–10), she continues by detailing the abuse of truth and wit for personal gain.

> "I seye by þo" quod she, "þat sheweþ by hir werkes
> That hem were leuere lond and lordshipe on erþe,
> Or richesse or rentes, and reste at hir wille,
> Than alle þe sooþ sawes þat Salomon seide euere.
> Wisdom and wit now is noȝt worþ a risshe
> But it be carded wiþ coueitise as cloþeres don hir wolle.
> That kan construe deceites and conspire wronges
> And lede forþ a loueday to lette þe truþe,
> That swiche craftes konne to counseil are cleped;
> Thei lede lordes wiþ lesynges and bilieþ truþe.   (B.10.13–22)

Wit has lost its place, and Kind Wit calls no one; rather, temporal lords implicitly call those with the craft of deception and conspiracy to counsel. The internalized Kind Wit's call is parodied: here the lords are called by covetise rather than charity.

Langland's invective against the clergy motivates narrative events, such as the trial of Lady Meed in the first dream (Passus 2–4), notably figured within another call associated with clerics, the call to law; but the very structure of *Piers Plowman* firmly connects the poem to the clerical *liflode* of sermon and penance. Langland replicates the mode of the penitential so the poem can replicate the livelihood of the clergy. The penitential literature of the fourteenth century, like John Acton's *Septuplum*, includes not only the seven deadly sins in a form similar to their confessions in B.5, but also reveals the emergence of the individual subject, the "who" which is added to the legal formulae of questioning penitents. Acton's book is divided into the same types of persons as the field of folk.[15] By using the clergy's own formulae Langland analyzes the clerical life, in its command to preach, as a social engine responding to Kind Wit's call. The clerical life should combine the individual with the divine, the theoretical with the actual, as the clergy are not only themselves "called," but must themselves call—preach—and ventriloquize the voice of God to the other estates.

The other question plaguing the issue of vocation is how to know the call of God, and the penitential literature naturally implicates Conscience, a major figure in the poem. The third dream's remarkable trio of mental faculties — Thought (Passus 8), Wit (Passus 9), and Imaginative (Passus 12) — distinguishes the pathway of Kind Wit's call. Langland anatomizes the mental faculties because they are the means for knowing the call: put another way, the mental faculties provide Kind Wit his vehicle. Furthermore, these allegorized mental processes are part and parcel of clergy's labor. The preacher's labor requires Thought, Wit, and Imaginative; his role as guide through penance necessitates the Thought, Wit, and Imaginative of the penitent. In Patience's disquisition, penance is the means by which Kind Wit, through the idealized clergy, calls the various *liflodes*. Penance, like the dream vision, connects the heavenly with the earthly. In this space, the penitential "who" — the individual — becomes paramount. For Langland, Thought is the self, as the Dreamer reports in Passus 8:[16]

> A muche man me þouȝte, lik to myselue,
> Cam and called me by my kynde name.
> "What art þow," quod I þo, "þat my name knowest?"
> "That þow woost wel," quod he, "and no wiȝt bettre."
> "Woot I?" quod I; "who art þow?" "þou ȝt," seide he þanne.
>   (B.8.70–74)

Thought is "lik to myselue": Thought is the pathway of the call, Kind Wit's conduit, and Thought is the Dreamer, the "I" of the poem, and thus its narrator.

Thusfar we have seen Langland dealing with God's voice in the clergy and in the individual. The way Langland uses the mechanism of "God's voice" reveals "the call" as social praxis of the sort outlined by Louis Althusser in "Ideology and Ideological State Apparatuses." In that respect, the call, while attached to particular "professions," serves as a foundational social mechanism, both within the class structure and outside it, conscious and unconscious.

> It is not their real conditions of existence, their real world, that men "represent to themselves" in ideology, but above all it is their relation to those conditions of existence which is represented to them there. It is this relation which is at the centre of every ideological, i.e. imaginary, representation of the real world. It is this relation that contains the "cause" which has to explain the imaginary distortion of the ideological representation of the real world. . . .[17]

The "cause" is labor; the imaginary represention is Kind Wit; the individual hears Kind Wit through Thought. According to Althusser the always already existing ideology is recognized by its subjects in the process of "hailing": "all ideology hails or interpellates concrete individuals as concrete subjects, by the functioning of the category of the subject."[18] "Hearing the call" is indeed the foundation of the division of labor, the foundation of "vocation," as it identifies the subject and internalizes its own mechanism.

The "call," then, in this broader sense, formulates itself in Thought — the individual conscience and its attendant penance — and in Kind Wit, which portrays itself as natural instinct and human reason. Kind Wit insures the success of this ideology of work, of the three estates and clergy's position especially as "the called." In the social and religious turmoil which characterizes the fourteenth century, Langland responds by naturalizing his metaphor for work, making it internal and inescapable. Langland's metaphor responds to what has upset the order of labor, the possibility of rebellion, as noted in David Aers's discussion of Thomas of Wimbledon's 1388 sermon:

> For ȝif presthod lacked þe puple for defaute of knowyng of Goddis Lawe [law being for Althusser a sign of subjectivity] shulde wexe wilde on vices and deie gostly. . . . And ȝif laboreris weren not, boþe prestis and knyȝtis mosten bicome acremen and heerdis, and ellis þey sholde for defaute of bodily sustenaunce deie.[19]

The voice of God is breathed into life: a voice to be heard, one implicated in the current ideology but which pretends to transcend it. In Althusser's words, "What really takes place in ideology seems therefore to take place outside it."[20] The call to labor is from God; it is heard within the individual who is, inescapably, a member of the whole society. The connection of subjectivity and labor, then, is created: the individual hears, through Kind Wit, the divine call to labor. "The reproduction of the relations of production can therefore only be a class undertaking. It is realized through a class struggle which counterposes the ruling class and the exploited class."[21] Langland strikes a mediating position between the classes in his preacher-plowman Piers; like the dream vision itself, this intermediary position attempts to negotiate social and theological distinctions, such as the division of labor, while at the same time it supports the ideology of a transcendant God's voice.

Thought is Kind Wit's vehicle for bringing the call to the individual, but the question of recognition, of "knowing" the call, still looms. Querulous clergy complicate the theoretical ease of Kind Wit's division of labor, "techynge or tellynge or trauaillynge of hondes": their garb, "this longe clothes," "signs" their labor, as the badge identifies the pilgrim, or the plow the farmer, or the millstone the miller.[22] But what provides the mark of the "true" calling of God? The necessity of the "marc," the "tokyn," comes from the social practice of identification, and false ascription motivates Langland's diatribe against the "wastours," those with false marks.[23] Such earthly impersonation disrupts heavenly harmony. For Langland the identifying mark results from labor: the labor of the pilgrimage, the labor of the plow, the labor of the clergy. For a poet like Langland, a producer of words, Kind Wit's call motivates holy words. But are all who write called? Conversely, are those who cannot write denied the call?

Critics have noticed not only Langland's satire on those who follow a religious vocation[24] but also *Piers Plowman*'s own difficult relationship to learning.[25] For the fourteenth century, vocation and education are related: to be an educated (i.e., literate) person in the Middle Ages is to be a member of orders. To read is to read of God. The Church owns writing and preaching. But as literacy moves through the culture, and as the culture itself changes in response to a rapidly changing social order, words become a commodity, and the production of words becomes a form of labor. Learning cannot alone serve as the pathway to the call: God's voice must always already be present via Kind Wit. For Langland, Kind Wit calls the laborer, whose labor itself "signs" his profession. Langland's poem, a product of labor, claims that all vocations are internally knowable, signable and ordained. His satire, while directed against those who fail their calling, attempts to recognize the track that can validate the call: the ability with words, God-given to the called. Langland attempts to vitiate hierarchy (as noted by Kirk and others): at times he does not want the call to elevate the priest, the monk, and the friar. Piers remains the preacher-plowman. Langland wants to subvert the extant hierarchy while at the same time underline the legitimacy of his own "vocation" as poet, and to identify the called with something new, a divinely-called preacher-plowman, and a divinely-called poet-cleric-narrator whose poem is his sign.

The signs of the call, the "tokyns" for surety, are the visions, the dreams of *Piers Plowman*, the call the dreamer creates, but naturalizes as recognition in order to verify his vocation. The dreamer reacts to the call, at both the beginning and end of the seventh dream, Passus 19, by writing what he has seen. He puts on paper the words of his vision; his labor, the response to the call, produces the poem. The plowshare of the tongue provides the *liflode* of preaching; the *liflode* of the poet resides in his written poem, the result of his call to labor. This grounding

of the metaphor for the poet's labor helps explain Wit's metaphor for
the Trinity as hand, pen and paper, in the third dream:

> Ac man is hym moost lik of marc and of shape,
> For þoruȝ þe word þat he warp[26] woxen forþ beestes,
> And al at his wil was wrouȝt wiþ a speche,
> *Dixit & facta sunt,*
> Saue man þat he made ymage to hymself,
> And Eue of his ryb bon wiþouten any mene.
> For he was synguler hymself and seide *faciamus*
> As who seiþ, "moore moot herto þan my word oone;
> My myȝt moot helpe forþ wiþ my speche."
> Right as a lord sholde make lettres; if hym lakked parchemyn,
> Thouȝ he wiste to write neuer so wel, and he hadde a penne,
> The lettre, for al þe lordshipe, I leue, were neuere ymaked.
>
> (B.9.32–41)

The holy ghost is the paper, the work of words is the physical product,
the "tokyn," if you will, that demonstrates the validity of the call. For
the poet, the poem and the call are identified with each other.

Commodification appears in the legal profession as well as the clerical, as Langland shows in Grace's arming the defenders of Unity again
in the seventh dream, Passus 19:

> And gaf ech man a grace to gide wiþ hymseluen
> That ydelnesse encombre hym noȝt, enuye ne pride:
> *Divisiones graciarum sunt &c.*
> Some wyes he yaf wit with wordes to shewe,
> To wynne wiþ truþe þat þe world askeþ,
> As prechours and preestes and Prentices of lawe:
> They lelly to lyue by labour of tonge,
> And by wit to wissen oþere as grace hem wolde teche.
> And some he kennede craft and konnynge of sighte,
> By sellynge and buggynge hir bilyue to wynne.   (B.19.227–235)

Kind Wit "wolde þat ech wiȝte wroȝte" (B.6.247); allied with Kind
Wit, Grace gives each word-laborer immediate understanding of his
liflode. The preachers, priests, and apprentices of the law, those who
labor with words, receive wit and "wynne wiþ truþe," earn their
livelihood through truth. "Giving" implies the direct call, something
directly apprehended, immediate, without mediation. Craft and cunning come from the gift of Grace, and surely Grace is identified with
God: the gifts of craft and cunning set the stage for all medieval labors.

But Grace specifically directs his gift to those who labor for belief — the logos — resulting in the "labour of the tonge," the commodification of words. Furthermore, if we are sensitive to the legal dimensions of such an ordering of labor, we see metaphoric connections among the calling to the religious life, the calling to court for the vouching of a surety, and the *clepinge* of social order itself. The call delimits labor as social order, as Althusser says.

The written word provides the token of the tongue's labor: the sermon book, the legal register, the poem. In helping to form his society's metaphor of vocation, Langland connects Kind Wit's call to the logos and to the self. Social organization is thus intimately bound to the veracity of the call, of the vocation of words. Langland, clearly concerned with social organization, reminds us in his alliterative formula of those who purvey words — preacher, priest, and 'prentices of the law — all three of which, it could be argued, describe Langland, who is preaching his poem. The Word comes into its own as a product of labor.

Langland attaches the call not only to the clerical but to the legal sphere in the triad of plowmen, priest, and 'prentices, those who labor with words and who hear and transmit the call. To this day we use the phrase "called to the bar," and the legal profession, growing up as it did in the late-fourteenth and early fifteenth centuries, uses this pregnant metaphor to portray itself. Althusser sees law as a dominant vehicle for ideology:

> Even if it only appears under this name (the subject) with the rise of bourgeois ideology, above all with the rise of legal ideology, the category of the subject . . . is the constitutive category of all ideology, whatever its determination (regional or class) and whatever its historical date — since ideology has no history."[27]

The call originates in ideology, especially as ideology informs law. Law, like Kind Wit, is often associated with instinct and reason, as in the opening chapters of the twelfth-century jurist Bracton and also in Gratian's *Decretum*.[28] But law's earthly practitioners abuse law's instinctual ideals, as the clergy abuses Kind Wit's call. The call can be ventriloquized by a bad king, by bad clergy, and by bad lawyers.

The ideal laborer, Piers the Plowman, embodies Kind Wit's call. What distinguishes Piers, however, is not simply his idealization. Piers, as the plowman-preacher, can be seen as a mystic, as having received a direct call from God, as hearing God's voice unmediated by

Kind Wit's agency. The metaphor of preaching and plowing as Langland figures it includes this mystical aspect. The discourse of the mystic and the prophet justifies the individualized, external call of God, which explains why Langland writes the mystical and prophetic so powerfully into the texture of the poem.[29] Regarding *Piers Plowman* in relation to mysticism and mystical practices, while not new, is not universally approved.[30] Despite reservations, however, the current interest in female mystics, especially in the Beguine movement, informs an analysis of how Langland deals with the verity of the "call."[31] The Beguines stand out because they are contemporary with Langland, they are connected to the Lollards, and they form a kind of ideal society based on manual labor and craft, such as weaving.[32] They also valorize the mystical experience and the direct apprehension of the divine. Insofar as their communities value manual labor, form independent, well-run, economically-viable centers (though not as small as a half-acre, I imagine), and value direct access to God's voice as enjoyed by the mystic, the Beguines provide a model for the right-running society with the called mystic at its base.

The call, the vocation, obligates the called to preach and to write. *Piers Plowman* identifies Kind Wit's call and recognizes the connection between labor and words. While "vocation" loses its exclusive associations with the religious life and its aspect of God's voice by the sixteenth century, its association with God's voice remains strong in Langland's poem and serves as a powerful metaphor for the "instinct" of labor. "Institutional legitimacy," as Anne Middleton calls it in referring to the mendicant/monastic debate, motivates "the call," and what kind of power the call gives the called. The call, both external and internal, cannot be escaped — this is Langland's audacious proposal, as audacious in its time as the valorization of the plowman. But the scriptural antecedents, the mystical *via* as the result of a call, and the way Langland anticipates professionalism, all point to the *vox* of God, Kind Wit's call, and the labor of the poet.

NOTES

1. William Langland, *Piers Plowman: An Edition of the C-text*, ed. Derek Pearsall (Berkeley and Los Angeles, 1979). All references to the C-text are from this edition.

2. It is implied that the poet-cleric-narrator entered his religious training early, which in the fourteenth century would normally have been the case: the minimum age for tonsure, the first of the minor orders, is eight; for the second, acolyte, the minimum age is fifteen; the minimum age for ordination as priest is twenty-four. See D. N. Lepine, "The Origins and Careers of the Canons of Exeter Cathedral 1300–1455," in *Religious Belief and Ecclesiastical Careers in Late Medieval*

England, ed. Christopher Harper-Bill (Woodbridge, Suffolk, 1991), pp. 89, 99.

3. According to the *Oxford English Dictionary*, "vouch" means "to cite, to call, or summon (a person) into court to give warranty of title." I am indebted to Paul Hyams for pointing out to me the connection between Latin *voco* and the English "vouch."

4. "1. The action on the part of God of calling a person to exercise some special function, especially of a spiritual nature, or to fill a certain position; divine influence or guidance towards a definite (especially religious) career; the fact of being so called or directed towards a special work in life; natural tendency to, or fitness for, such work," citing Lydgate's English translation of De Guilleville's *Pélerinage des ames* (1426), also to be cited in the *Middle English Dictionary*, vocacioun, l. 10808: "thapostles . . . As parfyt pylgrymes in ther way By choys and by ellecioun And also by vocacioun [F par sa vocation] . . . kam to hym." The *MED* also cites Henry VI, writing to the Bishop of Hereford in 1442: "Considre youre vocacion to youre said cure, not by you desired, but at the instans of oure noble progenitor after youre worth and holy labores." Paul Schaffner, who kindly shared this preliminary unpublished information with me, notes that the same document "Later refers to the same action as 'so gracyouse a callyng'." *Vocacioun* is thus used to mean specifically religious vocation. The meaning of vocation as the voice of God calling one to a "state of salvation" appears in Wynkyn De Worde's 1506 edition of *The Ordynarye of Crysten Men*.

5. For "2 b. One's ordinary occupation, business or profession," the *OED* cites Thomas Wilson's 1553 *The arte of rhetorique*, "By vocation of life a souldier is counted a great bragger, and a vaunter of hymselfe." Interestingly, the *OED* cites as 3 b. "The action, on the part of an ecclesiastical body, of calling a person to the ministry or to a particular office or charge in the Church," citing the 1578 *Second Book of Discipline*. In other words, by the mid-sixteenth century, what had been the word's primary meaning now needs special signifiers to denote any religious associations. Before the sixteenth century, such delineation would have been unnecessary.

6. *Clepinge* meaning calling or destiny is frequently associated with religious labor. *Vices and Virtues* (c.1200) notes the "sweet calling" for which one abandons the world, and takes upon himself Christ's mark: "For ðessere swete clepinge . . . lateð al ðe woreld, and nimeð Cristes marc uppen hem." This early use contrasts strikingly with another, contemporary with Langland's, from *The Cloud of Unknowing*, in which the author questions the token whereby the true calling of God is known: "By what o tokyn . . . ay I raþest wite . . . wheþer þis growyng desire þat I fele . . . be verely a clepyng of God to a more specyal worching of grace." For the late twelfth-century, early thirteenth-century author of *Vices and Virtues*, the "taking of Christ's mark" is apparent, indisputable, analogous to the right working of the universe, whereas by the turn of the fifteenth century the token of such a calling is unclear and ambiguous, and what seemed sweet must now verify its specialness.

7. 1 Cor. 7:20 reads "Uniusque in quo vocatione vocatus est, in ea permaneat"; at Ephesians 4:1 the Vulgate reads "Obsecro itaque vos ego vinctus in Domino, ut digne ambuletis vocatione, qua vocati estis."

8. All quotations from *Piers Plowman: The B Version*, ed. George Kane and E. Talbot Donaldson (London, 1975), unless otherwise noted.

9. The first place to look for definitions of professions when dealing with *Piers Plowman* is estates satire. Jill Mann, *Chaucer and Medieval Estates Satire* (Cambridge, 1973) delineates "social and occupational classes" (p. 3). As central issues of *Piers Plowman* criticism, poverty, manual labor, and class struggle are the subjects of David Aers, "*Piers Plowman*: Poverty, Work, and Community," Chpt. 1 in his *Community, Gender, and the Individual Identity: English Writing 1360–1430* (London and New York, 1988), pp. 20–72; on class conflict in the network of relations among the estates, see pp. 7–8, 36–40). See also Paul Strohm, *Social Chaucer* (Cambridge, Mass.,

1989), for the reality of estates in the fourteenth century, and also Allen J. Frantzen, "Prologue," and Britton J. Harwood, "The Plot of *Piers Plowman* and the Contradictions of Feudalism," in *Speaking Two Languages*, ed. Frantzen (Albany, 1991).

10. While others have noted the wrong running of the estates that Langland emphasizes in his satiric Visio, and while I agree with Aers' reading of Langland's conflict with received ideology, I here note *Piers Plowman*'s description of theoretical perfection as an anticipation of a coming ideal time: see Kathryn Kerby-Fulton, *Reformist, Apocalypticism and Piers Plowman* (Cambridge, 1990). Like her, I see these strands not as direct copying of source material, but still evident in the fabric of the poem (pp. 13–18).

11. Such a distinction perfectly suits the dream vision genre, and alludes to the dispute among medieval dream theorists about the quality of the mental faculties' operation during dreaming. See Steven Kruger's *Dreaming in the Middle Ages* (Cambridge, 1992) for a collection of the dream lore of the Middle Ages and an interpretation of its effect on the dream vision genre.

12. "The nature of the combination [of means to an income] would have serious consequences for the incumbent [rector], bringing to the fore basic tension within his position: that while he had a position of considerable status within the parish, and one of considerable latent power, he was nevertheless dependent on the parishioners for his livelihood, was essentially parasitic." Robert N. Swanson, "Standards of Livings: Parochial Revenues in Pre-Reformation England," in *Religious Belief*, p. 162.

13. "Langland's Plowman and the Recreation of Fourteenth-Century Religious Metaphor," *Yearbook of Langland Studies* 2 (1988): 1–21: "In other words, two of the most important innovative religious movements of the later Middle Ages [the Cistercians and the Franciscans], in striking contrast to more general social and literary attitudes, attributed major value to manual work as such, at least if undertaken voluntarily, and even considered it, under the conditions of such a vocation, as a centrally enabling condition of a redeemed life." (p. 18); she connects Langland's Piers to this development.

14. Stephen A. Barney, "The Plowshare of the Tongue: The Progress of a Symbol from the Bible to *Piers Plowman*," *Mediaeval Studies* 35 (1973): 276.

15. Michael J. Haren, "Social Ideas in Pastoral Literature of Fourteenth-Century England," in *Religious Belief*, pp. 45–46.

16. Thought has been traditonally understood, as Pearsall explains in his note to C.10.68, as "the first in a series of personifications who represent aspects of the dreamer's own mind and developing understanding; the first two, *Thoughte* and *Wit*, being innate, are portrayed as the dreamer's doubles." Such individuation as Thought provides also fits perfectly with Althusser's position of the "idea" in "ideology," of the idea/ideology as creating the individual: Langland would of course recognize himself in thought.

17. *Lenin and Philosophy and Other Essays*, trans. Ben Brewster (New York and London, 1971), p. 164. I am indebted to Clare Lees for this helpful insight.

18. Ibid., p. 173.

19. Aers, *Community*, pp. 7–8.

20. Althusser, p. 175. Althusser's assessment of the family's place in ideology supports Aers in *Community*, pp. 52–53: "Before its birth, the child is therefore always already a subject, appointed as a subject in and by the specific familial ideological configuration in which it is expected once it has been conceived."

21. Ibid., p. 184.

22. He bar a burdoun ybounde wiþ a brood liste,
     In a wiþwynde[s] wise ywounden aboute.
     A bolle and a bagge he bar by his syde.
     An hundred of Ampulles on his hat seten,

Signes of Synay and shelles of Galice,
And many crouch on his cloke and keyes of Rome,
And þe vernycle bifore, for men sholde knowe
And se bi hise signes whom he sou зt hadde. (B. 5. 517–25)

Open announcement and visual sign are woven into the texture of medieval society. Such openness is also apparent in the legal sphere, as evidenced in the word *apertly*, defined by John Alford in his *Glossary of Legal Diction* (Cambridge, 1988), as "clearly, plainly; also openly, without secrecy or concealment," p. 6.

23. Aers has "unpacked" these pretenders from the Prologue and Passus 10 in *Community*, pp. 36–37, revealing Langland's vexed relationship to them. The following observations are directly related to Aers' argument in *Community* that the turmoil in the fourteenth century's social institutions, and the turmoil within Langland's poem, reflect one another in their efforts to negotiate the labor nexus, as figured in the disquisition on *wastours*, pp. 20–53.

24. Penn R. Szittya, *The Antifraternal Tradition in Medieval Literature* (Princeton, 1986).

25. James Simpson, "The Role of *Scientia* in *Piers Plowman*," in *Medieval English Religious and Ethical Literature: Essays in Honour of G. H. Russell*, ed. G. Kratzmann and James Simpson (Cambridge, 1986), pp. 49–65.

26. *Warp* is alternatively *spak* in thirteen manuscripts, according to Kane and Donaldson.

27. Althusser explains "legal ideology" in a note: "Which borrowed the legal category of 'subject in law' to make an ideological notion: man is by nature a subject."

28. See the opening chapters of Bracton's *De Legibus et Consuetudinibus Angliae* (Cambridge, Mass., 1968–77) and Distinction One in James Gordley and Augustine Thompson's forthcoming edition of Gratian's *Decretum* (Catholic University of America Press, to appear in 1994). I am grateful to Fr. Thompson for sharing his edition proofs with me.

29. J. J. Jusserand, *Piers Plowman: A Contribution to the History of English Mysticism* (rpt. New York, 1965); Elizabeth Salter, "Piers Plowman and the Pilgrimage to Truth," in *Middle English Survey: Critical Essays*, ed. Edward Vasta (Notre Dame, 1965), pp. 195–215; Morton Bloomfield, *Piers Plowman as a Fourteenth-Century Apocalypse* (New Brunswick, N. J., 1961); David Aers, "Langland, Apocalypse and the *Saeculum*," chapter 3 in his *Chaucer, Langland, and the Creative Imagination* (London, 1980); and most recently Kerby-Fulton, who demonstrates the ineluctable connection between apocalypticism and mysticism as figured in what she terms the "reformist apocalypticism" of the fourteenth century, pp. 9–19, and "visionary" literature, pp. 76–132.

30. Referring to *The Spiritual Basis of Piers Plowman*, Derek Pearsall notes in *An Annotated Critical Bibliography of Langland* (Ann Arbor, 1990), "Vasta surely exaggerates the mystical element in *Piers Plowman*."

31. Kerby-Fulton's book is a masterful thesis on prophecy and mysticism (what she calls "the visionary") in *Piers Plowman*; her discussion centers primarily on Hildegard of Bingen and Joachim of Fiore. She does mention St. Bridget of Sweden and, in passing, the Brigittine order, but deals little with the Beguines and Beghards. On the history of the Beguines and the Beghards, see Edward W. McDonnell, *The Beguines and Beghards in Medieval Culture* (New Brunswick, N. J., 1954) and Jean-Claude Schmitt, *Mort d'une hérésie: L'église et les clercs face aux béguines et aux béghards du Rhin supérieur du XIVe au XVe siècle* (Paris, 1978).

32. Schmitt points out that records of the Beguines' "travail manuel" are lacking for the early period, but that by the mid-fifteenth century there was enough production to anger the local guilds. He notes for the Cologne *béguinage* in 1452 "une production textile variée et abondante: tissus de lin, filés, et tissus de soie, voiles mortuaires, draps liturgiques, voiles de religieuses, broderies" (p. 49).

11

DEFINING THE SERVANT: LEGAL AND EXTRA-LEGAL TERMS OF EMPLOYMENT IN FIFTEENTH-CENTURY ENGLAND

Madonna J. Hettinger

History seldom offers neat dividing lines between old and new attitudes toward such issues as work, identity, or status. Even such cataclysmic events as widespread famine or plague cannot serve as precise markers separating the traditional from the forward-thinking. While some elements of the population responded to the crises of the fourteenth century by embracing change, others responded by retrenching in familiar economic arrangements and social controls. Survivors of such disasters as the Black Death were not met by any medieval equivalent of the modern opinion poll-taker, eager to measure public views on labor and the changing relationships between masters and servants as the economy of scarce land and resources that predominated in pre-plague England was replaced by the economic challenges and opportunities of the late fourteenth century. If such evidence did exist, we might find that our modern questions about popular attitudes toward terms of employment in a time of shifting social and economic structures would be matched by medieval uncertainties about those same social re-alignments. Public opinion and private motives were as complex then as now.[1] Certainly, mobility and an increased demand for their services put skilled and unskilled laborers in a new bargaining position after 1348. It is equally clear that employers, ranging from small producers to the social-climbing gentry and the masters of significant urban enterprises, battled with wage earners and with each other in the scramble to reclaim a ready labor force.[2] What is less apparent is how this battle was part of a larger campaign to realign the social ranks and establish new social and legal definitions for "those who work." While the late fourteenth century witnessed social revolt on a grand scale in the Peasants' Revolt of 1381, the measures taken to quell that rebellion did little to address the tensions produced in daily disputes over wages and terms of employment. The continued calls for stricter enforcement of the Statute of Laborers in the generations after the revolt suggest that these employment disputes remained central to the struggle for order in the fifteenth century.

The hostilities between servants and masters in fifteenth-century England took place in several arenas. The most obvious and the most elusive of these battlegrounds is of course the household or place of employment itself. Our knowledge of what transpired in the employer's private realm is limited to the reports we have of instances when those disputes spilled out into the community and into the courts. Local courts and the Chancery itself were the public stages for the more advanced levels of labor disputes. By the term "extra-legal" in the title of this study, I do indeed intend a play on words. The measures implemented by both parties in servant-master disputes often used an extra helping of the legal system to go outside the intent of the law, a practice that some litigants seem to have raised to a fine art in the maze of corruptible local courts and disputed jurisdictions of late medieval England. It is through those extra-legal methods of resolving or perpetuating a dispute over terms of employment that we witness the most vigorous arguments on the proper position of the servant.

It is not the ambition of this study to define the servant. Rather, I want to look at the ways in which the government, employers, and servants themselves used the law to name, protect, restrict, and recognize — in other words to define — at least a segment of the growing class of free wage earners that emerged from the upheavals of the fourteenth century as a visible and vocal economic force. [3]

At the risk of stating my case too strongly at the beginning, I want to explore how the position of the servant was negotiated in post-plague England. On the part of the government and employers the intent of these contractual negotiations was to control the economic and political potential of a class relatively, but only very recently, free of the traditional constraints of servitude and/or poverty that had governed their lives before the Black Death. Conversely, servants negotiated their new positions in the post-plague social structure with an eye toward making the most of economic opportunities while maneuvering the shaky new ground of legal freedom.

Half of the task of exploring the relations between masters and servants is relatively straightforward. There is a variety of documents that reflect contract negotiations taking place on an individual level. Certainly the Chancery documents I use in this study illuminate the potential for misunderstanding or plainly malicious deception in every contract between employer and employee. I would like to take the issue further, however, by examining how those individual negotiations, and more pertinently the disputes over those contractual arrangements, reflected a larger social, perhaps even cultural, interest in defining the servant and encouraging wage earners to attach themselves to masters by means of annual contracts. This interest, I would argue, reflected a need to create a legal and economic place for a significant fraction of the population whose traditionally ordained place in medieval society simply did not work in the new economy. In other words, how did the employer's ostensibly economic interests converge with the government's ostensibly legal interests in the movement to place and keep servants, and in fact all types of wage earners, in standard contracts of service?

Servants, of course, are not an invention of the fifteenth century. Legal and economic developments, however, combined to make free but contractually attached servants the preferred arrangement, in both agricultural and urban households, from the late fourteenth century through the Tudor period.[4] Just as they are not an invention of the fifteenth century, neither are servants a narrow category in late-medieval England. The language of service was broadly applied to armed retainers as well as to low-paid, low-prestige domestic or agricultural help. For the purpose of this essay I will concentrate primarily on servants of low prestige engaged in households of relatively small size, although the circumstances of some cases suggest a household of the gentry. Kate Mertes has investigated the issue of the English noble household and its extensive retinue. Mertes very effectively argues that an image of the noble household drawn from accounts reflecting the organization of the royal household would be biased.[5] Similarly, I would assert that any picture of the middling urban or agricultural household would be deeply flawed by framing it in the language of service and loyalty that is more properly applied to the community of the noble household Mertes has so carefully defined. For the servant in the non-aristocratic household, service was part of a system of employment involving wages and contracts, not part of a system of patronage distinguished by livery and arms. While some of these contractual servants brought special skills into the household, many were unskilled workers whose appraised value and assigned tasks might vary widely from one yearly contract of service to the next, thus providing incentive to be on the look-out for more favorable terms of employment.

Because of the employers' growing preference for contractual service as a system of employment, I think it is also important to reverse the question of economic and legal interests: what interests did servants themselves have in establishing a standard understanding of the term "servant" and the terms of service? How did they use the label "servant" to claim a legal identity and legal protection? How did they use "servant" as a legal category to claim a minimum standard of treatment while in service?

In some respects, the interests of employers and the interests of the government (and to a much lesser degree the interests of wage earners) have already been spelled out in previous studies of labor and labor law in late fourteenth-century England.[6] Application of the labor laws in the fifteenth century, however, remains unexplored. Medieval historians have approached labor issues primarily as economic questions. In the context of England's demographic crises of the fourteenth century, scholars have found ready economic motives for landholders who sought government intervention in dealing with laborers. For employers, and especially for large-scale agricultural producers, a population loss of thirty to fifty percent due to the Black Death meant that they were threatened simultaneously by lower demands for basic agricultural goods and greater competition for the services of laborers. The laboring classes conversely enjoyed greater economic opportunity and the possibility of increased occupational, geographical, and social mobility as a result of their reduced numbers. For the government, judicial attempts to deal with errant workers meant an opportunity to raise much needed revenues in the form of fines for violations of the labor statutes.

The connection between economics and politics in the late fourteenth century is obvious if we consider the legislative agenda. The population loss due to plague, the erosion of traditional servile labor arrangements on large estates, and the wage demands of a newly free and mobile labor force, combined to make labor the chief concern of the landholders who dominated the parliamentary debates of post-plague England. Out of their concern, and the king's willingness to concede to landholders in return for their approval of taxes to support the Hundred Years' War, grew a body of labor legislation designed to stem the tide of rising wages and minimize the movements of free laborers and servants.

Scholars concerned with legal history have investigated the administrative and procedural developments that arose out of attempts to enforce the earliest and most notorious of the laws regulating wages, the Statute of Laborers of 1351. The effectiveness of such legislation, however, is usually measured in terms of its ability to keep wages low, thus returning again to economic measures as a gauge of legislative impact and judicial efficiency. Both the economic and the administrative investigations have found that the nature of the early records reflecting resistance to and enforcement of the labor law, especially through special Justices of Laborers and later the Justices of the Peace, lends itself most readily to an aggregate approach focusing on such measurable variables as wages, violations, and fines.

While such measures are useful in assessing the impact of wage and price regulations on the transitional economy of late medieval England, they leave aside questions regarding the nature of the relationship between employers and employees — "masters" and "servants" — and thus obscure, on both the personal and the national level, the social and political implications of laws regulating contractual labor. Between the individual contract negotiations and the trends reflected in the aggregate measures of labor law violations, I think something is being expressed about the position of labor in a shifting social structure. Before examining the documents that capture momentary slices of the on-going arguments through which employers and employees established the boundaries of their positions, it is necessary further to contextualize the problems of labor and labor law.

Questions regarding the social and political impact of labor laws are not usually raised until we examine the Tudor period, when the work force was again plentiful and the concerns about labor were inextricably tied up with concerns about vagrancy and the able-bodied poor. Most notable among the studies of this period that explicitly consider laws regulating labor as a means of social control are Kussmaul's work on servants in husbandry and Beier's aptly titled *Masterless Men*, although it is important to note that masterless women were considered dangerous too.[7] For this later period, the intent of the law to order society by making servants, in Kussmaul's words, "politically invisible," within a patriarchal social structure, is overt, and concerns about rank, social order, and the lawlessness of unpropertied and unattached persons dominate discussions about labor more than economic concerns.[8]

While these Tudor laws, especially those of the reign of Elizabeth, were innovative in their linkage of the issues of employment, idleness,

and crime, they drew heavily on the principles already put into practice by the fourteenth-century Statute of Laborers.[9] Foremost among
these principles were regulations that stated that the able-bodied must
work, that wages should be "reasonable" and that contracts must be
for one year of service.[10] While the statute was re-enacted, supple-
mented, or amended some twenty-one times, the basic principles remained intact.[11] Notable additions to the original statute provided for
the imprisonment, outlawry and branding on the forehead of laborers
who left their communities in order to avoid service (1360–61).[12] A
statute of 1388 determined that anyone who had served in husbandry
before the age of twelve should be compelled to continue in husbandry as an adult.[13] The same statute prohibited any servant in husbandry or laborer from wearing a sword, buckler or dagger.[14] In 1407
leet courts were given the responsibility of extracting yearly oaths
from laborers who were to swear to uphold the statutory wage.[15]
None of these amendments to the original Statute challenged the intent of the law, which was to restrict the wages and mobility, and thus
the economic independence, of laborers of all kinds. The Elizabethan
innovation was to tie these principles to practices regulating the distribution of poor relief and thus suppress sturdy beggars and other unruly elements by making it virtually criminal to exist outside of such
yearly contractual service.[16]

Between the famous labor crises of the fourteenth century and the
establishment of the rigidly paternalistic labor arrangements of the
Tudor period lies the fifteenth century, a period known more for its
chaotic politics and family feuds than for its economic or administrative developments. In that period, whether in spite of or because of the
chaos that ensued from constant land disputes and bickering among
the gentry, it is clear that one element of the central administration did
expand its authority, the Chancery. It is in the fifteenth century that we
first see the Chancery serving regularly as a court of equity, guided,
but not limited by the rules of Common Law. Legal historians have
established that the Common Law was becoming increasingly complex in its procedures and rules.[17] The language of the petitions to the
Chancery further suggests that evidence of corruption and a resulting
lack of faith in the lower courts were as important as the technical difficulties of the Common Law in adding to the growing case load of the
Chancery as a court of equity.

Chief among the concerns of petitioners to Chancery in the fifteenth
century were property disputes arising from the disastrous private
wars among the gentry. Also prominent in the Chancery's early work

as a court of equity, however, were cases in which the court intervened on behalf of petitioners who, through carelessness or ignorance of the Common Law's rules on deeds and written contracts, were unable to free themselves from disputed obligations. There is a real sense in the fifteenth century that the Chancery is obliged to intervene when the intricacies of the Common Law and the resulting professionalization of the courts have disadvantaged some litigants.[18]

Historians have mined sparsely the Chancery documents of the Tudor and Stuart periods for evidence of administrative developments and court intrigue. Similarly, the fifteenth-century documents of the Chancery have been used primarily for the purpose of corroborating the narratives of private warfare, piracy, and aristocratic feuds that are associated with the Wars of the Roses. Fortunately for historians more concerned with wage disputes than dynastic disputes, between the many contested enfeoffments that dominate the work of the Chancery in the fifteenth century we find a number of cases in which questions of labor and the appropriate relationship between employer and employee are being rehearsed if not resolved.

Unlike those who built national reputations through their use of retainers and the courts, the petitioners to the Chancery examined in this study are neither famous nor infamous. Evidence on these less distinguished petitioners is more fleeting and, at first, their concerns appear to reflect only the deceptively simple issues of wages and length of service. Collectively and singularly, however, the appeals of these petitioners call for that equity upon which Chancery built its unique reputation as a court removed from the Common Law. I want to consider how that appeal to equity was tied up with the circumstances and strains of social dislocation in the fifteenth century.

Before examining these Chancery petitions in detail it is important to note that they are far from perfect as sources. Dating is the most obvious problem with the writs. They are bundled according to the term of the chancellor to whom they are addressed with no further indication of a precise date. While I have transcribed over 200 petitions relating to servant-master disputes from the fifteenth-century records of Chancery, most of the cases presently under consideration date roughly from the period 1467 to 1493. Aside from the problems of dating, the petitions are frustratingly brief and typically give us only an entry into the dispute. Only rarely do the answers to the original bills survive, and attempts to verify the petitioner's complaint are obviously futile. Furthermore, some studies of the Chancery argue that the intermediary role of the Chancery clerk and the formulaic language of the petitions make it difficult to separate the standard and well-rehearsed complaints about the petitioner's "utter undoing" from the actual circumstances of the dispute.[19] Nonetheless, I would suggest that these cases might hold clues to the development of attitudes toward labor, law, and social order. Although the text of any given petition raises more questions than it answers, we should remember that these complaints did receive a hearing in the fifteenth century. With the appropriate cautions in mind, we can still look at the language of the petitions to explore how the petitioners constructed a personal history of employment relations before the court. Moreover, it is instructive to reflect on how the petitioners presented themselves and their foes before the court. Whether or not the petitioners' claims can be verified at this distance in time, the fifteenth-century Chancery saw fit to hear them. Furthermore, I would like to assert that the Chancery used the contractual disputes between servants and masters in shaping a larger administrative and social sense of the proper position of free but contractually governed servants.

I want to begin by focusing on four cases that are fairly typical of the nature of the contest between servants and masters. While unremarkable in terms of detail or circumstances, these cases clearly reflect the continuing influence of the Statute of Laborers in the fifteenth century. After examining these cases in detail I will broaden the discussion with reference to other cases.

In the Chancery records we do indeed see that the yearly contracts of service prescribed by statute were at least held up as standards, if not always respected.[20] The mandate of year-long contracts was intended to protect the employer by guaranteeing a regular supply of labor and restricting the wanderings of those who sought higher wages or better conditions. Ironically, in the fifteenth century it seems that servants themselves cited the standard yearly contract to protect themselves from interminable service. It was not uncommon for employers to try to stretch their claims beyond the covenanted year by various uses and abuses of the Common Law.

First, consider the case that Johanna Little of Canterbury brought to the Chancery. She had agreed to serve William Kyrkeby for one year. Complying with the law, she gave notice of her intent to leave his service a quarter of a year before the termination of her contract.[21] When she then tried to leave at the end of the year, William, in an effort to compel her to remain beyond the terms of the contract, had her arrested on charges of trespass. She asked the Chancery to examine the cause of her repeated arrests.[22] As a free woman without independent means, Johanna was indeed compelled to serve a master under the requirements of the Statute of Laborers. The standard of yearly contracts, however, freed her to negotiate with a new master as soon as her contract with William expired. William's attempt to retain her through a series of arrests effectively curtailed Johanna's free agency and presented her with a choice between continued service in his household or continual arrests, imprisonments, and impoverishment.

Often the servant's desire to leave at the end of a year of service was related to a dispute over what was considered the "reasonable wage" prescribed by law. Sometimes more conflictual than the wage itself was the time of payment or the calculation of food, drink, and clothing as a part of that reasonable wage. Notable in this connection is the case of William Hervy, who entered the service of Thomas Knyght of Maidstone on condition that he would receive 28 shillings for the year, payable quarterly. William not only fulfilled the year of service with Thomas, but stayed on eight months more. When William appealed to the Chancery he complained that he "hath diverse times desired of the said Thomas to have his wages at the said days according to the covenant abovesaid in so much as your said orator hath none other living but only by the means of his true and great labor." Thomas, however, refused to pay William either "penny nor halfpenny" and insisted that meat and drink were sufficient to keep William in his service. To retain William's services, Thomas took actions on the Statute of Laborers and actions of trespass against him, thus tying William up with a series of arrests that precluded any new employment for him. [23]

Less loyal than William, Johanna Chamberlyn of London told the court that she had spent a year in service with one Richard Swan and then left, with ten shillings of her salary still unpaid. Richard attempted to retain her services for another year by promising the payment of ten shillings in back wages and an increase in wages for the new contract. Johanna had had enough of promises and, "for as much as she hath often asked her said duty and cannot come by it nor by any part thereof, hath denied to be with him any more in covenant," whereupon Richard filed various charges of debt and trespass against her. [24]

More plaintive is the petition of Johanna Ruke who made a covenant to serve John Holme for one year for "a certain salary and wages between them accorded." The writ continues, "in which time your said oratrice well and truly served and kept without any payment or reward given unto her by the said John or any other person in his name. It is so gracious lord that your said oratrice understood that she might not live with only meat and drink [and] desired her wages according to the covenant between them made or else she might have license to depart out of his service." When John refused to let her leave his service she "still abode in his service half a year and more to the entent that she might have license to depart." Despairing of recovering her wages, Johanna finally left John's employ and found herself immediately arrested and imprisoned on charges of trespass. [25]

The first thing to recognize about these four cases is that they are all brought to the attention of the court by the servant. Thus it is the servant who tells us of the master's action, and to some degree of the master's intentions, as when Johanna Chamberlyn complains that her master "proposed to vex and trouble her . . . in accomplishment of his forward and malicious purpose . . . to the intent to make her fayn to entreat with him or to apply to his pleasure to serve him at his will." She further characterizes the repeated arrests and suits he brought through his friends as "sinister."[26] Likewise Johanna Little complains of William Kyrkeby's "pure malice" and "insatiable malice" in bringing trespass charges against her and maintains that he dropped the suits before they came to a jury "having knowledge that the said twelve men would have acquitted her."[27]

We might question how the servant/petitioner presumed to know the mind of the master. Perhaps there was a subtle sense that motive, or in the language of the records, "intent," and character, or in the language of the records, "disposition," were pertinent in the dispute. Some of these phrases occur often enough in Chancery petitions to be considered formulaic. Even so, we should ask why a particular formula was chosen in any given case. What moral suasion did the servant/petitioner hope to bring to bear by a particular characterization of his or her master?

Anyone who has struggled with the problem of piecing together peasant or working class history when we have only the records kept by manorial officials, monastic commentators, and other non-laborers to work with, will recognize the rarity of having documents in which history's usual losers get to report on the actions and the intentions of history's usual winners. While it is necessary to take into consideration the formulaic mediation of the Chancery clerk, there is still a way in which the Chancery petition retains the story behind the petitioner's plea. Some may argue that these records should not be taken at their word precisely because they originate in the employee's discontent with her or his treatment at the hands of an employer. The same argument, however, is seldom used to question the veracity of documents that reflect the concerns of those in power. Having been told tradition-ally from the perspective of the winners, history may have made us overly suspicious of the losers. Suspicion of the narrative seems to run even higher when those who have been portrayed traditionally as ill-born, unworthy, or crushed by an oppressive social system present a story that recognizes their economic condition and vulnerability in the system, but refuses to capitulate to any of the stereotypes imposed by contemporaries or historians.

Even if we entertain questions regarding the reliability of the ser-vants who seemed to be putting words in their masters' mouths, we can still take the narrative of the dispute and the trail of suits and non-suits as an indication of the master's efforts to keep an individual in service. In all of the cases cited above, the servant's reportage of a dis-pute over wages, length of service, or benefits, although suggestive of the employer's desire to retain the servant, and the servant's reluc-tance to submit to contracts that kept him or her economically depen-dent, tells only half of the story. The other half of the story suggests the complexities and corruptibility of the local courts and the employer's familiarity with the powerful weapon of legal delays.

In the petition of the above-mentioned Johanna Little, whose master tried to keep her after the year's contract expired, we see the avenues open to employers who wanted to press their claims to the service of a given individual. The employer, William, first took an action of tres-pass against Johanna. When she answered the charge and requested a jury trial William "let his said action be nonsued and immediately thereupon commenced a new action of trespass before the mayor of Canterbury." The scenario continued for several rounds of charges, nonsuits, and new actions, "the space of an whole year and much more," effectively impoverishing Johanna.[28]

Similar legal delays complicated the case of William Hervy. When he offered surety to stand against the charges of trespass and violation of the Statute of Laborers brought by the employer he had served an extra eight months, he found himself instead languishing in Maidstone prison without the case ever coming to court.[29] Likewise Johanna Chamberlyn stood ready to meet the charges of debt and trespass filed by Richard Swan but could not get her day in court because Richard used his influence as an officer in the city to initiate a series of charges and nonsuits. Johanna stood ready to wage her law but Richard's friends stood "always ready to attach her and take of her the fees for the arrests," while Richard let every action be nonsued.[30] Johanna Ruke similarly found herself outnumbered and out-maneuvered when her employer John Holme "caused an Alderman to lay his command-ment upon her so that she can in no wise be had to bail to her utter-most undoing."[31]

Even this micro-sample of four cases reveals the wide variety of extraordinary legal actions employers were willing to take in an effort to retain servants. We might ask, was it really worth it for a master to use up favors and influence simply to "vex and trouble" a reluctant servant? The demographic picture tells us that the population loss after the Black Death was both severe and protracted, but did that make it sensible to keep servants languishing in prisons and tied up in lawsuits in an effort to keep them in service? The economic logic does not work. Other concerns must have motivated these protracted legal battles over service.

Complex though the legal maneuvers were in the four cases cited above, the petitions were by no means spectacular. Before leaving these four unspectacular cases to examine a few of the more unusual ones, I should note that in their petitions the servants were as careful in describing themselves as they were in describing their employers. "Your poor oratrice" or "your poor orator" are standard formulaic methods of address that appear at the beginning of virtually all Chancery documents. But in the battle of adjectives and character it gets more personal. Johanna Chamberlyn sets herself against the "pure malice" of her employer by emphasizing that she is "a poor maiden and nothyng hath to live by but only by her true service."[32] Likewise Johanna Ruke presents herself as a covenanted servant who had "well and truly served" her employer without the covenanted payment until she was compelled to leave because she "understood that she might not live only with meat and drink."[33] William Hervy reminds the court that he "hath none other living but only by the means of his true and great labor."[34]

Far from denying their legal status as servants, these petitioners appear to be self-consciously claiming it, emphasizing both the true value of their labor and the economic fragility of their position. While it could be argued that they were merely playing on the sympathies of the court with these humble self-descriptions, I would suggest that they were establishing their claim to legal protection by embracing the law's definition of servant. That definition put great stock in the indi-vidual's dependency on labor. I will return to this question of how in-dividuals accepted or rejected the definition of servant before the courts later. For the moment I want to turn to the position of the masters and examine some of the more remarkable cases.

The employers' use or abuse of the law and their positions in the local community speaks both to the notorious problems in the local courts of the time and to the proprietary claim these employers made over the lives of servants. Even when the story was told by the servant, as in the cases cited above, the relationship between the master and the reluctant servant appears to be one that assumes and attempts to perpetuate the servant's economic dependency. Did that economic dependency imply a social dependency as well? Was that economic dependency at the root of the servant's political invisibility in the master's household?

Indeed, much of the Chancery material gives us not only a vivid portrayal of the material conditions under which people worked but also a sense of how intimate and familiar the relationship between servant and master could be. I think it would be wrong, however, to assume that the familiarity that grew from this dependency translated into a personal or protective relationship. In spite of the fact that servants appear in the same section as wives and children in Blackstone's famous *Commentaries on the Laws of England*, the word "familiar" should evoke no romanticized notions of extended family here.[35] Indeed, in the Chancery cases it seems that the more familiar the servant-master relationship, the more likely it was that the servant would come to be treated as a commodity rather than as family.[36]

Most telling of the master's claim over a servant are the cases in which the services of an individual are treated blatantly as a property right belonging to the master.[37] On occasion the master's claim over a servant is taken to its most extreme conclusion and servants are offered for sale or hire. These extraordinary examples of the proprietary nature of the master-servant relationship are more likely to occur when the relationship is of long standing than when servants move from one yearly contract to another, a fact that may have provided incentive for servants to move on when their masters exhibited an excessive desire to extend contracts beyond the covenanted year as we saw in some of the cases cited above. There are a number of Chancery cases in which an apprentice or bond servant is offered for sale without his or her consent. In the case of a bond servant this is, unfortunately, not surprising; selling the remaining contract of a bond servant would raise no more medieval eyebrows than selling the right to collect a debt. In apprenticeship arrangements, however, wherein the apprentice or his or her guardian has paid for the position and instruction in the master's household it is considerably more problematic. Because both apprentices and bond servants represent special categories of servitude, I have left the many cases of their complaints to Chancery out of this study. Nonetheless I would suggest that examples of the sales of apprentices and bond servants stood as sober witness to the vulnerability of those who lived only by their labor.

Leaving aside the extreme proprietary attitude exhibited toward apprentices and bond servants, we can still get at the issue of the master's property rights if we consider cases wherein masters were pitted against each other in competition for servants. In spite of the Statute of Laborers' explicit prohibition of the procurement of workers by offers of higher wages or better benefits,[38] the Chancery records reveal numerous circumstances in which servants already under contract were sought, and at times besieged, by other employers using legal, illegal, and extra-legal means to draw them into their employ or at least deprive the rightful master of their services. In these cases too the services of a given individual are spoken of as a commodity to be acquired or reclaimed.

In some cases servants seem to be only the pawns in a dispute that is really between two rival members of the middle class. In these cases it is the master who complains to the Chancery and the masters' petitions exhibit strong evidence of the proprietary claim that the court recognized over contractual servants. Unusual in its detail but typical in the attitude it demonstrates toward the servant is the petition of Nicholas Warynges, whose servant, Stephen, was the victim of an armed attack led by John and Richard Salford. Stephen, "then being there in the peace of God and our sovereign lord in his bed," was roused from sleep when John and Richard set the house on fire to draw him out. Waiting outside with John and Richard were a number of other "riotous" persons who "beat, wounded, hurted and maimed him and him there left for dead so that he stood long and yet standith in danger of his life, by the which your said beseecher hath lost by long time the services of his said servant." The writ continues, emphasizing the loss of valuable services and the compensation Nicholas sought.[39] Although the violent circumstances in this case suggest some strain of the private warfare that characterized rivalry among the gentry in the fifteenth century, the legal language remains the language of property and contract. The issue in this case was not assault and we should not confuse Nicholas' legal pursuit of the attackers with a protective stance toward his servant. Nicholas was not asking for criminal charges to be brought against the riotous persons who attacked Stephen; rather he wanted recompense for having "lost by long time the services of his said servant," that is, for having lost a commodity.

Similar concerns over lost service and the challenged claim to a given servant are reflected in numerous cases in which one employer charged another with stealing a servant. Some of these cases are common, intriguingly vague, and some of them contain remarkable detail. On the vague side is the case of Alexander Shepard of Kent who, being a stranger in London, had no friends to stand for him when Thomas Whitehead of London accused him of stealing a servant, Johanna Bolton, whom Alexander had met briefly in a tavern. Although Alexander claimed that he did nothing to lure the servant away, and in fact had little acquaintance with his accuser, he had slim hopes of pleading his case successfully in London because Thomas was "a man that is well acquainted with the common jurors of London and hath impanelled an inquest that he is sure will pass with him in the said wrongfull plaint."[40] Alexander's case speaks again to the weight of local influence in the legal system but also raises questions about the popular understanding of the labor law. What we don't know about this case makes the imagination work hard. Had Johanna actually left Thomas' household? Were strangers an easy target for servant-stealing scams? These we cannot answer. But we can note that servant stealing was readily interpreted as essentially a property trespass. Neither Alexander nor Thomas needed to explain the circumstances in order to present the concept of the master's property rights to the court.

The lack of detail in Alexander's case contrasts sharply with the rich detail in the case of a foreign merchant who found himself similarly charged with taking away a servant. It seems that Herman Ryng encountered one Johanna White "singlewoman" who by her own confession "was wont to dance and make revelry in her master's house, sometimes in man's clothing and sometimes naked." According to Herman, Johanna offered herself "to be at his commandment" and would not take no for an answer until Herman ordered one of his servants to chase her away with two or three stripes. When the "misliving" Johanna reported this treatment to her master, Stephen Reygate, he laid a charge of trespass against Herman "surmitting that he had taken away his servant to the damage of twenty pounds."[41] The remainder of the case is a treasure trove of loaded language referring to Stephen's reputation and influence in the community and Herman's pitiful position as a foreigner before the local courts. To explore this issue of the master's rights, however, it is more important to focus on the disparity between Herman's story and the charges brought by Stephen. Johanna was clearly a prostitute, Stephen was clearly her pimp. In spite of Herman's vivid references to these occupations in his petition to Chancery, these facts seem to have been ir-relevant to the principles of the case. The most notable feature of this case is that, while Herman admitted to having beaten Johanna via his servant, the charge Stephen brought against him had nothing to do with this attack, but rather was a charge of taking away a servant and denying the rightful master of the commodity of her services. Again I would suggest that this charge was a sort of legal convenience. Courts and citizens easily understood the concept of the master's property right over the servant. A charge of taking away a servant was recog-nizable from the Statute of Laborers and thus was readily prosecutable in the local courts. The wronged party was Stephen, not Johanna, and the damages he sought were to replace the loss of her services. The courts were asked to rule on these issues rather than on the more in-triguing circumstances of the case. In accepting the master's claim of property rights over the servant, the courts and popular opinion up-held the master's economic control over the individual labors of a con-tractual servant. I would argue that they were also upholding the master's social control over that servant.

The concern for social control that became so blatant in sixteenth-century discussions of labor was already present in many of the fifteenth-century Chancery writs. When William Gregory of London complained about the freelance activities of his servant, Alice Shevyngton, his concern was not merely economic. Alice had served him on yearly contracts for three years for the sum of sixteen shillings a year, which, William carefully pointed out, he had "paid and con-tented unto her . . . and more above." Recently, however, Alice ab-sented herself from his household for days and weeks, "pretending herself to have cunning in the healing of sore eyes." William sought "reasonable amends" for the time that Alice spent in the sore eyes business. Alice, perhaps enjoying new-found confidence and promi-nence in the community as a result of her recent success as a healer, prevented William from pressing his claims on her service or her money by bringing an action of debt against him. William insisted that he would be unable to wage his law fairly because of the popular sup-port his erstwhile servant had won in the community.[42] While Alice had indeed broken her contract with William by leaving his service when other, more lucrative opportunities presented themselves, the tone of the petition suggests that William was more upset by the eco-nomic independence and social clout Alice demonstrated than by the loss of a few days of her service.

Other cases similarly suggest that the master was disturbed as much by the audacity of a servant who manipulated local and legal influence as by the initial dispute. Notable is the case of Philip, who had had his former servant, John, arrested for certain unstated offenses. To Philip's dismay the servant, John, "through the comfort, maintenance, and stirring of diverse kinsmen and friends inhabitant within the city of London," brought a counter charge of trespass against him, claiming that Philip had unlawfully beaten and ill-treated the servant. To this charge Philip answered that "he never so did, otherwise than a master should do to a servant." Philip's appeal to the Chancery reflects both indignation at being charged for ill-treating a servant and fear that Philip would not fare well in this dispute because of the influence of his servant's kinsfolk and friends. Philip's defense, that "he never did so otherwise than a master should do to a servant," speaks volumes about the acceptance of a norm of master-servant relations. [43]

Before concluding I want to raise once more the issue of the employee's acceptance of the label "servant" and the correlary claim to legal protection as one who had no other living than by his or her true and great labor. Just as telling as the acceptance of that status by some individuals is the rejection of the label "servant" by those who could maintain their economic and social independence. Robert Sherman asked the court of the Chancery to relieve him from imprisonment on a Statute of Laborers charge brought against him by John Ashely. John maintained that Robert was a covenant servant, which according to statute meant that he owed a year's service. Robert protested that he had "never made covenant with the said John but only he was with him but four days and that was solely upon liking." [44] Robert could not have made this argument about his "liking" to the court with such confidence unless he had sufficient means to live outside of a yearly contract.

Aleyn Jane was even more explicit in her attempt to establish economic independence before the court. She described herself as "a widow . . . and honest woman . . . and a good spinster." When Robert Crueys offered her two nobles more than any other master would give her for a year's service Aleyn flatly refused, maintaining that "she would never serve him nor be no man's servant in no mannerwise." [45]

If one could not prove the economic independence that Robert and Aleyn claimed above, then one was subject to accusations of idleness, or worse, suspected of being a vagabond. A broad-based fear of individuals who could demonstrate neither independent means nor safe governance in the household of a master is echoed in the accusations of vagrancy that appear in the preludes to other Chancery cases. The language of both the accusation of vagabondage and the petition that attempts to establish the alleged vagabond's economic legitimacy reflects again the necessity of being attached, placed, governed, in the eyes of the courts and the community.[46]

Even those who in fact did have independent means seem to have been vulnerable to false charges of vagrancy when they travelled on business and their transactions went sour. Richard Payne, a tailor of Hornedon, walked with "great amity and love . . . with certain special friends of his" to the town of Waltham. His friends continued on their way to Our Lady of Walsingham while Richard stopped to collect payment for some garments he had made. When he ran into trouble collecting his payment, an argument ensued and the local bailiff, "a kinsman and special lover" of Richard's customer, arrested him "for a misgoverned man and a vagabond." Richard offered ample evidence that he was a man "of honest rule."[47] Note the care he took in identifying himself in relation to his friends. Nonetheless, Richard had difficulty proving his honesty and his economic legitimacy because his witnesses were not residents of Waltham.

While personal influence and vendetta on the part of Richard's reluctant customer made the circumstances of his arrest complex, those complexities were irrelevant to the local court that first heard the case. Like the understanding of service as a commodity and servants as property, a charge of vagrancy needed little explanation in a fifteenth-century court. The constable of Maidstone similarly needed little justification when he arrested John Lamb, a servant travelling on behalf of a London tailor. John was labeled a vagabond and kept in Maidstone prison "because he was not there retained in service with any man."[48] A vagabond was an individual who could not be named, defined in relation to a known master — an individual who, by virtue of living outside of local service, lived outside good governance. To the community at large, as to the master of a household, the issue of service was an issue of governance, an issue of social and economic control. An individual without independent economic means was either a servant or a vagabond — either an individual who well and truly served, or a misgoverned human being.

The use and abuse of laws regulating relations between servants and masters in the fifteenth century already reflected the concern for social order that is so explicitly stated in later Tudor legislation. Ironically, the disputes between master and servant in the fifteenth century also reveal a further way in which that notorious period, as concerned about social order as it was, can be characterized as lawless or even, perhaps, over-lawed. Every charge of a Statute of Laborers violation or breach of contract had the potential to spin out its own series of subsequent charges of trespass or debt. These extra helpings of legal actions and nonsuits produced delays intended to impoverish and often imprison a reluctant servant. The time and expense devoted to these legal and extra-legal measures says as much about fears of the ungoverned laborer as it says about the complexity and corruptibility of the Common Law courts.

Although it was typically the master who exerted such power over local constables and juries, some servants successfully brought the clout of their own social networks to bear upon charges against their masters in the local courts. Even the formulaic refrains of the Chancery writs make it clear that the supplicant had found no redress through the Common Law and that familiarity with local officials often weighed more heavily than any arbitrary standards of justice in determining whether master or servant would be protected by the law. The line between what was legal and what was extra-legal in servant-master relations was probably crossed with impunity in the local courts far more often than it was crossed and captured in the records of the Chancery. Servants who claimed their own access to the strategic delays and countersuits available through the Common Law were in a sense claiming a much more public arena for their grievances than the quietly governed household to which they were contractually assigned.

In the Chancery documents, the labor laws first articulated in the fourteenth century were applied to establish the positions of both servants and masters in a given household and in a larger social structure. While both parties in servant-master disputes took part in this defining of the servant, neither accepted the restrictions or guarantees of the labor laws without trying to protect their personal interests. Certainly that "politically invisible" definition of the servant that was embraced and mandated in the sixteenth century was developing throughout the fifteenth century. The Chancery writs initiated by both masters and servants, however, suggest that, even when servants admitted economic dependency, at least some attempted to claim legal identities far more independent than those their Tudor successors would be able to exercise. The fact that they met their masters in court and appealed to the law's own definition of "servant" to free themselves from intolerable conditions and interminable bonds of servitude, speaks to the servants' acute awareness of both the economic restrictions and the technical freedom of their status. The fact that their employers and the larger community invested so much time and legal energy in keeping these servants governed in a master's household suggests that they too were acutely aware of the technical freedom, and thus the political potential, of this growing element in the laboring classes.

NOTES

This paper began as an exercise in legal history and I am grateful to Sue Sheridan Walker for her helpful comments on the workings of the Chancery. David Wallace and Barbara Hanawalt of the Center for Medieval Studies at the University of Minnesota also provided valuable feedback on my reading of the Chancery documents. I would also like to acknowledge the roles of Kathleen Biddick and Allen Frantzen played in bringing the project to its present form.

1. The complex issues of community and identity in post-plague England have been explored most thoroughly by David Aers in *Community, Gender, and Individual Identity: English Writing, 1360–1430* (London, 1988). Aers also addresses the problems of periodization and master narratives that deny the complexity of identity in the Middle Ages in his essay, "A Whisper in the Ear of Early Modernists; or, Reflections on Literary Critics Writing the 'History of the Subject' " in *Culture and History, 1350-1600: Essays on English Communities, Identities and Writing,* ed. David Aers (Detroit, 1992), pp. 177–202.

2. The history of the peasantry and its response to the demographic disasters and tax impositions of the fourteenth century has received extensive treatment in national and local studies of the English economy. The most important of these studies in relation to the social tensions that culminated in open rebellion are R. H. Hilton, *Bond Men Made Free: Medieval Peasant Movements and the English Rising of 1381* (London, 1973); and *The English Rising of 1381,* ed. R. H. Hilton and T. H. Aston (London, 1984). The role of wage earners in the agricultural economy is further articulated in two collections of articles by Hilton: *The English Peasantry in the Later Middle Ages* (Oxford, 1975), especially Chapter 2, "The Social Structure of the Village," pp. 20–36; and *Class Conflict and the Crisis of Feudalism: Essays in Medieval Social History* (London, 1985), especially Chapter 17, "Some Social and Economic Evidence in Late Medieval English Tax Returns," pp. 180–91.

3. For comments on the distinction between servants and laborers see: Christopher Dyer, *Standards of Living in the Later Middle Ages: Social Change in England, c. 1200–1520* (Cambridge, 1989) pp. 211–33; see also Hilton, "Some Social and Economic Evidence," p. 188. The preference of employers for servants in husbandry on annual contracts over wage laborers is dealt with by R. M. Smith in his introductory essay, "Some Issues Concerning Families and Their Property in Rural England, 1250–1800," in *Land, Kinship and Life Cycle,* ed. Richard M. Smith (Cambridge, 1984) pp. 1–86; see especially pp. 36–38. Smith's article on "Human Resources" in *The Countryside in Medieval England,* ed. Grenville Astill and Annie Grant (Oxford, 1988) pp. 188–212, similarly associates the growth of service with periods of labor shortage, p. 210. Just as defining the servant is not the focus of my current project, so too, enumerating the servant in proportion to other types of wage earners is not a concern of this essay. The difficulty of quantifying servants and laborers in the post-plague economy is immense due to their mobility and to the strong incentive for evasion in the poll-tax lists that attempted to count and tax them in their masters' households. See Hilton, *The English Peasantry in the Later Middle Ages,* pp. 31–36 and "Some Social and Economic Evidence," pp. 181–82,

188, on the problems of evasion in the poll-tax returns of 1380–81.

4. The compulsory service clause of the original Ordinance of Laborers of 1349 (23 Edw. 3 st.1, c. 1) and the stipulation in the Statute of 1351 that laborers in husbandry should work by the year or the term rather than for lucrative daily wages (25 Edw. 3 st. 2, c.1) set the legal ground for the employers' preference for annual contracts.

5. Kate Mertes, *The English Noble Household, 1250–1600: Good Governance and Political Rule* (Oxford, 1988) pp. 3–5. Scholars of Old-Regime France have investigated servant and master relations in considerable depth and provided a valuable focus on the vulnerability of the servant. The emphasis, however, remains on larger and wealthier households. Sarah C. Maza has pointed out the problem that contemporary literature on servants reflected primarily the interests of the aristocracy and their concern for public image in *Servants and Masters in Eighteenth-Century France: The Uses of Loyalty* (Princeton, 1983). Although Maza's work deals with the servant in the urban aristocratic household, she presents a rich discussion of the threat even these liveried servants presented to the larger urban community. "Servants were despised and feared because they were different, but above all because their social status was ill-defined, because they were marginal creatures" (p. 136). Building on the theories of anthropologists Mary Douglas and Victor Turner, Maza describes the domestic servants of the Old-Regime aristocracy as "liminal beings" who lived on the threshold of their masters' establishments (ibid). See Mary Douglas, *Purity and Danger* (London, 1966) and Victor Turner, *The Ritual Process: Structure and Anti-Structure* (Chicago, 1969). Although unliveried and, for the most part, unburdened by the language of loyalty that framed the servant in the noble household, contractual servants in small English households of the fifteenth century might well have shared the marginality that Maza identifies with servants in the Old Regime. Another example of the explorations of the topic of servants in France is Cissie Fairchilds, *Domestic Enemies: Servants and Masters in Old Regime France* (Baltimore, 1984). For northern England, P. J. P. Goldberg provides a regional study of female servants in "Female Labour, Service and Marriage in the Late Medieval Urban North," *Northern History*, 22 (1986): 18–38. Goldberg also includes female servants in his "Women in Fifteenth-Century Town Life," which appears in *Towns and Townspeople in the Fifteenth Century* , ed. J. A. F. Thomson (Gloucester, 1988), pp. 107–28. See also "Marriage, Migration, and Servanthood: The York Cause Paper Evidence," in *Woman is a Worthy Wight: Women in English Society c. 1200–1500*, ed. P. J. P. Goldberg (Gloucester, 1992), pp. 1–15. Goldberg sees a continuity between the life-cycle stage pattern of service for women in late medieval and early modern England. Barbara A. Hanawalt devotes a chapter to servants, particularly those for whom service was a life-cycle stage before establishing their own households, in *Growing Up in Medieval London: The Experience of Childhood in History* (Oxford, 1993), pp. 173–98. With the exception of these sources little attention has been paid to contractual servants in late medieval England compared to their counterparts in later periods. Perhaps it is again the marginality of servants in the late medieval period, their stance outside the more familiarly constructed category of "peasant," that has discouraged more extensive work on medieval servants. Kathleen Biddick's discussion of the constructions of "peasants" by historians and anthropologists appears in "Decolonizing the English Past: Readings in Medieval Archaeology and History," *Journal of British Studies* 32 (1993): 1–23.

6. Bertha Haven Putnam's early work on the enforcement of the Statute of Laborers remains indispensable. See "Courts Held Under the Statutes of Labourers," in *Medieval Archives of the University of Oxford*, ed. H. E. Salter, vol. II (Oxford, 1919); "The Justices of Labourers in the Fourteenth Century," *English Historical Review*, 21 (1906): 517–38; and *The Enforcement of the Statute of Labourers During the First Decade After the Black Death, Columbia Studies in History, Economics and Public Law*, 32 (New York, 1908). See also Hilton's work on labor in the agricultural economy

cited above, note 2. More local treatments of labor issues in the fourteenth century include: N. K. Ritchie, "Labour Conditions in Essex in the Reign of Richard II, " in E. M. Carus-Wilson, ed. *Essays in Economic History*, vol. II (London, 1962) pp. 91–111; L. R. Poos, "The Social Context of Statute of Labourers Enforcement," *Law and History Review* 1.1 (1983): 27–52; and Elaine Clark, "Medieval Labor Law and English Local Courts," *American Journal of Legal History* 37 (1983): 330–53. My own investigation of the impact of the statute in the fourteenth century appears in my Ph.D. dissertation, "The Role of the Enforcement of The Statute of Labourers in the Social and Economic Background of the Great Revolt in East Anglia in 1381," Indiana University, 1986.

7. Ann Kussmaul, *Servants in Husbandry in Early Modern England* (Cambridge, 1980); A. L. Beier, *Masterless Men* (London, 1985). See also Marjorie K. McIntosh, "Social Change and Tudor Manorial Leets," in *Law and Social Change in British History*, ed. J. A. Guy and H. G. Beale (London, 1984) pp. 73–85.

8. Kussmaul, *Servants in Husbandry*, p. 9.

9. *Statutes of the Realm*, 23 Edward III (Records Commission: London, 1810).

10. Blackstone's discussion of menial servants echoes the principle of a yearly contract established by the Statute and further articulates the practice whereby such contracts could be imposed by two justices on any male between the ages of twelve and sixty and any female between the ages of twelve and forty who was unable to demonstrate an independent means of support. Sir William Blackstone, *Commentaries on the Laws of England*, ed. Edward Christian (London, 1818), p. 422. J. H. Baker further outlines the covenant implied by the Statute of Laborers in *An Introduction to English Legal History*, 3rd ed. (London, 1990), pp. 378–79. Elaine Clark gives a succinct breakdown of the various clauses of the Statute in the Appendix to "Medieval Labor Law and English Local Courts," cited in note 6 above.

11. Wilhelm Hasbach, *A History of the English Agricultural Labourer* (London, 1908), pp. 422–24.

12. *Statutes of the Realm*, 34 Edw. 3, c. 10.

13. *Statutes of the Realm*, 12 Ric. 2, c. 5.

14. *Statutes of the Realm*, 12 Ric. 2, c. 6.

15. *Statutes of the Realm*, 7 Hen. 4, c. 17.

16. William S. Holdsworth, *A History of English Law*, vol. 4 (Boston, 1924), pp. 279–380. The degree to which service was assigned by status as much as by contract is discussed in Baker, *An Introduction to English Legal History*, p. 382.

17. Holdsworth, p. 276. For further discussion of the development of the Chancery see Margaret Avery, "The History of the Equitable Jurisdiction of the Chancery Before 1460," *Bulletin of the Institute of Historical Research* 42 (1969): 129–44; and William P. Baildon, *Select Cases in Chancery, A.D. 1364–1471* (London, 1986). C. K. Allen provides a discussion of the development of equity in *Law in the Making* (Oxford, 1964), pp. 399–413. Marjorie Blatcher investigates the movement of disputed enfeoffments from Common Law courts to Chancery in *The Court of the King's Bench 1450–1550* (London, 1973), pp. 25–27. Alan Harding presents a succinct discussion of the development of Chancery as a court in *The Law Courts of Medieval England* (London, 1973), pp. 100–102. The later development of the Chancery and its procedures is explored in W. J. Jones, *The Elizabethan Court of Chancery* (Oxford, 1967).

18. Baker suggests that the Chancery's informality, lack of jury, and flexible schedule, made it more accessible to the poorest and most vulnerable elements of society, thus increasing its case load as the Common Law courts became more rigid. See Baker, *An Introduction to English Legal History*, pp. 119–20. Jones discusses the chancery principle of *in forma pauperis* in *The Elizabethan Court*, p. 323.

19. See John H. Fisher, "Chancery and the Emergence of Standard Written English,"

Speculum 52 (1977): 870–99; Malcolm Richardson, "Henry V, the English Chancery, and Chancery English," *Speculum* 55 (1980): 726–50; also Mark Beilby, "The Profits of Expertise: The Rise of Civil Lawyers and Chancery Equity," in *Profit, Piety and the Professions in Later Medieval England*, ed. Michael Hicks (Gloucester, 1990), pp. 72–90.

20. *Statutes of the Realm*, 25 Edw. 3 st. 2, c. 1.

21. Blackstone affirms the quarter's notice as standard, p. 422, while a later commentator, R. Campbell, cited one month's notice as standard. R. Campbell, *Principles of English Law (Based on Blackstone's Commentaries)* (London, 1907), p. 91.

22. PRO, C1 64/1077.

23. PRO, C1 61/510.

24. PRO, C1 61/377.

25. PRO, C1 46/117.

26. PRO, C1 61/377.

27. PRO, C1 64/1077.

28. PRO, C1 64/1077.

29. PRO, C1 61/510.

30. PRO, C1 61/377.

31. PRO, C1 46/117.

32. PRO, C1 61/377.

33. PRO, C1 46/117.

34. PRO, C1 61/510.

35. Blackstone, *Commentaries*, ed. Christian, pp. 422ff.

36. Ibid., p. 429.

37. Baker discusses the legal options available to a master who had lost services in *An Introduction to English Legal History*, p. 517.

38. *Statutes of the Realm*, 25 Edw. 3 st. 2.

39. PRO, C1 178/18; see Blackstone's discussion of the employer's rights to service, *Commentaries*, ed. Christian, p. 429.

40. PRO, C1 224/37.

41. PRO, C1 158/47.

42. PRO, C1 66/264.

43. PRO, C1 67/137.

44. PRO, C1 47/266.

45. PRO, C1 66/52.

46. Marjorie K. McIntosh has raised the issue of the manorial community's concern with vagabonds and the poor in "Social Change and Tudor Manorial Leets" in *Law and Social Change in British History*, ed. J. A. Guy and H. G. Beale, pp. 73–85; and in *Autonomy and Community: The Royal Manor of Havering* (Cambridge, 1986). See especially part 3, "Community, Conflict and Change, 1352–1500," pp. 181–264.

47. PRO, C1 61/246.

48. PRO, C1 64/421.